WING LEADER

WING LEADER

Air Vice-Marshal 'Johnnie' Johnson
CB, CBE, DSO & Two Bars, DFC & Bar

Top-scoring Allied fighter pilot of World War Two

Published in 2000 by Stoddart Publishing Co. Limited
34 Lesmill Road, Toronto, Canada M3B 2T6

Distributed by General Distribution Services Limited
325 Humber College Blvd, Toronto, Canada M9W 7C3
Tel (416) 213-1919 Fax (416) 213-1917
Email cservice@genpub.com

First published in hardcover in Great Britain by Chatto & Windus, 1956
Published in paperback in Great Britain by Crécy Publishing Limited, 2000

The Author asserts his moral right to be identified as the author of this work.

04 03 02 01 00 1 2 3 4 5

Canadian Cataloguing in Publication Data

Johnson, J. E. (James Edgar)
Wing Leader

ISBN 0-7737-3240-3

1. Johnson, J.E. (James Edgar). 2. World War, 1939-1945 – Aerial operations, British. 3. World War, 1939-1945 – Personal narratives, British. 4. Fighter pilots – Great Britain – Biography. 5. Great Britain. Royal Air Force – Biography. I. Title.
D786.J63 2000 940.54'4941'092 C00-930202-6

Photographs reproduced with kind permission of
Air Vice-Marshal 'Johnnie' Johnson

We acknowledge for their financial support of our publishing program the Canada Council for the Arts, the Ontario Arts Council, and the Government of Canada through the Book Publishing Industry Development Program (BPIDP). This book was made possible in part through the Canada Council's translation grants program.

Printed by Interprint, Malta

Air Vice-Marshal 'Johnnie' Johnson's decorations include the DSO and two Bars, the DFC and Bar, the Légion d'Honneur (France), the Légion of Merit (USA), DFC (USA), Air Medal (USA), the Order of Leopold (Belgium) and the Croix de Guerre (Belgium).

On his retirement from the Royal Air Force in 1966, Air Vice-Marshal Johnson founded *The 'Johnnie' Johnson Housing Trust*, which provides sheltered accommodation for the elderly and disabled.

CONTENTS

FOREWORD

By
GROUP CAPTAIN DOUGLAS BADER
C.B.E., D.S.O., D.F.C.

DEAR JOHNNIE,

I did not know that you could read and write! In spite of what you say about me I think this is a splendid book, apart from your dissertation on Battle of Britain strategy, with which I cordially disagree!

I like your style, which is in the tradition of our famous predecessors of World War I, Ball, McCudden, Mannock and Bishop. Never let it be forgotten that our generation of fighter pilots learned the basic rules of air fighting from them. When I was a cadet at Cranwell I used to read their books time and time again and I never forgot them. I am sure this book of yours will be read with the same enthusiasm by future generations of cadets. I commend it to them.

Yours,

Douglas

LONDON
7th June 1956

God send me to see suche a company together agayne when need is.

LORD HOWARD OF EFFINGHAM

Chapter One

THE VOLUNTEER RESERVE

When the war ended in Europe I commanded a Spitfire wing and we were based at Celle, the most easterly of our airfields in Germany. Since the Rhine crossing, some six weeks before, we had met the Luftwaffe almost every day, and although they were in a hopeless position, short of fuel and spares and their airfields under constant bombardment, let it be said to their credit that they continued the fight until the end.

During these past few weeks when we patrolled their airfields and harried them from dawn till dusk we had shot down over a hundred enemy aircraft, including the latest jet- and rocket-propelled types, the well-proved Messerschmitt and Focke-Wulf fighters, pilotless aircraft, pick-a-back contraptions, lumbering transports, bombers and light communication aircraft. The Luftwaffe did not ask for quarter, and we flew hard against them until the morning of V.E. day.

We had lifted our Spitfires from the flare path into the black night and watched the dawn paint the earth with colour when we flew towards the rising light in the east. At low level we curved across Berlin, sparred cautiously with large gaggles of Russian fighters and saw the surging tide of men and armour pouring through the open flood-gates of eastern Europe.

Now that it was all over, the Germans flew in from Norway and Denmark to surrender. One arrogant young pilot landed his brand-new bomber at Celle and saluted smartly when I met him as he dropped from the cockpit. He was very pleased, he told us, now that the Luftwaffe no longer fought the Royal Air Force. But a common foe remained, and if we could fix him up with a few bombs and perhaps a Spitfire escort... He was still looking pained when we bundled him off to the nearest prisoner-of-war stockade.

During the next few months there was the difficult transition period from war to peace ahead of us, and my chief responsibility would be not so much the flying but to make sure that upwards of a thousand airmen left the Service with pleasant memories. For the off-duty hours the local streams were well stocked with brown trout, and in the autumn there would be some excellent wild-fowling. There was blackgame to be flushed and shot on the wild, barren heathlands, red deer and roe buck to be stalked in the brooding pine forests and wild boar to be ambushed in the fields beneath the hunter's moon. All this for the asking, and for the first time in six years there was the opportunity to get properly organised for such things.

The day after it was all over I drove slowly round the perimeter track and tried to get accustomed to the rare sight of fifty-odd Spitfires squatting idle on the grass while the sun blazed down from a blue, clean sky. Suddenly a lone aircraft, a captured Fieseler Storch bearing our own markings, swung into view just above the tree-tops and glided in to land. This could only be our group commander, Air Vice-Marshal Harry Broadhurst, and I was on the tarmac to meet him before he switched off the engine.

"Well, Johnnie, how do you like the piping days of peace?" he asked.

"I'm not sure, sir," I answered. "Seems odd to be sitting on the ground in this weather. But I suppose we'll get used to it."

"You won't have to get used to it just yet," said the air vice-marshal. "I've got another job for your chaps. Any idea what it is?"

"Not the faintest, sir," I replied.

"I think you'll like this one. We've been asked to send a token British force to Copenhagen. It should be great fun, and since your chaps have done so well recently I'm giving you the job as a sort of bonus. Make the most of it, for I shall replace you after a month or so with another wing. You'd better get off to Copenhagen today and have a look at the accommodation. Get your chaps up there as soon as you can. I'll fly up in a few days' time to see you."

I thanked the group commander, and after he left I collected my wing leader and one or two other officers, jumped into an Anson and set course for the airfield at Kastrup, which lies on the southern flank of Copenhagen. We had enjoyed the liberation of Paris and had lived in some style in Brussels. A few weeks in Copenhagen would provide a fitting end to our trek across Europe.

After a flight of about ninety minutes I put the creaking Anson down on the smooth asphalt surface of the Kastrup runway. Crowds of people swarmed the tarmac: police, soldiers, resistance personnel, newspaper men, photographers and attractive blondes. When we stepped out we were immediately besieged by a battery of interrogators.

"Are the Spitfires coming here?"

"Where are the Russians?"

"The Germans are still here. They will not surrender to us. Perhaps you..."

"Where is Monty?"

"The Russians are at Bornholm. Our island! Are they coming here?"

"Please take these flowers."

And so on.

Eventually some sort of order was restored. I explained the purpose of our visit. The Spitfires would soon arrive, probably tomorrow. A detachment of the famous Sixth Airborne Division was on its way to Copenhagen and would take care of the German troops, who would soon leave Denmark. The Royal Navy would sail into the harbour within the next few days and a Military Mission would soon be established to solve the various problems. All would be well!

Meanwhile, if we could borrow a car to have a quick look at the airfield and the buildings, it would help to speed up the arrival of the Spitfires. A pre-war Buick was soon produced and we decided that the airfield contained more than adequate accommodation for our modest needs. Food was not a problem; for, even if the supply organisation did not catch up with us for a day or two, the well-fed appearance of the Danes told us that here was an abundance of food. Our reconnaissance was therefore very brief and we prepared to leave, for the quicker we got back to Celle the sooner we should be firmly entrenched in pleasant Copenhagen.

On the next day it was a fairly long flight for the limited range of our aircraft, so we flew to Kastrup by squadrons. I led the first formation and we flew over Lower Saxony and Schleswig-Holstein in a loose, easy fashion. But when we approached Copenhagen I put the boys into a tight formation and we roared over the capital. I thought the Danes would appreciate the gesture.

When we taxied to the large expanse of concrete in front of the administrative buildings at Kastrup, the crowds were greater than before and several of the pilots were almost dragged from their cockpits by the excited Danes. Perhaps it was a good thing that the fighting was over!

Personally, I was ready for a rest from operations. The past was remembered not by the years but by the events – the Volunteer Reserve, the Battle of Britain, our gradual reaching out across the Channel and over France, Dieppe, my first Canadian wing, Normandy, Paris, Brussels, Arnhem and so finally across the Rhine and into Germany.

After a great deal of hard work and cramming, and some luck in the professional examinations, the year 1938 found me, at twenty-two, a fully qualified civil engineer and holding an appointment at Loughton, on the edge of Epping Forest. I joined the nearby Chingford Rugby Club, enjoyed some excellent games and the company of a very spirited collection of young men, most of whom were already serving in one or another of the various Territorial organisations. In one game, against Park House, I was brought down heavily on a frozen surface and broke my right collar-bone. Although I did not know it at the time, the break was improperly set and the nerves to the forearm were imprisoned below the bone. Later, in 1940, this incident almost ended my active flying career.

I tried to become a pilot in one of the squadrons of the Auxiliary Air Force. After some time I was seen by an officer, who, I learnt, was a very keen fox-hunting type. He asked me the usual questions, school, profession, sports, and whether or not I had any flying experience. Naturally, I laid great stress on the fact that I had already started flying instruction at my own expense. However, he didn't appear to be impressed and I had the distinct feeling that the interview would soon be concluded with the usual "We'll let you know if we are likely to have a vacancy." But his flagging enthusiasm revived a little when he learnt that I came from Leicestershire and that my home was at Melton Mowbray. "That's a jolly good thing," he said. "I know the country very well as I hunt there quite a lot. Tell me, which pack do you follow?" When I tactfully explained that all my spare cash was devoted to flying, not hunting, the interview was speedily ended, and my services with an Auxiliary squadron were not required until the shooting war had begun.

The crisis of Munich gave way to a period of rapid rearmament and expansion of the Auxiliary and Territorial units. Once more I tried to join the Auxiliary Air Force. I was curtly informed that sufficient pilots were already available but there were some vacancies in the Balloon squadrons. Was I interested in this vital part of the defence organisation? I replied, with similar brevity, that I was not at all interested in flying balloons!

One or two of my rugby friends had already joined the R.A.F. Volunteer Reserve, had been taught to fly, and were well on their way to gaining the coveted wings, only worn by qualified pilots. The V.R. had been formed in 1936 and its aim was to recruit a reserve of pilots. All entrants were at first in non-commissioned rank and a reasonable number were commissioned when they got their wings. The V.R. was far less of a *corps d'élite* than the socially inclined Auxiliary Air Force, and it was with great expectations that I submitted my application to the Air Ministry. In due time it was acknowledged, but they regretted that for the time being they had far more candidates than vacancies in the V.R. training schools. However, should the scheme be expanded, then they would communicate with me in due course.

Any hopes I had of ever joining one or the other of the part-time flying organisations of the R.A.F. were now firmly put aside. I decided that I must join some other Territorial organisation, as my civilian appointment was a reserved occupation and, should war come, I could not work up any great enthusiasm for building air-raid shelters or supervising decontamination squads. Despite my lack of interest in the hunting field I had learned to ride at an early age, and on my next visit to see my people at Melton Mowbray I applied to join the mounted Leicestershire Yeomanry. I was interviewed by the local troop commander and was pleased to find that he did not think it was necessary to know how to fly in order to ride a horse.

Service with the Yeomanry was a very happy affair and we spent many enjoyable days charging over the countryside on our various manoeuvres. After all the long hours and the hard exercise I returned to Loughton, a few pounds lighter in weight, to find an official looking letter from the Air Ministry. It had been decided to expand the V.R. scheme and they referred to my application of the previous year. If I was still interested would I present myself at Store Street, the London headquarters of the V.R., for the necessary medical examination in two days' time? I was outside the doors when they opened. Together with a dozen other types I was processed through the various stages of the stiff and lengthy medical examination. After lunch, having successfully negotiated the medicos, a few of us were ushered into the presence of a group captain and without further ado were sworn in as sergeant-pilots under training in the R.A.F. Volunteer Reserve. I was told to report to a flying training school in Essex, Stapleford Tawney, for my week-end flying and that they would also welcome my attendance on the long summer evenings. We were informed that in addition to the flying we were expected to report to Store Street on Tuesday and Thursday of each week for lectures in navigation, airmanship, armament, signals and the like. We were warned in no uncertain terms that ground lectures and flying instruction had to proceed simultaneously and should we neglect the classrooms then our flying would be stopped immediately.

Attendance at Store Street on two evenings of each week, together with flying tuition on suitable evenings and every week-end, meant that my time was fully occupied. Our flying instructors were, in the main, released short-service R.A.F. pilots who earned a pleasant livelihood by offering their services to those firms who had contracted with the Air Ministry to train various numbers of V.R. pilots. Our ranks were made up from every walk of life, including farmers, engineers, stockbrokers, articled pupils, bank clerks and young men who were beginning their professional careers.

Competition was very keen, and at frequent intervals in our

flying training we were tested for progress and general ability by competent flying instructors from the R.A.F. proper. As a result of these tests it was not an uncommon occurrence for a pupil to be washed-out; so were those of us who either failed consistently to attend the ground lectures or fared badly in the various examinations. Despite the expansion of the V.R. there was still a great pool of waiting candidates, and for every one of us who fell out there were a dozen applicants ready to take his place.

At Stapleford Tawney we newcomers received our instruction in Tiger Moths while the veterans, who spoke a different language, were watched with some reverence as they walked across the grass airfield to their waiting Hawker Hart aeroplanes. Sometimes the relative serenity of our small area of sky over Essex was shattered by the appearance of small formations of Hurricanes from the nearby airfield at North Weald as they tore through the sky.

"Keep a sharp look-out for those brutes," warned my instructor. "They come at you at a terrific speed and, head on, look no bigger than a razor blade."

In late August we received our mobilisation orders. We reported to Store Street, where we were simply told to return to our various homes, where detailed instructions would be sent. For a few days we kicked our heels and idled away the time as best we could. All doubts that this was yet another scare were put aside when, on 1st September, the German Army and the Luftwaffe combined to demonstrate to the rest of the world a new technique of warfare, the 'Blitzkrieg'. The Royal Air Force was now fully mobilised and already our fighter and light bomber squadrons had landed in France to form the Advanced Air Striking Force. Once more we reported to Store Street, but this time we were warned to bring our personal belongings. After listening to the broadcast by the Prime Minister and hearing London's sirens for the first time, several hundred of us were put on a train to Cambridge.

On our arrival we disgorged on to the platform and stood about in uncertain groups, for we had no inkling of the next move. Suddenly there arrived upon the scene an extremely neat, portly, red-complexioned warrant officer whom we later discovered to be Mr. Dalby. We heard him muttering to himself as he fussed about the platform:

"Never seen so many sergeants in all my life. Sergeants!
Sergeants! They're all sergeants. Not a corporal among 'em!"

From this interesting soliloquy we gathered that Mr. Dalby was
not greatly impressed by his first contact with the Volunteer
Reservists. He grabbed me by the arm.

"Sergeant," with due emphasis on this important rank which
doubtless had taken him many long years to reach, "you're section
leader of this crowd here," and he waved a deprecating hand in the
direction of a mere two hundred of my colleagues. "Can you,
sergeant, form them up in fours and follow the first bunch which I
shall lead? Are you capable of this, sergeant?" With the amount of
dignity necessary for the occasion I assured him that I could and I
was careful to call him 'sir', a courtesy invariably rendered to one
of warrant rank by a lesser mortal. And so, with Mr. Dalby buzzing
up and down our long column, we marched through Cambridge to
Jesus College, which was to be our home for the next few weeks.

Enthusiastic aircrew of the Volunteer Reserve continued to
move into the various colleges, and Magdalene, St. John's, Trinity
and others soon received their quotas of wingless sergeant-pilots.
We were told that we should remain at Cambridge until such time
as we could be absorbed by the various flying training schools.

Early in December some thirty of us were called together and
told that on the following day we were to march to Marshall's
airfield, on the outskirts of Cambridge, where we would resume
our flying training on Tiger Moths. Before the war, Marshall's had
been a civilian flying school and, under contract to the Air
Ministry, had trained a number of locally recruited V.R.s. Most of
the peace-time instructors, now either officers or sergeant-pilots,
still remained, and for the next few months our destinies would be
in their hands.

Instructing is a great and difficult art and it does not necessarily
follow that a good pilot will make a satisfactory instructor. Some
types we had the misfortune to fly with claimed to be so anxious to
get on operations that their talents were wasted on a bunch of ham-
fisted pupils. This attitude was reflected not only in their approach
to their jobs but also in the product they turned out. An untimely

and ill-conceived criticism, when a word of encouragement would have been more appropriate to the occasion, often dismayed and retarded a nervous beginner. It was not uncommon knowledge that some washed-out pilots would have graduated had the right bond of understanding and confidence been established, in the first instance, between pupil and instructor.

Personally I was lucky at Marshall's, since four of us were assigned to Sergeant Tappin and 'Tap', although to his face we addressed him with a respectful 'sir', was the very best type of instructor. A gentle, unassuming man, he flew beautifully and went to great lengths to foster a good spirit with his pupils. Tap could always find time to explain a tricky point of airmanship, and when we walked across the tarmac at the end of a period of dual instruction he would retrace the pattern of the flight and make certain that the various lessons were driven home.

Our course at Marshall's finished in the spring at about the same time as the squadrons of the Luftwaffe and the armoured columns of the German Army struck across the frontier of Germany into the territories of the optimistic neutrals. My log book records that I left Marshall's with the modest total of eighty-four flying hours, and I had passed the various ground examinations. On our last evening a few of us clubbed together and invited our instructors to dine at a local hostelry. We had a good party, but I detected a wistful air about the instructors when it was time to say good-bye. We were to move on to Service flying training schools, where we would fly monoplane aircraft, and in ten weeks' time, if all went well, we could anticipate joining our operational squadrons. But the instructors would remain at Marshall's, training batch after batch of beginners and with little opportunity of flying modern aircraft. Some of the keener types eventually badgered their way to the combat squadrons, but the majority remained anchored to the training machine, where they carried out their essential tasks throughout the war.

Chapter Two

TRAINING DAYS

With 'Butch' Lyons, who was Jewish and operated a butcher's shop in a fashionable quarter of London, we drove from Cambridge to the flying training school at Sealand, near Chester, where we were to continue our flying. We arrived at the guardroom late one Saturday evening and experienced some difficulty, for we were not included in the list of pupils to be accommodated in the sergeants' mess. After some enquiries we found that a few of us had been recommended for commissions and during our time at Sealand we should be rated as officer-cadets and live in the officers' mess. This was an important milestone in our progress and we walked to the mess, where an aged servant conducted us to our quarters. Although we slept in wooden huts, the mess itself was a comfortable, permanent building where the food was superb and the service beyond reproach. The majority of the mess servants had served here for a number of years and bore themselves with a quiet dignity. Soon we were assembled by a young, self-assured flight lieutenant, who took some pains to point out that as cadets we were very much on probation and our behaviour would be carefully watched.

Once again I was fortunate to have a good instructor, and Sergeant Broad sent me off solo in a Miles Master after two dual trips. The Master was a pleasant aircraft to fly, being reasonably fast and having a higher ceiling than anything we had flown so far. On grey, leaden days when the overcast hung low across the Cheshire plain I thrilled to the sensation of climbing through the cloud formations into the dazzling beauty of the sun-drenched cloud-tops.

Our time at Sealand was in marked contrast to the leisure of our Cambridge days. Towards the end of June we scanned the headlines of the papers and listened to the momentous bulletins of the B.B.C. What remained of the squadrons of the Advanced

Striking Force had been withdrawn from a prostrate France. The epic withdrawal of the B.E.F. had taken place and high above the Dunkirk beaches fighter squadrons of 11 Group had challenged the domination of the Luftwaffe's Messerschmitts All these great events were reflected in the tempo of our life at Sealand, and we flew throughout the week-ends and from dawn until dusk in a determined attempt to speed up the complicated progress of the training machine.

I had one unpleasant experience at Sealand. The Luftwaffe had made an accurate reconnaissance of the airfield and once or twice we were attacked whilst night flying was in progress. It was therefore decided that in future this training would be carried out from an isolated, satellite airfield where it was improbable that a dimly lighted flare path would attract the enemy intruders. Late one afternoon we climbed into the back of a lorry and were driven, in some discomfort, to the distant base. Just before it got dark, half a dozen Masters, flown by our instructors, appeared from the west and landed. A fair amount of thick haze and smoke drifted down-wind from industrial Lancashire and the visibility was very limited and getting worse. After some discussion the senior instructor decided that night flying would take place.

I was detailed to fly dual in the programme, and before we took off I remembered the basic problem of instrument flight. Most of the flying on this dark, moonless night would be carried out on instruments and I must take care not to fly 'by the seat of my pants'. Once in the air, the 'feel' of the aircraft as interpreted through one's natural senses bears absolutely no relationship to its actual attitude, which is always displayed correctly by the various instruments. Until one is fully experienced on instrument work and procedures, one is sometimes bewildered by the mental confusion arising from this conflict of feel and the true attitude of the aircraft. Such confusion can easily lead to a disturbed mental state, when dangerous and fatal mistakes are made.

My first few circuits, with the instructor in the back seat giving a running commentary on the form together with our position in relation to the flare path, were uneventful enough, and after an hour of this we taxied in for a break and a cigarette before my solo effort.

The industrial smoke from the north had increased and when I trundled the Master across the grass I noticed, with some dismay, that the visibility had worsened since our previous flight. I had a strong urge to turn back and simply say that the conditions were too bad for my limited night experience, but the winking green light from the end of the runway urged me on. Full of apprehensions, I tore down the uneven surface of the flare path. A bump or two and we were airborne. Wheels up. Throttle back to climbing revs. Concentrate on the instruments. 500 feet and all's well so far. A slow, climbing turn to port through 180 degrees and level out at 1,000 feet. Throttle back again, this time to cruising revs. Trim the Master to fly with the least pressures from feet and hands. All set. The flare path is about 1,000 yards distant on the port side. Or is it? I peered from the cockpit, but all I could see were the eerie opaque reflections from the red and green wing-tip lights on the swirling cloud. This was my third trip at night in a Master, and my second solo experience, and to make matters worse I suddenly hit some turbulent air. The Master didn't feel right, and in a moment of panic I had the most vivid sensation that she was plunging earthwards in a steep twisting dive and automatically I began to take corrective action. But the instruments revealed that she was flying straight and level with a slight tendency to climb. Concentrate on the instruments! I concentrate to such an extent that my grip on the stick is like a vice and my feet are braced against the rudder pedals as if they were steel struts. Relax! Sing or swear or shout! But relax, and with only the slightest pressures from feet and hands climb through the cloud for safety. And time to think.

At 3,000 feet, we lurched out into a clear sky. There was no moon but the stars seemed bright and friendly after the cold, treacherous belly of the cloud. Soon I could make out a vague but real horizon and obtained some relief from the strain of the unaccustomed instrument work. Remote in a world bounded by cloud and stars, I found time to determine the next step, and reasoned judgement gradually replaced the near panic of a few moments ago. I had no radio to guide me back to the airfield, which was now shrouded in cloud down to about 600 feet. The local countryside was hilly; the foot-hills of the Welsh mountains were but a few miles away and to the east the Pennine Chain reared its formidable bulk. I had sufficient petrol for about half an hour, and in this time I had to be on the ground in one piece, either with the 'Master or in my parachute. I was careful to fly for five minutes on one course and then to turn on to its exact reciprocal for a similar period. In this manner I wouldn't drift from the vicinity of the airfield, which I must try and find. I would make my let-down to the west, for this course would take me away from the hills to the flat Lancashire coast. I would descend to 500 feet, try to pick up my position, and if this proved to be impossible I would climb and bale out. Now that I had a definite course of action I felt considerably better and I tightened the harness straps, checked my parachute webbing, and began the descent.

The stars vanished as the Master slipped into the top of the cloud and once more we were imprisoned in a hostile world of clammy, swirling vapour. Now we are descending at 500 feet a minute. Rather gentle but still fast enough to make a nasty hole in a hillside! Nonsense! Concentrate on the job. Still in the 'clag'[1] at 1,000 feet. Once more tremors of fear wrestle with logic and training. 800 feet! At 600 the cloud thins and I see a glimmer of light from some remote farmhouse. Now, a square search for the airfield. Two minutes on each of the four legs and then if I haven't found it back through the clouds for the jump. Two minutes to the south – no luck. Two minutes to the west and not a sign of activity. Then to the north and I see a wavering pencil of light playing to and fro on the base of the cloud. I speed towards it and as I circle over the thin beam I see the lights of the flare path below. I have to repress a wild instinct to smack the Master on to the flare path there and then. Deliberately, I carry out a wide, slow circuit and flash out the identification letter of my aircraft. My signal is acknowledged from the ground. I put her down and taxi in to our dispersal, feeling quietly elated at having reached the ground without breaking either myself or the Master.

[1] Pilot's jargon for cloud.

The senior instructor intercepted me as I walked away.

"What happened to you?" he exclaimed.

"I straightened out at 1,000 feet, sir, and couldn't see the flare path. I was in cloud."

"Yes you were, you idiot! The cloud had dropped to 600 feet. Why didn't you stay below it?"

I answered defensively: "I was briefed to fly circuits at 1,000 feet. I didn't know the cloud had dropped until I was in it."

"I realise that," he said. "But surely you have enough sense to fly below cloud. It's obvious to me that you require far more night flying practice." It was equally obvious to me that he should have exercised better judgement than to permit an inexperienced pupil to fly solo under such conditions, so I smothered the strong resentment that flared up in me against this stupid man, and went to bed. But we never flew again at night except when there was a clear sky.

Our course at Sealand ended during the last few days of July. Six or seven of us were interviewed by the commanding officer and recommended for commissions. We ordered our new uniforms and a few days later we reported to an operational training unit at Hawarden, only a few miles from Sealand, where we would fly Spitfires for a few hours before joining our squadrons.

The day I flew a Spitfire for the first time was one to remember. To begin with the instructor walked me round the lean fighter plane, drab in its war coat of grey and green camouflage paint, and explained the flight-control system. Afterwards I climbed into the cockpit while he stood on the wing root and explained the functions of the various controls. I was oppressed by the narrow cockpit for I am reasonably wide across the shoulders and when I sat on the parachute each forearm rubbed uncomfortably on the metal sides.

"Bit tight across the shoulders for me?" I enquired.

"You'll soon get used to it," he replied. "Surprising how small you can get when one of those yellow-nosed brutes is on your tail. You'll keep your head down then! And get a stiff neck from looking behind. Otherwise you won't last long!" – and with this boost to my morale we pressed on with the lesson. After a further half-hour spent memorising the various emergency procedures and the handling characteristics, the instructor checked my harness straps and watched while I adjusted the leather flying-helmet.

"'Start her up!"

I carried out the correct drill and the Merlin sprang into life with its usual song of power, a sound no fighter pilot will easily forget. The instructor bellowed into my ear:

"'You're trimmed for take-off. Don't forget your fine pitch, otherwise you'll never get off the ground. Good luck." And he ambled away with a nonchalant air, but I knew that he would watch my take-off and landing with critical eyes.

I trundled awkwardly over the grass surface swinging the Spitfire from side to side with brakes and bursts of throttle. This business was very necessary, for the long, high nose of the aircraft made direct forward vision impossible and more than one pupil had recently collided with other Spitfires or petrol bowsers. I reached the very edge of the airfield, and before turning into wind carried out a final cockpit check. No aircraft was in sight on the circuit and I had the whole airfield to myself. I swung her nose into the wind. No more delays now, get off. Throttle gently but firmly open to about four pounds of boost. She accelerates very quickly, much faster than the Master. Stick forward to lift the tail and get a good airflow over the elevators. Correct a tendency to swing with coarse rudder. No more bouncing about. We can't be airborne yet! Yes, we are, and already climbing into the sky. Things move fast in the Spitfire! Wheels up. Pitch control back and throttle set to give a climbing speed of 200 m.p.h. Close the hood. After a struggle, during which the nose rose and fell like the flight of a magpie, I closed the perspex canopy and the cockpit seemed even more restricted than before. I toyed with the idea of flying with the hood open, but I could not fly or fight at high altitudes in this fashion and I must get acquainted with every feature of the plane.

Now it was time to take a firm hand with this little thoroughbred, for so far she had been the dominant partner in our enterprise. I carried out an easy turn and tried to pick up my bearings. Not more than four or five minutes since take-off, but already we were more than twenty miles from Hawarden. I flew back, gaining confidence with every second. A Master looms ahead and slightly below. I overtake him comfortably, and to demonstrate my superiority attempt an upward roll. I forget to allow for the heavy nose of the Spitfire with sufficient forward movement of the stick and we barrel out of the manoeuvre, losing an undignified amount of height. Better concentrate on the handling characteristics and leave the aerobatics for another day. Over Hawarden again. Throttle back to a circuit speed. Hood open. All clear ahead. Wheels down and curve her across wind. Now the flaps and a final turn into wind. 120 m.p.h. on the approach and we are too high. Throttle back and she drops like a stone. 100 m.p.h. and over the boundary. Stick back and head over the side to judge the landing. Too high and in a semi-stalled condition we drop out of the sky to hit the unyielding ground with a hefty smack. As I suspected, my instructor had seen it all and was there when I switched off the engine.

" I saw the Spit get you into the air! And given a fair chance she would have carried out a better landing than yours! If you make a mess of your approach, open up and go round again. You've been told that with every plane you've flown. Get into the front seat of that Master and I'll show you a Spitfire circuit."

To be relegated back to the second team, as it were, was a severe jolt to my pride.

"'Right, I've got her, Johnson. We're on the down-wind leg. The Spit is heavier than the Master and soon loses height when you cut the power. So make your circuit tight and try to get a steady, continuous turn from here. It looks good. You're down quickly, and if you're turning you can watch the sky behind. Remember that when you're down south, for you're a sitting duck on the circuit! Wheels down and adjust the trim. Flaps down. Continue the turn. Now into wind. Plenty of height – perhaps a little too much so we side-slip a bit off – so! Throttle right back. Ease back the stick and check her. She's sinking. Stick right back and she's down. Piece of cake, isn't it?"

Four days later I made a mess of the approach, but this time with disastrous results. I had been instructed to land at Sealand and deliver a small parcel of maps which were stuffed into my flying-boot. The circuit at Sealand was crowded with Masters and I weaved amongst them for a favourable into-wind position. There was a stiff wind across the short, grass airfield and I aimed to be down close to the boundary fence so that I had the maximum distance for the landing run. I came over the fence too high and too slow and the fully stalled Spitfire dropped like a bomb. We hit the ground with a mighty crash and I had a little too much slack in the harness straps, for I was thrown violently forward and pulled up with a nasty wrench across the shoulders. For a few yards we tore a deep groove in the ground, then she slithered to a standstill in a ground loop which tore off one under-carriage leg and forced the other through the top of the port mainplane. I switched off the petrol cocks and the ignition switches and stepped out. The duty officer, an immaculate flight lieutenant complete with webbing and revolver, stepped out of a car and eyed me coldly:

"It was quite apparent you were going to prang. You were too high, too slow, not enough power, a poor approach..." And so on. "Don't you know the country's short of Spitfires? What do you want here anyway?"

"I was told to deliver these," I replied. And handed him the maps.

I found my way back to Hawarden and reported the dismal facts to the flight commander. He was a good type and made allowances for the fact that I was trying to get into a short airfield. He had me airborne in another Spitfire very shortly afterwards and I heard no more of the incident. But I was suspect and knew that my flying was watched closely. Another prang and I would certainly be washed-out.

At this time the problem of Fighter Command was not so much the replacement of Hurricanes and Spitfires as the maintenance of a steady, continuous flow of pilots to the operational squadrons. The number of trained pilots was far less at the beginning of September 1940 than at the corresponding time in August. A further reason for some anxiety was the fact that we V.R.s who were replacing casualties were not of the same high quality as the dead and wounded pilots. Our time at Hawarden was spent in learning how to fly the Spitfire; during my few days there I never fired the eight guns or took part in any tactical training. This would come later, if there was time.

Our instructors were a seasoned bunch of fighter pilots, most of whom had fought in France, over Dunkirk or in the preliminary phases of the Battle of Britain. One or two of them wore the mauve-and-silver ribbon of the Distinguished Flying Cross, but they rarely spoke to the pupils of their combats against the Messerschmitts. The unit at Hawarden had only been formed a short time and lectures on combat tactics had not yet been devised. How we longed for this knowledge! What went on when flights of Spitfires and Messerschmitts met? When squadron met squadron and wing encountered wing? Could the 109s turn inside us? What about their new cannon that fired through the hub of the propeller? What happened when they hurtled down from out of the sun? Were they aggressive, these fighter pilots who had inherited the traditions of Von Richthofen[1], the 'Red Knight' of the First World War? And what about their formation leaders who had tested their aircraft and tactics in the Spanish Civil War? What was the most important asset of a fighter pilot – to shoot straight, to keep a good look-out or to be able to stay with his leader at all times?

All these and a hundred other questions remained unanswered, for the handful of instructors hung together and had their work cut out to keep the sausage machine turning. But occasionally, after a few beers, they struck up an animated conversation amongst themselves and we heard of 'tail-end Charlies' and 'weavers'. These conversations only served to confuse me, and I left Hawarden with anything but a clear-cut idea of what took place when Spitfire met Messerschmitt. I think this was true of every inexperienced fighter pilot who joined his squadron at this stage of the war. Perhaps there was no short-cut, no easy way, to the lessons that could be learnt by hard experience alone. Certainly

[1] Baron Manfred von Richthofen; Germany's ace fighter pilot of the First World War, called the 'Red Knight' because he fought in an all-red fighter.

with me it was only after many flights against the enemy that I could begin to trace the fabric of an air battle with all its intricate and swift-moving patterns.

Towards the end of August I was called into the adjutant's office and told to report to 19 Squadron at Duxford, near Cambridge. I packed my few possessions and set out to travel across England by train. I had a total of 205 hours in my log book, including twenty-three hours on Spitfires.

Chapter Three

HUN IN THE SUN

I met two other replacement pilots for 19 Squadron in the station adjutant's office at Duxford. We were told that the squadron operated from Fowlmere, a satellite airfield five or six miles distant, and after completing the usual formalities the three of us were driven to our new unit.

Fowlmere proved to be little more than a large grass meadow, and when we arrived only one or two Spitfires were dispersed on the airfield. We learnt that the squadron had been scrambled[1] half an hour previously.

The nearest Spitfire looked different from those we had flown at Hawarden, and I walked across the grass for a closer inspection. I found that a radical change had been made, for although the Merlin engine and the airframe were the same, the usual eight machine guns were replaced by two cannon.

Several armourers were busy stripping and cleaning these weapons and a young flying officer watched these proceedings and discussed various technicalities with a harassed-looking N.C.O. At an opportune moment I introduced myself and said that I was a newcomer to the squadron. He replied in an offhand fashion and began a long discourse about the new weapon. They had received their first cannon Spitfires at the beginning of July and had been trying to iron out the bugs ever since. They were the guinea-pigs of Fighter Command! Personally he wished he'd never seen the cannon. And so did every other member of the squadron. When they fired properly they were very effective against enemy bombers, for they possessed greater hitting power, a higher muzzle velocity and a longer range than the machine guns. But they seldom worked correctly. Only a few days ago, seven Spits had attacked a large mixed formation of enemy fighters and bombers. Three twin-engined Messerschmitt 110s

[1] Order to take-off immediately.

were destroyed, but six of the Spits had cannon stoppages, otherwise more Huns would have been clobbered.

On another occasion the whole squadron fought individual combats, but only two Spits succeeded in firing off their full load of shells. It was a hell of a bind and not altogether healthy when you had to fight your way out of a mob of Messerschmitts. All the pilots would far sooner have their eight-gun Spits. "I don't know how we shall find time to train you chaps. We've simply got to get these things working first." His woeful tale was interrupted by the roar of fighters and a bunch of Spitfires arrived overhead in a loose but neat formation.

"No scrap this time," said my companion more to himself than me "or they'd be coming back in ones and twos. Let's go and meet them."

The pilots left their aircraft and were soon grouped round the tall figure of their squadron leader.

They had just completed their third patrol of the day and so far had not met the Luftwaffe. Already for the two flight commanders were chalking the names of pilots for the next flight on a large blackboard. A wingless officer joined the group and said that Fighter Command had been on the blower[1]. The pilots fell silent and listened intently. The speaker went on to say that the squadron probably would be withdrawn from the battle until the faulty cannon were put right. They would move to an airfield farther north and would be replaced at Fowlmere by an eight-gun squadron.

The angry pilots loudly exclaimed their displeasure. Why couldn't they have their eight-gun fighters back? There were eight-gun Spitfires at Hawarden for training pupils? The young flying officer turned to me for confirmation and I nodded my head vigorously – glad to contribute something to this bitter discourse. All right, send the blasted cannon Spitfires to Hawarden and exchange them for the training Spitfires. Now the squadron leader who had remained silent stepped into the breach and soothed them with a promise that he would get on to the station commander at Duxford that very afternoon. Meanwhile, chaps, where was the tea?

While they were lounging about waiting for the telephone call

[1] Telephone.

from operations that would send them climbing to the south, the C.O. found time to greet us.

"Let me get your names straight. Forshaw, Johnson and Brown?" We nodded agreement. "How many hours on Spits?"

"Eighteen, sir."

"Twenty-three, sir."

"Nineteen, sir."

"Huuumph. We'll give you a few hours locally before we take you on ops. And we're having all this cannon trouble. Find a bed in the mess and come and see me tomorrow."

Soon the scramble came, and we watched the slender Spitfires when they tore across the airfield and rose into the early evening sky. They were to patrol Debden and in a few minutes might well be tangling with the high-flying Messerschmitts. We three newcomers made our way back to Duxford in a gloomy silence. On paper we were members of 19 Squadron, but a great gulf separated us from the handful of pilots who had disappeared into the infinite southern horizon.

Over our dinner we worked out our campaign. After the meal we would corner one or two experienced pilots and over a pint of beer we would try to learn something of the form.

Our little ruse succeeded, and soon we were listening to graphic accounts of dog-fights between Hurricane and Messerschmitt. Our new acquaintances were well qualified to speak with authority, for they were Czechs who, after the fall of their own country, had fought their way across Europe and now were members of 310 Squadron. Fortunately for us, they were not so reticent as their British contemporaries and soon we were with them – five miles high and breaking into Messerschmitt attacks which always seemed to streak out of the sun!

At that time the Luftwaffe were coming across southern England in large mixed numbers of fighters and bombers. Their bombing targets were our fighter airfields. The enemy formations generally consisted of between fifty and one hundred bombers – Heinkel 111s, Dornier 17s or Junkers 88s – escorted by gaggles of Messerschmitt 110 twin-engined 'destroyers' and the single-engined Messerschmitt 109s. The ratio of escorting fighters to bombers was about three to one, so that a bomber formation would often be accompanied by upwards of two hundred Messerschmitt 110 and 109 fighters. The Czechs went on to say how their sturdy Hurricanes were slower and less manoeuvrable than the Spitfires. Ideally, then, they should take on the heavy, slow Dorniers and Heinkels while the Spitfires held the high-flying Messerschmitts at bay. A good plan – yes. But so often it didn't work, for their Hurricanes were nearly always hammered by the 109s before they could get to the bombers.

The 109? They glanced at each other quickly with a suggestion of apprehension. A good fighting aeroplane with a better ceiling than either the Hurricane or the Spitfire. And very good guns in the Messerschmitt 109E, two 20-mm. cannon mounted in the wings and two machine guns. Led by veterans of the Spanish Civil War who knew a thing or two, including the value of surprise and the tactical importance of height and sun. The 110 didn't give you any trouble. In fact, it was slower than the Hurricane and was of little account. As soon as they were bounced, the 110 pilots formed a defensive circle. But this was easy to break up, as long as the 109s weren't lurking above. The 109s! Yes, you soon knew when they were about!

I ordered another round of beer.

What about our tactics? we demanded What sort of formations do we fly in? Line-astern or line-abreast?

When they first joined the R.A.F., the Czechs were told that they had to practise a number of set-piece attacks devised by Fighter Command. The book laid down various techniques whereby fighters attacked the bombers from various positions, including dead astern, directly below, below and astern, from the beam and ahead. Various formations were adopted by the fighters as they manoeuvred for the correct tactical position and the leader gave several orders when they swung into a precise co-ordinated attack. These types of textbook attacks called for accurate flying and lots of time. Time! This was the key to the whole business. For the presence of the aggressive hard-hitting 109s would not permit our fighters the time necessary to carry out elaborate manoeuvres. Tactics must be simple. Surprise if possible, and a straight-in attack – from the sun. Always with your number two guarding your tail. Always keep your head turning. It takes about four seconds to shoot down a fighter – so look round every three!

Squadron formations varied from unit to unit. There was no set rule, and the squadron commander of a unit decided how his chaps should fly. In peace-time the fighter squadrons had trained their formations on the basic and well-known 'vic' of three aircraft. Some squadrons still operated in this fashion and went into battle in four vics. Other squadrons had adopted a more open style and the pilots flew in three sections, each containing four aircraft. The four aircraft flew in line-astern and followed their leader, who weaved his aircraft laterally so that he could cover the blind spot to the rear; from immediately above the three sections looked like three writhing snakes. The great fault with this formation, continued the Czechs, was that when the leaders weaved violently the number fours, the tail-end Charlies, had all their work cut out to stay in formation and had little time to look behind. And so the tail-end Charlies were often the first to be clobbered, especially as they were invariably the newest pilots.

Had we heard of Douglas Bader, the legless pilot who commanded 242 Squadron? Most of his pilots were Canadians. Bader's squadron was based at Coltishall, in Norfolk, but he often brought his boys to operate from Duxford. The Czechs had heard Bader voice his strong opinions concerning the tactical value of large numbers of fighters. Bader had proposed that the two Duxford squadrons, 19 and 310, together with his own should form a wing. He would lead at the bottom of the gaggle. 310 would fly up-sun and some 2,000 feet higher, and 19 would guard the Hurricanes from a high, down-sun position. Thirty-six fighters. Yes, they would like to fight like this. It would be far better than the nibbling attacks of today.

The Czechs fell silent and finished their beer. They glanced at their watches. It was not yet ten o'clock, but they were on at dawn and wanted bags of sleep. Abruptly, and with some discreet heel-clicking, they withdrew from the ante-room.

After breakfast on the following morning we drove out to

Fowlmere; the squadron was already engaging upwards of 60 bombers escorted by 150 fighters high over North Weald.

They dribbled back in ones and twos and we listened to their accounts of the fight. Two of the enemy were destroyed and a further aircraft was severely damaged. It was the same unhappy story as before – cannon stoppages again, otherwise more Huns would have been sent down.

But there was some excellent news from Fighter Command. The commander-in-chief had decided that their cannon Spitfires were to be replaced by eight-gun fighters. These would arrive late that day and the squadron was to be fully Operational as soon as possible. This was not a major undertaking, but there would be plenty of work for both the ground crews and the pilots. Squadron identification letters to be painted on the Spitfires. Radios to be recrystalized. Guns to be tested if there was time, and the cannon Spitfires checked before they were flown away.

Two more days of this cloudless autumn dragged by and I had not even got near the cockpit of a Spitfire. Once again I watched the scramble and the return, some forty minutes later when, singly, they swung in to land. They had run into a bunch of bombers escorted by a strong force of Messerschmitts. Although the Spitfires were at a serious height disadvantage, the squadron leader had climbed B Flight into the bombers whilst A Flight struggled into the sun to ward off the Messerschmitts. But the enemy fighters ignored the highest Spitfires and concentrated on heading off B Flight before they could get to the bombers. Two Spitfires were badly shot up and the squadron leader had not returned.

Later that morning the squadron adjutant sent for us. "You chaps are to report to 616 Squadron at Coltishall at once. They've just been pulled out of the front line and will have time to train their new pilots. It's probably the best thing. You can see what the form is here. We must have experienced pilots who can take their place in the squadron." The phone rang and the adjutant listened for a few moments before he slowly replaced the receiver.

"They've found the C.O. Probably dead when he crashed."

For a moment he brooded.

"Well, good luck with 616."

Once again we took to the trains and made our way to the airfield at Coltishall in Norfolk. Soon we were ushered into the sparse office of the squadron commander and gave him brief details of our flying careers. Billy Burton was a short, well-knit young man of about my own age. He was a regular officer who, as a Cranwell cadet, had won the Sword of Honour in 1936. The war had brought him rapid promotion, but deservedly, for he was an outstanding product of the Cranwell system. Somewhat exacting in his demands, he was always full of vitality and enthusiasm. I liked him at first sight and have never served under a better or more loyal officer. From the outset he took us into his confidence.

"The squadron had a rough time at Kenley. They were only there a couple of weeks and lost quite a few chaps. They were pulled out of the front line two days ago and I was given the command. My job is to get it fully operational within the next few days, for we may go south again any time. Any questions?"

We remained silent.

"Right," continued the C.O. "You, Johnson, will fly with me in half an hour and we'll see what you're like. Wait for me in the car outside and I'll take you all down to our dispersal."

I tucked my Spitfire alongside the C.O.'s starboard wing and together we climbed over the stubbles and broads of East Anglia. It was a perfect evening for flying. Unlimited visibility and not a tremor as our Spitfires swung through the sky. After a few easy turns in close formation Burton tapped the back of his helmet and I slid into a line-astern position. Now the real business of the flight began. Fast power-dives when the air-speed indicator registered well over 400 m.p.h. Then up into a soaring climb at full throttle followed by a roll off the top of the loop. Slow rolls and barrel-rolls. Half-rolls and dives. Aileron-turns and stall-turns. And then a waggle of his wings – the signal to re-form in line-abreast formation.

After about an hour of this we landed at Coltishall, and although my right shoulder was painful my spirits were high because, after the set-backs of the previous week, I felt I was making some progress. I fell into step beside the C.O., who began to talk about tactics.

"Not bad, Johnson. Not bad at all. But you'll have to keep a better look-out. You'll have to learn to keep that thick neck of yours turning! Look round all the time. Your life depends on spotting the 109s before they bounce you. It's no use simply looking at the sky. Learn to focus your eyes on a particular area and scan it thoroughly. Every time you fly, look for any movement in the air and try and identify the type of aircraft you see. With practice you'll find that you can improve your eyesight tremendously."

We had reached the door of the dispersal hut, but the C.O. was not finished with me. He talked of the necessity for strict radio-telephone discipline at all times; the difficulties of deflection shooting and the technique of the killing shot from the line-astern or near line-astern positions; the duty of the number two whose primary job was not to shoot down aircraft but to see that the sky behind his leader was clear of enemy fighters; the importance of keeping a good battle formation and the tactical use of sun, cloud and height.

Inside the dispersal hut I was introduced to some of the original Auxiliary members of the squadron, who rose to their feet as Burton entered. I was immediately impressed by a thick-set pilot officer, with a ruddy, expansive complexion, who seemed considerably older than the rest of us. This character was Ken Holden, who had played rugby for Yorkshire on many occasions – and looked the part. Like Burton, he was married, although their wives lived some distance away. Ken had learnt to fly with the Auxiliary Air Force, at the ripe old age of 29. During the following years I came to know him well. Whatever the state of the war, he always insisted on his Saturday evening excursions. These consisted of changing into a good uniform immediately flying was over, a drive to the nearest sizeable town, plenty of good ale followed by a variety show, then dinner and more ale. Ken was a good mimic, always full of humour and a most lively and entertaining companion. But during our first few weeks together this side of his character was not revealed, and I thought he was inclined to be dour and cautious. His north-country wisdom tended to frustrate us younger chaps, who soon thought we knew all the answers and were dead keen to get at the Huns. Later, Ken became our flight commander and some of us who saw the war through owe our necks to his thoroughness and the lessons we learnt from him.

I met some other Auxiliary members of the squadron, including Buck Casson, who before the war was in the steel business in Sheffield. One or two of the sergeant-pilots had served with the unit for some time, and after the C.O. had left they sprawled about the hut reading magazines.

I did not like the atmosphere. The veterans kept to themselves and seemed aloof and very remote. Even to my inexperienced eye it was apparent that the quiet confidence of a well-led and disciplined team was missing from this group. There was a marked difference between the bunch of aggressive pilots I had met at Fowlmere and these too silent, apprehensive men. But my conjectures were interrupted by the approach of a stooping, donnish young officer who addressed me:

"My name is Gibbs. I am the squadron intelligence officer. If you have half an hour to spare you should read this. It is the operations record book of the squadron and will give you some food for thought!"

I thanked him and took the heavy volume to a seat near the window. For a few moments I flicked over the pages of this official history of the squadron. Before I began to read, I glanced again at the other occupants of the room. One or two of them watched me with curious eyes for here, between the drab covers of the volume I held, registered in terse and sometimes brutally abrupt language, was the credit and loss ledger, the life and death accounting of the squadron throughout the past twelve months.

No. 616 (South Yorkshire) Squadron, Auxiliary Air Force, was formed at Doncaster in 1938 under Squadron Leader the Earl of Lincoln. Some trained Auxiliary pilots from local squadrons were transferred to 616 and other pilots were recruited locally, as were the great majority of the ground crews.

Shortly after the outbreak of war a regular officer was posted to command the squadron, but he only remained a few months and Billy Burton became the fourth C.O. in little more than twelve months. The young and relatively raw Auxiliary pilots had never benefited from a continuous period of leadership and command.

During the winter of 1939, the Hawker Hinds and Avro Tutors were replaced by Spitfires, and the pilots first fired their guns in anger when they patrolled Dunkirk to help cover the evacuation of the B.E.F. During the withdrawal they operated from Rochford, but early in June they returned to their airfield in Yorkshire. They had quite a field day when the squadron intercepted a formation of about fifty Junkers 88s off Flamborough Head and destroyed eight without loss to themselves. The long North Sea crossing, flown by the enemy bombers, was far beyond the range of the Messerschmitt 109s, and on this occasion the pilots found that the unescorted bombers were fairly easy game.

In mid-August the squadron was sent to Kenley, which together with Biggin Hill protected the eastern flank of London. In early September they were withdrawn from the front line to Coltishall and during the previous fifteen-day period of fighting four pilots were killed, five were wounded and one became a prisoner of war. At Kenley the commission of one officer was terminated and another was posted away from the squadron. Of the original twenty pilots who made the journey south, only eight flew back to Coltishall, although some of the wounded pilots eventually rejoined the unit and fought again.

No unit could continue in the face of such losses, and, although the remaining pilots acquitted themselves well, it was inevitable that they should be withdrawn from the front line to gather their strength and train the replacements. This was Billy Burton's task. To restore the confidence of the older members and with the new arrivals weld the mixture into a fighting, aggressive team. How this was all achieved, and how Burton combined with Douglas Bader to build 616 into a tradition and a unit which holds an honoured place in the annals of Fighter Command is the early part of my story.

On the following Saturday, Burton walked into the dispersal hut after tea and said that the squadron readiness state could be reduced to one section of two aircraft. The rest of us were free for the remainder of the day, but before we left some pilots were detailed for the next morning's dawn readiness. After a bath and a quick change into a respectable uniform, a small party of pilots were soon jammed into an ancient car and bounced along the narrow, winding road which leads to Norwich.

Some hours later we were still wedged together in the crowded, stuffy bar of the 'Bell' when a posse of Service police stalked in and announced that all R.A.F. personnel were to report back to their airfields at once.

At Cottishall we found that Alert No. 1, 'invasion imminent and probable within twelve hours', had been declared by the responsible authorities and the defences were to be brought to the highest state of readiness. The scene in the mess could only be described as one of some confusion. Elderly officers, mobilised for the duration, darted about in various directions. Our own C.O. was not to be seen, and we tried to get a coherent explanation of the situation. We soon heard half a dozen different versions, the most popular of which was that the invasion was under way and some enemy landings were expected on the east coast. Perhaps the C.O. and the flight commanders were already at our dispersal, and I left the ante-room to make a telephone call from the hall. As I hastened along the corridor, I almost collided with a squadron leader who stumped towards me with an awkward gait. His vital eyes gave me a swift scrutiny, at my pilot's brevet and the one thin ring of a pilot officer.

"I say, old boy, what's all the flap about?" he exclaimed, legs apart and putting a match to his pipe.

"I don't really know, sir," I replied. "But there are reports of enemy landings."

The squadron leader pushed open the swing doors and stalked into the noisy, confused atmosphere of the ante-room. Fascinated, I followed in close line-astern because I thought I knew who this was. He took in the scene and then demanded in a loud voice, and in choice, fruity language, what all the panic was about. Half a dozen voices started to explain, and eventually he had some idea of the form. As he listened, his eyes swept round the room, lingered for a moment on us pilots and established a private bond of fellowship between us.

There was a moment's silence whilst he digested the news.

"So the bastards are coming. Bloody good show! Think of all

those juicy targets on those nice flat beaches. What shooting!" And he made a rude sound with his lips which was meant to resemble a ripple of machine-gun fire.

The effect was immediate and extraordinary. Officers went about their various tasks and the complicated machinery of the airfield began to function smoothly again. Later we were told that the reports of the enemy landings were false and that we could revert to our normal readiness states. But the incident left me with a profound impression of the qualities of leadership displayed in a moment of tension by the assertive squadron leader. It was my first encounter with the already legendary Douglas Bader.

Early the following week we flew to Kirton Lindsey, a new airfield some ten miles from Scunthorpe on the Lincolnshire plain. We were moving farther away from the air battle in the south, but we possessed only five or six experienced pilots and as a squadron were not yet ready for intensive operations. Sooner or later our turn would come, and personally I was grateful for this respite, for I gained confidence and learnt something of tactical value on every flight.

At Kirton Lindsey we were met and welcomed by the station commander, Stephen Hardy, who drove our C.O. and his flight commanders to the mess. Eventually we arrived there with our personal belongings. A dapper, bowing little man met us in the hall and introduced himself. He was Mr Smith, mess steward, and late of the Majestic Hotel at Harrogate. Indeed, a few potted palm-trees decorated the hall in the tradition of the spas. I felt that perhaps a string orchestra playing softly in the background would have fitted the occasion. Our C.O. and the two flight commanders, said Mr Smith, had already been conducted to their rooms. Were any of us flight lieutenants or flying officers? No, we answered, we were all pilot officers. Mr Smith looked distressed. He had a room for each of us, but only one possessed a wash basin with hot and cold water. Perhaps we could settle this delicate matter between ourselves? Ken picked up his bag and spoke to Mr Smith. It was not a question of negotiation but merely one of seniority, and the senior pilot officer took off in search of his wash basin!

The C.O. took full advantage of those cloudless autumn days

and kept us hard at it. More replacement, but inexperienced, pilots arrived and we built up to our quota of pilots. To the south the squadrons of 11 Group were meeting large mixed numbers of German fighters and bombers, but we were not sent into these dangerous skies. For the moment the squadron was held in reserve. Occasionally a section of Spitfires was scrambled to investigate 'bogey'[1] aircraft over Lincolnshire and the North Sea, but these turned out to be friendly.

On 15th September, Fighter Command's greatest day, I flew several times, but my efforts, like those of the remainder of 616 were confined to practice battle climbs to high altitude and firing my eight Brownings at a drogue towed behind another aircraft. Late that night we heard the tremendous news that our fighter pilots had shot down 185 German aircraft. This figure was of course subsequently reduced to 56 on the evidence of the official German Air Ministry figures which were made available after the war. Between 10th July and 31st October we claimed the destruction of 2,698 enemy aircraft, but, according to German records, actually shot down 1,733. Throughout the Battle of Britain we claimed about three aircraft for every two brought down. But it is interesting to see that the claims of the German fighter pilots were far less accurate than ours. During this period they claimed no less than 3,058 R.A.F. aircraft destroyed, but our actual losses were 915. The Germans claimed more than three victories for every aircraft they brought down.

Why should there be such discrepancies between the claims of fighter pilots and the actual losses inflicted on the enemy? During the Battle of Britain the hard-pressed intelligence officers had little time to sift and check the various claims. Our regulations prescribed that before an enemy aircraft could be claimed as destroyed it must be seen to crash, or going down in flames, or its pilot bail out. But the burning wreck of one aircraft or one white parachute spilling out against the sky were often glimpsed by many pilots when they twisted and turned five miles high. Very few of our Spitfires and Hurricanes were fitted with ciné cameras at this time, which again added to the difficulties of subsequent confirmation. And the pilots

[1] An unidentified aircraft.

themselves were often flying and fighting too hard to be bothered with accurate and detailed combat reports.

There can be no doubt that in the confused and intricate air fighting many of our claims were duplicated, but, wisely, those in authority were not concerned with mere numbers, but with the greater issues of whether or not the Luftwaffe was being held at bay.

Every fighter pilot has experienced the swift transformation from the confused mix-up of a dog-fight to the dangerous solitude of a seemingly empty world. For the sky is a big place. Its horizons are infinite and a man's capacity in its vastness is very limited. I was to learn from hard experience that in one moment the air space can be saturated with a hundred twisting Spitfires and Messerschmitts. Two or three parachutes blossom open and drift towards the earth below. The wing of a Hurricane, or is it a 109, spins lazily down like an autumn leaf. A plume of dark smoke draws a parabolic curve against the backcloth of the sky whilst high above the impersonal sun glints on the perspex canopies of the 109s.

Throughout it all the radio is never silent – shouts, oaths, exhortations and terse commands. You single out an opponent. Jockey for position. All clear behind! The bullets from your eight guns go pumping into his belly. He begins to smoke. But the wicked tracer sparkles and flashes over the top of your own cockpit and you break into a tight turn. Now you have two enemies. The 109 on your tail and your remorseless, ever-present opponent 'g', the force of gravity. Over your shoulder you can still see the ugly, questing snout of the 109. You tighten the turn. The Spit protests and shudders, and when the blood drains from your eyes you grey-out . But you keep turning, for life itself is the stake. And now your blood feels like molten lead and runs from head to legs. You black-out! And you ease the turn to recover in a grey, unreal world of spinning horizons. Cautiously you climb into the sun. You have lost too much height and your opponent has gone – disappeared. You are completely alone in your own bit of sky, bounded by the blue vault above and the coloured drapery of earth below.

My right shoulder was causing me a great deal of anxiety. At this time I didn't know that the rugby injury had been improperly set in 1938, and the crash at Sealand had given it a nasty wrench.

The old break at the collar-bone was tender and sore. I had to be careful when I swung the parachute straps over my shoulder and when I tightened the harness straps in the cockpit. I began to pack the shoulder with a wad of cotton-wool, which I wore next to the skin and held in place by strips of adhesive tape. But the trouble did not finish with the shoulder, for sometimes the fingers of the right hand seemed cold and lifeless and had little feel in them. Our Spitfires possessed fabric ailerons, and the stick pressures in a steep dive were so high that they aggravated the condition of the shoulder. Whenever I could, I held the control column with my left hand, but when the C.O. or Ken put me through my paces I had to resort to the right hand, for dog-fighting a Spitfire was a two-fisted affair. I began to land the aircraft with the left hand so that I had some degree of feel, but this was a dangerous procedure, for if I held off too high I couldn't use my left to ease her down with a burst of throttle.

I wanted to avoid an official examination by the doctors. Each day brought an added and welcome sense of acceptance by the veteran members of the squadron. Johnson had given way to a warmer contraction, Johnnie, and I was anxious to prove myself in combat and mix on equal terms with men. Life could offer no more at present than this simple ambition.

I remembered that before I played rugby again after the injury I had a long course of heat treatment and massage. Perhaps this would do the trick again.

In the mess I approached a young doctor, a flying officer, who also wore the small brass V.R. symbols on the lapels of his tunic. He was very solicitous when I told him of the trouble. When did I have the rugger accident? And the prang in the Spit? And when did the numbness start? We had better walk across to sick quarters and have a look at it.

I hedged at this suggestion, for it probably meant a searching examination with all the details on one's medical record. But the young doctor scorned the suggestion of such a breach of confidence and soon he was examining the shoulder and forearm. He carried out some small experiments with a needle, which he jabbed into the fingers of my right hand.

Even this treatment brought little response although some of the pricks left faint smears of blood. In the midst of all this another and more senior medical officer entered. What was the trouble? The young doctor explained, and his colleague also carried out a searching examination.

Both docs were charming. Yes, the shoulder would probably feel better after heat treatment and massage. But it might be a good thing to have an X-ray sometime. Just to be certain. For the present they would pack the shoulder with cotton-wool and I was to avoid straining the arm. Come back in a couple of days, they told me, and we'll have another look at it.

On the following morning I was about to fly when Burton strode into the dispersal hut.

"There you are, Johnson. The station commander wants to see you at once. You'd better come with me. He wants me there too."

The C.O. was silent when we drove round the perimeter track to station headquarters. I muttered something about wondering what it was all about, but he would not be drawn.

We were shown into the station commander's room. Stephen Hardy shifted his six-and-a-half-foot frame in his chair and acknowledged my salute with a faint nod. He did not invite me to stand at ease, and even Burton stood rigidly at attention a pace behind. It was a formal interview and the atmosphere was cool. Hardy came straight to the point:

"Well, Johnson, the docs tell me that you are suffering from some affliction to your right shoulder." He glanced through the window at a couple of Spitfires which were climbing into the clean September sky. "So I am grounding you. All our pilots must be 100 per cent. fit. As I see it, there are two alternatives open to you. Apparently your shoulder didn't trouble you during your training when you flew light aircraft. So I could have you transferred to Training Command, where you could instruct on Tiger Moths."

Hardy paused and looked out of the window again. He eased the neckband of his shirt with some irritation and I suddenly knew why the incident was so distasteful to him. He suspected that I was suffering from a not unknown malady known officially as 'lack of moral fibre'. We pilots had another name for it. No doubt he thought I was using my shoulder as an excuse to escape operations.

"Or you can take your chance on the operating table. The docs think that if your shoulder was opened up and re-set there would be a good chance of getting it right once and for all. The choice is yours."

I did not hesitate.

"When can I go into hospital, sir?"

The tension broke, and the wing commander stretched his tall frame and grinned. Even Billy Burton forgot his Cranwell training and produced a battered pipe.

"Well, Johnnie, I'll get on the blower straight away and fix it up. It will be some time before you fly again. Do you want him back, Billy?"

For a second my future hung in the balance, either to rejoin the squadron or to be sent to a fighter pool and posted to the first vacancy.

"I think we can make something of him, sir," answered Burton. "He's not shaping too badly."

At the R.A.F. hospital at Rauceby, in Lincolnshire, my shoulder was fixed up by a brilliant young surgeon serving for the duration of the war. At the end of the year I was pronounced fit for full flying duties and made preparations to rejoin the squadron, grateful to the Service and the understanding officers in it. They had afforded me a second chance and the opportunity to live and fight with men of the calibre of Billy Burton and the senior pilot officer.

Chapter Four

FIGHTING TALK

When I returned to the squadron in December the golden autumn had given way to the grey shroud which cloaks our island during the winter months. The weather had closed in and with it the daylight offensive of the Luftwaffe had come to a complete standstill. But the enemy Air Force was far from being defeated, as the strength of their formations and their subsequent campaigns bear witness. Rather had they been held by the R.A.F. and prevented from gaining their immediate objective of air superiority over southern England, the essential prelude to a successful Nazi invasion. The margin by which they had been held was a very slender one, and at one time the elimination of Fighter Command as an effective force had been more than a possibility. That the Command survived this crucial period was due not only to the superior fighting qualities of our pilots but also to gross errors of strategy and tactics by the Germans.

It was interesting to watch the well-known German rigidity of mind at work in their approach to the battle with the R.A.F. Their plan against the Polish Air Force had been gloriously successful, so why, with a few modifications here and there to allow for the greater strength of the R.A.F., should such a plan not succeed equally brilliantly against us? Thus we saw the Luftwaffe switch from one target system to another after a given period, apparently regardless of the success or otherwise of the attack. Finally, at the insistence of Hitler himself, the attack was switched to London, thereby affording Fighter Command the respite it so desperately needed, and which it was unable at the time to get for itself. From then on the outcome was no longer in doubt.

Undoubtedly the Germans failed to appreciate the effort needed to knock out our well-trained and scientifically backed Air Force, and they also failed to allow for the recuperative powers of the R.A.F. Undoubtedly, too, had the Luftwaffe persisted with attacks against our airfields in southern England, the result would have been different. But it is not my intention to analyse the Battle of Britain in all its phases; this has already been done, and by abler pens than mine. To us fighter pilots this period is full of interest from a tactical point of view because the tactics developed by both sides formed the basis upon which our air battles were fought for the remainder of the war. It is worth examining these tactics and some of the differing opinions held by those in authority at the time, since they form an essential back-ground to the rest of my story.

The Luftwaffe possessed some excellent aeroplanes, and the Messerschmitt 109E had a higher ceiling and better guns than either the Spitfire or the Hurricane. The enemy fighter carried either four machine guns or two machine guns and two cannon; the latter compared very favourably with our eight Browning machine guns. The 109F, which was soon to make its appearance over England, had one cannon which was centrally mounted and fired through the hub of the air-screw, and later versions of this splendid fighter had three cannon.

During the fighting over Dunkirk our pilots found that their Spitfires had slight margins of speed and climb over the 109E. But most of these fights took place below 20,000 feet, and later, when we had to fight well above this height, it was soon discovered that the enemy fighter was decidedly superior because its supercharger was designed to operate more efficiently at the higher altitudes. When the Messerschmitt took evasive action by half-rolling and diving vertically for the deck, we found that we couldn't stay with it in this manoeuvre. Certainly the Spitfire was more manoeuvrable, but manoeuvring does not win air battles, and tight turns are more of a defensive than an offensive tactic. The Spitfire's rate of turn would get you out of trouble if you saw your attacker in time, but only superior height would save you from the 'bounce'.

The Luftwaffe pinned great hopes on the stable companion of the 109, the twin-engined Messerschmitt 110D, 'destroyer' fighter. It had a greater range than the 109 and was accordingly often employed as a close escort to the bomber formations. It carried a formidable number of cannon, but it could not hold its own against either Spitfire or Hurricane. On more than one occasion the 109 had to help the twin-engined fighters out of a tight spot.

The Junkers 87 dive-bomber, the Stuka, had enjoyed great success as a close-support weapon in the recent campaigns. It was little more than a piece of flying artillery and it could dive very steeply at a low forward speed. This meant that the pilot could line up his diving aircraft against a ground target with great accuracy and release his bombs when he pulled out at low level. But one of the basic principles of the employment of close-support aircraft is that they must be capable of holding their own against contemporary fighters. The Stuka contradicted this simple truth and paid the price in full when it met our Spitfires.

Of the three types of enemy bombers, the Heinkel 111, the Dornier 17 and the Junkers 88, the last named was superior to the other two and quite the most difficult to bring down. It had a high top speed, and when it dived with wide-open throttles our Spitfires couldn't catch it.

Morale was high in the Luftwaffe. Their young fighter leaders had fought in the Spanish Civil War and had then blazed their way across half Europe. Their fighter tactics were more advanced than ours and they were highly critical of our tight fighter formations.

Before the war our own fighter squadrons, together with those of other countries, flew in compact formations built up from tight elements of three aeroplanes. Such formations were ideal for spectacular fly-pasts, and although every fighter pilot must be able to 'formate.' closely on his leader to climb through cloud, this close style was to be of little value in the great air battles.

In Spain the German fighter pilots soon realised that the speed of their 109s made close formations impracticable for combat. The large turning circle of the curving fighters dictated that a loose pattern was the only method in which individual pilots could hold their position in the turn and keep a sharp look-out at the same time. The high closing speeds, especially from head-on positions, made it essential to pick out and identify enemy aircraft as soon as possible, so that the leader could work his way into a good attacking position.

The simple requirement was for a loose, open type of combat

formation with the various aeroplanes flying at separated heights which would permit individual pilots to cover each other and search a greater area of sky than before.

Credit must be given to the Germans for devising the perfect fighter formation. It was based on what they called the *rotte*, that is the element of two fighters. Some two hundred yards separated a pair of fighters and the main responsibility of the number two, or wingman, was to guard his leader from a quarter or an astern attack. Meanwhile the leader navigated his small force and covered his wingman. The *schwarme*, four fighters, simply consisted of two pairs, and when we eventually copied the Luftwaffe and adopted this pattern we called it the 'finger-four' because the relative positions of the fighters are similar to a plan view of one's four finger-tips.

Let us examine the outstretched finger-tips of the right hand and assume that the sun is shining from well above on the left side. The longest finger represents the leader and the index finger is the leader's number two, whose task it is to search the down-sun area of the sky. The wingman flies lower than his leader so that the pilots can see him well below the direct glare of the sun. An attack will usually develop from the sun, so we must have a constant search maintained in this direction. This is why numbers three and four fly on the right side of the leader, but slightly higher, so that we have two pairs of eyes always scanning the danger area.

When you fly your Spitfire five miles above the earth you will find that your wings hide a good deal of the ground and sky below. Suppose you are crossing the coast and Margate is just disappearing under your nose. The port wing-tip is over Clacton, the starboard wing-tip slides across Dungeness, and Maidstone is just reappearing from the trailing edge of the wing. In other words, an area of about one thousand square miles is always hidden from your view at this height. But the finger-four, if properly flown in varying height intervals, is the best means of covering these blind spots below individual aircraft. The formation is loose and manoeuvrable. The three pilots following the leader can search their respective areas of sky and keep him in sight without a great deal of uncomfortable neck twisting. The finger-four is easy to fly and far less tiring than the line-astern style. It permits an excellent all-round view, and the two wingmen, numbers two and four, separated by a distance of five or six hundred yards, can guard the vital area above and behind. It is easily split up into its basic elements of two aircraft, the smallest fighting unit in the air, since a lone pilot cannot protect himself from all quarters at the same time. It is a simple matter to build it into a squadron or wing formation. It is a great boost to morale, for the number four in a line-astern formation, tail-end Charlie, knows full well that if his section is bounced he will be the first to take a beating. But his equivalent in the abreast formation is well up with his comrades and stands an equal chance of survival.

Some critics of the finger-four claimed that frequent turns made it difficult for the two wingmen to hold their flanking positions, but our pilots simply slipped into line-astern positions behind their leaders during tight turns and combat manoeuvres. We found this criticism to be unjustified, and it is an interesting fact that towards the end of the war the finger-four was flown by fighter aircraft throughout the world. It has survived the test of time and the jet age, for it was used by both Sabre-jets and Mig 15s during the near-sonic fighting over Korea. Today, supersonic fighters carry out their operational training at speeds of over 1,000 m.p.h. in this well-proved fashion.

Upon his return to Germany after a tour of operations in Spain, that great fighter pilot Werner Mölders advocated that the open formation should be standard throughout their fighter arm. Tactically the German fighter squadrons were ahead of us, for our two types of formation were either built up from a tight vic of three aircraft or four in line-astern. The vic of three had little to recommend it and was an unfortunate legacy of peace-time flying, for the two wingmen had all their work cut out to stay near their leader and little time to search the sky. The high casualty rate of the wretched tail-end Charlies was a grim measure of the vulnerability of the line-astern formations. A further disadvantage of both these patterns was that the tightly packed aircraft were far more conspicuous in a clear sky than the widely spaced fighters of the finger-four.

Some of our squadrons provided two weavers in an attempt to guard themselves from the bounce. The weavers flew above the squadron and continually weaved and criss-crossed. They were usually the first to be picked off by the Messerschmitts, and the practice was stopped.

Apart from our combat formations we lagged behind the Luftwaffe in our methods of attacking enemy aircraft. At Coltishall we were taught various types of attack in which we carried out a series of lengthy and complicated manoeuvres before firing at the bombers. We were not told how the high Messerschmitts were supposed to be occupying their time whilst we carried out these lengthy procedures.

The fighter is simply a flying gun, and its basic qualities of speed and surprise should always be used to the greatest advantage. The outstanding pilots of an earlier generation than ours soon found that the leader with the height advantage controls the battle. With height the fighter leader can use the sun or cloud cover to the best tactical advantage. Those fighter pilots of earlier days had coined an apt phrase, 'Beware of the Hun in the sun', and its warning was no less potent today.

In the thirties there was a growing body of opinion that manoeuvres at high speeds were impossible because of the effects of 'g' on the pilot. Dog-fighting at speeds over 400 m.p.h., said the critics, is no longer possible. And so we had to learn, the hard way, that fighter tactics must be simple in character because elaborate techniques are not possible within the critical time available. A leader cannot retain control of even a small formation through a lot of complicated manoeuvres, because the force is soon split up into individual, ineffective packets. Tactics must be simple, and the leader's task is to bring all the guns of his fighters to bear against the enemy in the shortest time. Leadership in the air consists not in scoring a personal kill but in the achievement of a decisive success with the whole force.

During his interrogation by the Allies at the end of the war and subsequently in his book[1], Adolf Galland, one of Germany's greatest fighter pilots, accused his commander-in-chief of faulty

[1] *The First and Last*, published by Methuen & Co.

direction and tactical misemployment of their fighter forces during the Battle of Britain. Galland asserts that Göring cut down the offensive power of his fighter squadrons by ordering them to act in an escort rôle and not permitting them to leave the bombers even when they could see Spitfires or Hurricanes manoeuvring for attack. Before examining the validity of Galland's claims it is necessary to know something of the theory of bomber support and escort by fighters.

The bomber is the true instrument of air power, and the fighter, when used offensively to assist the bomber, is merely a means to an end. In any fight for domination of the air it is the bomber, assisted by the fighter, which will decide the issue. When used alone, fighters can challenge the defenders to combat, but the number of aeroplanes shot down in such clashes will rarely decide the main issue.

There are two methods by which fighters can assist bomber operations. Ranging formations of fighters can sweep ahead on the flanks, and behind the bombers. Usually they are well out of sight of the bombers, for they may be fifty or a hundred miles away. Their leaders should have complete freedom of action to vary their planned flights so that they can take full advantage of the local tactical conditions. This type of fighter operation usually pays good dividends and is known as 'bomber support by fighters'.

Bomber 'escort' by fighters is quite different from support, for here the fighters provide protection within sight of the bombers, and the nearest fighters, those of the close escort squadrons, are never allowed to break away and chase the enemy. The escort-cover squadrons guard both the close escort and the bombers, and we later found that to get the best results two of the usual three squadrons of the escort-cover wing should be free to leave the bombers. Against stiff opposition high cover and top cover wings were used, but two-thirds of these forces were always free to break away.

It is not possible to lay down hard and fast rules about the proportions of fighters to be used in the support and escort rôles. The allocation of fighters to these two tasks will depend upon the efficiency of the enemy's defence system and the type and number of his defending fighters. If the enemy chooses to ignore the free-lance fighter sweeps, which he should, and concentrates his fighters against the bomber formations, then it would be a mistake merely to increase the number of escorting fighters. The most effective remedy would be to plan the fighter sweeps to patrol the enemy airfields and from their superior height bounce the defenders when they climbed up. During 1941 our bomber pilots were greatly encouraged by the sight of masses of wheeling Spitfires, but there is no doubt that we tied far too many fighters to the bombers.

Fighters should always be used as offensively as possible and there is no doubt that Göring realised this, for after a conference with his air commanders before the Battle of Britain he issued clear instructions about their employment. Only part of the fighter arm, the Reichmarshal instructed, was to be employed as escort to the bombers; the remainder must be employed on free-lance operations in which they could come to grips with R.A.F. fighters and indirectly protect the bombers.

No student of air warfare can find fault with the broad directive issued by Göring. Indeed, the Americans adopted the same tactics when they developed daylight operations to a high standard with their ranging fighter sweeps, which covered the length and breadth of Germany. But we know that the Luftwaffe fighter squadrons were by no means used in the tactically correct and flexible manner decreed at the time.

During the vital phase of the Battle of Britain when the bombing attacks were aimed at our airfields and aircraft factories, the Luftwaffe assembled massed formations of bombers with a close escort of 110s and large formations of 109s in the escort cover, high cover and top cover rôles. The timing of these heavy attacks was such that they usually followed a diversionary raid thirty or forty minutes earlier against a coastal target. Although these tactics made life difficult for our controllers, who had to distinguish between the feint and the main thrust, we found that the 109s flew too high above the bombers and so gave them little protection.

During late August and early September it was obvious that Göring's doctrine about the freedom of action of the 109s was not being followed, for the fighters were rarely seen unless they accompanied the bombers. Formations of fighters flew above, on the flanks and behind the bombers, and sometimes the 109s were seen weaving well below. Great gaggles of 109s were stepped up behind the bombers, and some idea of the size of these escorts can be judged from a great New Zealand fighter pilot, Al Deere, who reported that when the bombs from the leading Heinkels were falling on North Weald the rising screen of 109s stretched to Gravesend, a distance of more than twenty miles. These were poor tactics, for the lengthy assemblies of these unwieldy formations over the Pas de Calais often gave our radar ample warning of the approach of large raids. These large gaggles could be seen by our pilots from a great distance, and the high proportion of fighters tied to the bombers denied to the Messerschmitt squadrons that flexibility and freedom so essential to fighter operations.

After the war Galland told us that because of heavy Stuka losses the bomber pilots complained to Göring about the failure of their fighters to provide reasonable protection, and that the Reichsmarschall issued different instructions from those already mentioned. When the fighter leaders objected and pointed out the difficulties of escorting the relatively slow bombers and that the poor flying of the bomber pilots resulted in straggling formations impossible to protect, Göring ordered them to cease weaving and to fly straight and level close to the bombers. Galland bluntly pointed out that it was quite impossible for the 109s to operate efficiently at the speed and height of the bombers. When Göring sarcastically asked him just what he would like to have as an ideal fighter, Galland retorted: "Give me a squadron of Spitfires!" This remark was to become legendary in the Luftwaffe.

In early September the enemy abandoned his attacks against our airfields, which had met with a great deal of success, and concentrated his attention on London. For the second time in this comparatively short campaign the Germans demonstrated that same lack of single-mindedness, that failure to maintain the aim, which caused them to abandon, earlier on, the attacks against our radar sites.

These daylight attacks against London were marked by a change in the tactics used by both enemy fighters and bombers. The bombers penetrated on a wider front in numbers which varied between twenty and forty. A similar number of 110s provided close escort and large flocks of 109s wheeled above and on the flanks of the bombers. These formations were sent across in two or three waves, and some attacks lasted up to an hour. Other gaggles of 109s made high diversionary raids ahead of the bombers in an attempt to draw off our fighters, but it was apparent that the greater proportion of 109s were flying in the escort rôle.

Apart from the high-altitude superiority of the 109 over our Spitfires, which only the introduction of a more powerful engine could redress, our squadrons had largely resolved the tactical inferiority which had marked the beginning of the fighting. We had recognised the principle that two fighters constitute the smallest element which can fight, and survive, in the air. The vulnerable vic of three was fast disappearing, and pilots who found themselves alone knew that there was no future in a hostile sky.

Although some of our squadrons still clung to the line-astern formation, the individual sections of four aircraft were separated by greater horizontal distances and we were evolving a more flexible line abreast style of fighting. Our leaders had re-learnt the value of height in the air battle, and even on the few occasions when they possessed an apparent height advantage over the 109s they now rarely failed to leave a covering force of Spitfires high in the sun. No longer were we always outnumbered, for whenever time and weather permitted the 11 Group squadrons joined together in pairs and 12 Group often sent a wing to reinforce the southern area.

The most suitable size of our formations to oppose the large enemy gaggles was the subject of a lively argument between Air Vice-Marshal Park, the 11 Group commander who fought the battle, and Air Vice-Marshal Leigh-Mallory, the 12 Group commander whose contribution was largely confined to reinforcing the southern area. Park held that the critical time factor did not permit the assembly and subsequent climb of more than two, or at the most three, squadrons into a wing. Leigh-Mallory, on the other hand, was a staunch advocate of the larger wings and often sent a

'Balbo'[1] of three, four, five and once seven squadrons to reinforce the south. Park stated that the time taken to scramble, assemble, climb and move these mass formations across country meant they arrived on patrol almost one hour after the request from 11 Group, and by this time the bombers had dropped their load, had lost some of their Messerschmitt escort, had already been attacked by the southern-based squadrons and harried by heavy flak and were on their way home.

This difference of opinion was, of course, not confined to the group commanders, for Leigh-Mallory was merely supporting the tactical views of his fighter leaders which were not, in this case, unanimously supported by the 11 Group leaders.

Day after day the 12 Group wing assembled at Duxford, four or five squadrons strong, and their wing leader was for ever demanding to be let off the leash against the Huns. Our radars were picking up the enemy gaggles building up over the Pas de Calais. Scramble the wing and meet the invaders well south of London. Look at the map! It was only a question of simple arithmetic! Scramble the outlying wings at Duxford, Tangmere and Middle Wallop and the Huns would be broken and scattered before they reached London. But if they were always held back until the last moment they couldn't intercept with a height advantage before the bombers reached London.

Park's main task was to decide when to react to the information presented to him by our radars and the Observer Corps. This task was not easy, for although our radars usually presented fairly accurate range and position information, they were unreliable about the number and height of the enemy formations. To make matters worse, there was some positive evidence that the Germans were learning how to spoof our early-warning network; although a considerable number of large enemy gaggles were displayed on the radar screens, they were never actually seen in the air by our pilots.

Enemy raids suddenly appear on the 'table' in the 11 Group operations room at Uxbridge. Raid number one is shown as fifteen-plus at 6,000 feet over Cape Gris Nez, but experience has taught

[1] Marshal Italo Balbo, who led large formations of Italian aeroplanes before the war.

the controllers that fifteen-plus could be a formation of three or four times that number. Raid number two is twelve-plus over Dunkirk (no height), but a few minutes later it is increased to fifty-plus, which probably means that the bombers have joined with their fighter escort. Raids three, four and five are plotted over the Arras area, small numbers to begin with and no height in information. Raid number two is seen by the Observer Corps in the Dungeness area, but a wing of Spitfires is climbing to intercept and others are gaining height over their own airfields. Where is raid number one, for it has disappeared from the table? Was it a decoy meant to lure up our squadrons or a wing of Messerschmitts flying well above our radar screen? Or will it develop into a low-level attack against our forward airfields?

More counters are placed on the table. Raids six, seven and eight are building up over the Pas de Calais. This means that a second strong wave of fighters and bombers will follow the first attacks and the enemy has recently shown a tendency to put in three distinct waves at intervals which vary between twenty minutes and one hour. Move the Debden Wing to Maidstone. Kenley to patrol Brooklands. 222 Squadron from Hornchurch over their airfield at 15,000 feet; hardly enough, so reinforce them with 92 Squadron from Biggin. A good reserve so far, but what is this? Three more raids, numbers nine, ten and eleven, are plotted by the Observer Corps in the Tonbridge area. Another 100-plus over England without a vestige of radar warning, and the air battle swings in favour of the enemy. Move some of the patrolling wings and squadrons to the south to meet the attack. Replace them with the North Weald Wing, the Hornchurch Wing, 74 Squadron and 229 Squadron. The third wave is building up over France. But some of our squadrons are already landing after the first clash. Will there be time for them to refuel and get up again to meet the new threat? What's ready now? The Tangmere Wing, the 10 and 12 Group Wings and a few squadrons here and there. Ask the 12 Group Wing to patrol Sheerness and the 10 Group Wing to guard the west flank of London. And hope that the Hun doesn't put in a fourth wave over the Midlands or Southampton. He would meet with little opposition!

This, then, was the task of the group commander; to analyse and sift the various bits of information; to fill in the gaps; to distinguish between feint and real threat and to oppose it at the right time, height and place. Our fighter pilots were often in the right place but at an inadequate height, and they were often highly critical of the fact that they usually suffered from a height disadvantage. it could have been said of Keith Park that he was the only man who could have lost the war in a day or even an afternoon. Too strong a commitment of his fighters might only too easily have resulted in the vast majority of his precious squadrons being caught by the enemy on the ground refuelling.

The majority of fighter leaders who fought the Battle of Britain contend that Park's tactics were right at the time, if for no other reason than the unreliability of our radars. The flying log book of one of our greatest fighter pilots shows that during the Battle of Britain he flew on more than fifty scrambles, in addition to many patrols. On these scrambles, which were all carried out in perfect weather, the enemy was met on about half the occasions; this interception rate proved to be higher than that of the average squadron pilot. These records stress the profound tactical error that would have been committed had Park sent off nothing less than a Balbo on all such occasions, as advocated by the proponents of the larger formations.

Time is one of the most important factors in air fighting. During the Battle of Britain the requirement in terms of time was to intercept with our fighters before the bombs fell. Far better to have one squadron above the Huns than half a dozen below!

There are other strong reasons for not committing fighters in too large formations. The vital element of surprise was often lost because the tight formations of Hurricanes and Spitfires could be seen from a great distance by the Luftwaffe's escort fighters. In addition, the leader's soon found that the larger the formation the more unwieldy it is in the air and the more difficult to control. My own later experience on both offensive and defensive operations confirmed that two squadrons of fighters was the ideal number to lead in the air. On some subsequent operations, when large numbers of enemy fighters opposed our fighter sweeps over

France, I led a Balbo of five squadrons, but we got in each other's way in a fight and only the leaders were able to bring their guns to bear. Our common radio frequency was insufficient to control the activities of sixty pilots, especially in a fight. Finally there was the weather to contend with, for when we climbed our Balbo through layers of cloud we sometimes spent more time searching for each other than looking for the enemy.

It is interesting to note that the pattern of the great daylight air battles fought over Germany between the United States Army Air Forces and the Luftwaffe vindicated the tactics used by Park during the Battle of Britain. The German problem in 1944 was the same as ours four years previously: to stop large bomber formations, escorted by fighters, from reaching their targets in daylight. The Germans fell into the trap of trying to operate their fighters in formations of up to sixty strong, the same size as one of our Balbos of five squadrons. These cumbersome gaggles denied to the enemy fighter pilots those essential and inherent qualities of their aircraft speed, surprise and manoeuvrability – and they fell easy prey to the ranging and aggressive American fighters.

It would obviously be wrong to suggest that massed formations of fighters and bombers should not be opposed by strong concentrations of defending fighters. I have tried to describe some of the difficulties of leading and controlling the Balbos and to make the point that a wing of two squadrons proved to be the ideal size for flexible operations of both offensive and defensive character. It is the task of the ground controller and not the wing leader to achieve concentration of fighters in time and space. Thus we can understand the reluctance of Keith Park to experiment with large formations during the heat and stress of battle; the passing years have undoubtedly proved the tactics of this distinguished field commander to have been correct.

Chapter Five

TO THE SOUTH

It was after Christmas when I rejoined the squadron at Kirton Lindsey They had spent a quiet autumn in Lincolnshire and we did not expect to move south before the spring. During my absence one of our flight commanders, the ex-boy apprentice Jerry Jones, intercepted a Heinkel 111 over the North Sea one bleak winter evening, just as the gathering dusk joined clouds and ocean together in dark shades of neutral tints and made it impossible to distinguish between sea and sky.

Jones shot down the enemy bomber, but the rear gunner put a bullet through his elbow as he broke away. He flew the Spitfire through the darkened sky to land safely on the flare path and walked into the dispersal hut to make out his combat report before reporting to sick quarters for medical attention. He was suspended from flying until his injured arm was fully recovered. His place at the head of A Flight had been taken by Ken Holden, and the burly Yorkshireman was now of some consequence in the squadron.

Two of the pilots, Dundas and Marples, who had been shot down and wounded whilst operating from Kenley had also returned to the squadron. 'Cocky' Dundas was a lanky, freckle-faced youth of nineteen who, after leaving Stowe, began to serve his articles to a Yorkshire solicitor. We were to fight together for a long time and became the best of friends; later Cocky was best man at my wedding and godfather to my younger son. Even at this early stage of his life he had developed an astonishing aptitude for expensive living. Once or twice each week he insisted on dining out of mess, when a bottle of wine with the meal, together with an assortment of drinks before and after, was the order of the day. Once, stranded at Brighton, he chartered a taxi all the way to Tangmere because he disliked buses. His hair oil came from an exclusive address in Bond Street. His uniforms were tailored in Hanover Square and lined with red silk, a custom followed by the Auxiliary pilots. To show his status as a member of the Auxiliary Air Force he should have worn two small brass 'A's, one on each lapel of his tunic. These symbols were present on Cocky's everyday uniform, but the left 'A' was much larger than its opposite number. This gave him a curiously lop-sided appearance and was apt to irritate some of the more serious minded senior officers. He was a devout champion of what he called the 'Auxiliary attitude'.

Cocky never became a good shot, either when poking a twelve bore at driven game or lining up the multiple guns of his Spitfire, but he was always a determined and courageous pilot and he possessed a rare ability to lead, either in the air or on the ground. The keystones of his simple creed were honour and duty, and to enjoy life to the full at the same time.

Cocky's brother, John Dundas, was one of the younger journalists of the *Yorkshire Post* who, after leaving Stowe and Oxford, specialised in European affairs. He was a flight commander in another Yorkshire Auxiliary unit, 609 (West Riding) Squadron, but he had failed to return from a fight over the Isle of Wight in late November. Spitfires had tangled with Messerschmitts when the elder Dundas jubilantly shouted over the radio:

"I've finished a 109 – whoopee!"

His squadron commander had answered, "Good show, John," but Dundas was never seen again.

Later the German press reported that one of their foremost aces, Major Helmut Wieck, who was credited by the enemy with fifty-six victories, had been killed in action during this engagement and that Wieck's wingman had in turn shot down a Spitfire. Cocky was left to carry on the Dundas tradition, which task he achieved with great distinction throughout the following four years.

Roy Marples, a stocky, assertive boy from Manchester, although not an Auxiliary member, had served with the squadron for some time. With his blond, wavy hair and good looks he fitted the popular conception of a fighter pilot and had a fatal fascination for the opposite sex. He was to have a long and distinguished career as a pilot and leader both at home and in the Desert.

A newcomer to the squadron was Pilot Officer Heppell from Newcastle. 'Nip', as he was generally known, belonged to a well-known flying family, for his father had fought in the Royal Flying Corps and his sister ferried various aeroplanes across the country. Nip, not yet twenty, was apt to be absent-minded and something of a dreamer, but once in the air he seemed to assume an entirely different personality, for he pressed home his attacks in no uncertain fashion. Since he was the youngest and most junior member of the squadron, he was subjected to somewhat more than his fair share of leg pulling, which he accepted with a considerable amount of patience and good humour.

On the opposite side of the airfield the pilots of the first Eagle Squadron were busy training on their Hurricanes, and we saw a great deal of these buccaneering Americans who had come across the Atlantic to join the fight. Their squadron commander was an R.A.F. officer, as were the two flight commanders, but the rest were a very odd assortment, including a Hollywood set designer, a professional parachutist who had made several hundred jumps including some at night, a Mormon from Salt Lake City and an officer who spoke fluent Polish. They were all tremendously keen to come to grips with the Luftwaffe and it was interesting to watch their widely different personalities combine to serve a common purpose. They were an exhilarating company to live with, and some of them could almost salute.

One day Cocky Dundas and I were detailed as the readiness section, and with our mae-wests tied securely we lounged about the warm, comfortable dispersal hut, talking, reading flying orders or magazines, waiting for the jangling of the telephone bell that would send us streaking to our Spitfires.

Two telephones served the dispersal hut. The bell of the operations instrument had an entirely different note from the administrative line, and whenever it rang we fell silent while the operator answered. Perhaps the lad was more keyed up than we were, for almost before the bell rang he would jump to his feet and yell into the receiver. On two occasions I had manoeuvred to the door to get a flying start, but these were false alarms. Some operations clerk wanted to know the number of pilots and the serviceability state of our Spitfires. So we settled down to our reading and tried not to hear the disturbing clamour of the bell.

It jangled again. This time the airman dropped the instrument like a hot potato and bellowed "Scramble, red section," so loud that the Eagle Squadron on the other side of the field probably heard him!

I settled down after the wild scramble into the cockpit, after the hurried start and after the lurching, bouncing take-off run which was not helped by a stiff cross-wind. Now there was time to collect myself, to draw up alongside Cocky and to listen to the calm, impersonal voice of the controller.

He sent us climbing over the white snow-sheeted fields and well out over the North Sea, and always climbing into the cloudless sky. We were after a lone raider, probably a twin-engined bomber, and far below I caught a glimpse of a straggling convoy of twenty ships heading south – the target of the bomber.

It was a perfect interception. We were up-sun and higher than the Dornier 17. But he saw us when we streaked down, and wheeled round for Holland in a fast, diving turn.

Cocky went in first and I followed as he broke away. I thought that I was well within range, but opened fire too far out – always the fault of a beginner. The enemy gunner fired long bursts from his cabin position behind the pilot, and the tracer left his barrel in seemingly slow orange clusters, but suddenly they separated and streaked over the top of the Spitfire. I broke away when I was at a good killing range of 200 yards and swung the Spitfire round for another attack. I bored in closer before opening fire, for the undercarriage of the Dornier was hanging down, wisps of whitish smoke came from the port engine and there was no return fire from the gunner. This time I went in much closer and the Spitfire was violently rocked in the bomber's slipstream when I broke hard to starboard.

We reefed our Spitfires round in a greying-out turn to finish off our badly damaged opponent, but a layer of sea-fret persisted up to about 1,000 feet and the crippled Dornier slipped into this concealing mist. Although we strained our eyes and flew low over the smooth surface of the sea, we didn't catch another glimpse of the bomber.

We flew back to Kirton, where we made out our combat reports and handed them to Gibbs. Already our listening service had intercepted a distress signal from the Dornier to its base in Holland and it seemed doubtful if it could struggle back to the Dutch coast. But we had not seen the aircraft plunge into the sea, neither had we observed any signs of fire, and the bomber could not even be claimed as probably destroyed. So I was officially credited with half one Dornier 17 damaged, and this incident marked the beginning of my personal score against the Luftwaffe.

Late one February evening Billy Burton walked into the dispersal hut with welcome news. We were to fly south in a few days and, if all went well, would remain in 11 Group for the spring and summer. We gathered round and plied him with questions. Where was our new home? Biggin, Kenley, North Weald, Hornchurch or Northolt? But he shook his head at all these guesses. Then someone said Tangmere and the C.O. laughed and nodded and a ripple of excitement ran through our small company.

We all knew Tangmere. A pleasant sunny airfield which crouched at the foot of the South Downs and was only separated from the coast by a small span of flat Sussex land. It was one of Fighter Command's established airfields and for many years had provided a home for fighter squadrons. In our world Tangmere was already a tradition, for its squadrons had gained great distinction during the fighting of the previous autumn, when they had routed many an enemy raid. Now we would strive to add to that tradition and at the same time gain a reputation for our squadron. These were our thoughts on that bleak February evening in Lincolnshire. But they were unspoken.

"I'll take the squadron down to Tangmere next Wednesday," said the C.O. "We're relieving 65 Squadron, who will bring our Spit 1s back here. We'll take over their Spit 2s at Tangmere. We'll have a better aircraft and be right in the front line. If the Huns come across again like last year, we'll have all our work cut out. If not, the form is that we'll carry our offensive to France. So there'll be plenty of excitement."

The South Yorkshire Squadron was popular both with the members of the Eagle Squadron and the permanent staff at Kirton

Lindsey, and everybody wanted to have a suitable opportunity of wishing us *bon voyage* for our return to 11 Group and the fighting. The popular station commander, Stephen Hardy, was also leaving to take up a staff appointment at the Air Ministry, so the mess committee held a party to mark both events.

I left the ante-room when the party was in full swing, for I was in charge of the ground crews and the train left at some unearthly hour. Apart from the troops, I was responsible for the safe conveyance of a pack of dogs, including Cocky's surprisingly unintelligent yellow retriever, so that I was not going to have a leisurely journey. The champagne corks were still popping, and along the length of one corridor the defeat of Cornwallis at Yorktown was being re-enacted with some spirit. Numerous fire extinguishers were deployed by the Americans, whilst the inferior British fire was restricted to soda syphons from behind a defensive screen of Mr Smith's potted palms. Once again, as in 1776, the Americans had the upper hand and both the palms and the British were decidedly the worse for wear.

Our first day at Tangmere was spent in a visit to the operations room to meet the controllers and staff upon whom we were so dependent once we were in the air. Then we were conducted to the senior intelligence officer, who gave us a long talk on the Luftwaffe's order of battle, on the escape and evasive techniques we ought to adopt should we be shot down over France; he concluded with an appraisal of the qualities of the Messerschmitt 109F.

This latest product from the skilful designs of Willi Messerschmitt, although similar in appearance to the 109E except for its rounded wing-tips, had improved armament, a higher ceiling of 36,500 feet and a top speed of 396 m.p.h. at 22,000 feet.

The chief difference between the Spitfire 2 and the 1 was the installation of the Rolls Royce Merlin 12 engine in the former, which provided extra power and incorporated the Coffman cartridge starter. In addition, the recent experiences of fighter pilots had made it abundantly clear that the original two-position airscrews of the Spitfire 1 were inadequate for modern conditions of combat. Either De Havilland or Rotol constant-speed airscrews were fitted to our present aircraft, which gave us a marked improvement in climb and ceiling. It remained to be seen how the Spitfire 2 would match up against the Messerschmitt 109F.

Tangmere still bore the scars of last autumn's bombing attacks, and flat expanses of rubble indicated the previous positions of hangars and administrative buildings. On an average throughout the year Tangmere was favoured with better weather than the majority of our airfields, and since it lay just to the east of the creeks and estuaries of West Sussex it was always fairly easy to find from the air, even in doubtful weather. This feature had one drawback; the Luftwaffe rarely failed to put in a nightly attack against the airfield, and although it was never put out of commission, the enemy bombers succeeded in knocking down more buildings, including a wing of the officers' mess. It came as no surprise, therefore, when the C.O. told us that we were to leave the Tangmere mess and in future would be accommodated in the nearby village of Oving. 'Rushmans' was an old, low, rambling house of some character and we moved in with great enthusiasm, for a fighter squadron is very self-contained and its morale is greatly influenced by the manner and style in which its members live together.

One of our squadron armourers, Fred Varley of Nottingham, had been injured when his barrack block was hit by a bomb. The first thing Varley remembered about the incident was when he came to in hospital with a burst ear-drum. He soon recovered, but his medical grading was reduced so that he was unable to continue his work on our guns. Since he was a cheerful fellow with a keen sense of humour and plenty of initiative, we moved him into Rushmans as a batman, where his services eventually became invaluable. As it later turned out, we were to serve together for several more years.

Except for an occasional high-flying reconnaissance flight, the single-seaters of the Luftwaffe were rarely seen over England during these early months of 1941. But their twin-engined bombers were active by night; there were sharp attacks against Birmingham, Southampton, Liverpool, Bristol and Plymouth. The dreadful inadequacy of our night defences at this time can well be imagined from the stark fact that for every 1,000 bombers that crossed our coasts only six were brought down by ack-ack or night fighters. For instance, on 14th November 1940, when Coventry was attacked by more than 300 bombers, only one Blenheim was able to open fire against the invaders. Later in the month, when Birmingham and Liverpool were fiercely attacked at night, not a single bomber was intercepted.

In order to augment the slender night defences the day fighter squadrons had already been instructed to train pilots in the 'fighter-night' rôle. The theory behind the fighter-night concept was that Spitfires or Hurricanes would patrol over the target areas in a height band of medium altitude. Individual Spitfires were separated by small height intervals and the heavy ack-ack guns only had freedom of fire well below our lowest altitude. The controller, we were assured, would see to it that our own prowling twin-engined night fighters were kept well clear of the Spitfire patrol lines. In theory we were only supposed to fly on fighter-nights when the moon would give us a fair chance of seeing enemy bombers, but in practice we flew on some dirty nights and were sometimes badly frightened in the process.

The regular night fighter pilots possessed their own radar equipment and skilled radar operators, who usually combined with the controller on the ground to bring about a night interception. Generally speaking, the controller passed a broad picture to the Beaufighter crew and gave the pilot several 'vectors' until the target was picked up on the radar screen of the night fighter. The radar operator then passed his pilot various vectors until a visual sighting was obtained, and, after identification, the pilot attacked the enemy with his four cannons. This technique was a stealthy, scientific affair and was in marked contrast to our own relatively clumsy and uninformed operations.

Whenever the enemy beam[1] was directed against Portsmouth or Southampton, usually during the late afternoon preceding a raid, we were warned to detail six or eight pilots for a fighter-night and we were usually sent off after the fore-runners of the attack, the incendiary-carrying bombers, had illuminated the target. Often we could see the raging fires below, and the bursting flak, and sometimes the dark canopy of the night was broken by an arc of fire

[1] Radio beam system for blind navigation.

when some Beaufighter scored a success. But no member of our squadron ever claimed a victory at night, and few fired their guns.

Nip had an experience which well illustrates the short-comings of day pilots who tried to fight at night. The outline of the sheltering hills was already growing blurred and dim when he took off, but he climbed to the west and the light, for the high cloud tops were still brushed with a red and golden fire. For half an hour he flew high above a series of deep ravines formed by the cumulus clouds until these flaming arches of the sky grew dim and only a dull, red band was left on the far horizon to mark the sun's descent. When the sky finally lost its colour the first stars appeared, and with them the first enemy bombers winged their way across the Channel, the harbingers of a heavy attack against our air-fields.

Everything seemed to happen at once. Nip's petrol was getting low and he called Tangmere for a homing. The controller said that he was very busy with the Beaufighters and would the Spitfire pilot stand by and call again in five minutes? Nip stood by, but a bank of industrial smoke drifted across Tangmere from Southampton and although the full moon was high, the forward visibility was less than a mile. Now he had to fly on instruments for most of the time. Bombs were exploding on the ground below him and strings of flak drifted up from the gunners. At first they came up very slowly, almost too slowly to be real, like uncoiled necklaces of glowing amber. Suddenly they became real and dangerous, for they tore past the Spitfire, very close and disconcerting.

Five thousand feet above Nip a young Beaufighter pilot, Johnnie Topham, stalked an enemy bomber. Topham closed to firing range and opened up his four cannons. He hit the Heinkel in one engine, which began to burn, but the enemy pilot dived away into the murk. Topham followed in a fast dive, determined to finish off the Heinkel. Ahead of him was a glowing light which he thought was the burning engine. The Beaufighter was travelling very fast and Topham opened fire at Nip's white tail light! As the Beaufighter swerved past the Spitfire, Topham recognised the other fighter and thought: Now I'm in front of him he's bound to think I'm a Hun and let me have it!

But both pilots got down safely. Topham called the controller, who told him the identity of the Spitfire pilot. He jumped into a van and drove to our dispersal, where a thoughtful Nip was stowing away his parachute and flying gear. Topham held out his hand and said:

"I'm sorry, Nip. I thought you were my Heinkel in that clag up there! And when I got in front of you I thought my time had come!"

"No, I didn't fire at you," replied Nip. "What with the flak and the bombs and the clag I only wanted to get down."

He paused for a few moments and then said:

"That's the last bloody time they get me up at night!"

We never became proficient in this type of work, largely because the requirement itself was a basic contradiction of all our training. During the day we fought and lived as a team, and this was the very essence of our squadron and wing formation. When we climbed our Spitfires into the darkness we were oppressed not only by the strange loneliness of our solitary flights but by the thought of our own severe limitations in the task ahead.

But there was one fighter pilot who flew a Hurricane at night and achieved outstanding success. This was the fearless R. P. Stevens of 151 Squadron, and I make special mention of him in this chronicle of day fighting because he, like us, flew a single-seater and had none of the scientific aids available to the Beaufighter crews.

Before the war Steve was a commercial pilot and flew newspapers to Paris. He joined his squadron in early 1941, and to those who flew with him it seemed as if life itself was of little account to him, for the risks he took could only have one ending. He never concerned himself about the mechanical condition of the Hurricane that carried him through the darkened skies night after night to continue his own very personal war. We heard that his wife and children had been killed in one of the Manchester blitzes and it was said that he screamed, like a man demented, at the sight of the enemy bombers.

He found the bombers by the simple method of following the flak bursts of our own gunners. He could always be found in that part of the sky where the flak was heaviest, prowling and searching for the hated enemy. On one occasion he blew up a bomber, and pieces of human flesh and blood stained his own aircraft. He refused to have these removed and they remained on his aircraft for all to see – a symbol of his private war. He was quite fearless and attacked his opponents at such close range that on some occasions his own Hurricane was badly damaged by the force of the explosion. His end was inevitable, and after destroying at least fourteen enemy aircraft at night he failed to return from a patrol over enemy territory and was never seen again. We have the fondest memories of him.

Apart from the Beaufighter squadron we shared the airfield at Tangmere with 145 Squadron, who also had Spitfires. The Cheshire Auxiliaries of 610 Squadron were based at the satellite airfield of Westhampnett, and these three Spitfire units comprised the Tangmere Wing. Soon after our arrival we began to operate together and sometimes felt our way cautiously across the Channel and over Normandy, the Cherbourg peninsula and the Pas de Calais. One or other of the available squadron commanders led these wing shows and determined the tactics of the day. So that our tactics varied from day to day according to the whims of the leader. A most unsatisfactory arrangement.

Towards the middle of March our C.O. strode into the dispersal hut with some momentous news:

"Listen, you chaps. Fighter Command are appointing wing commanders to lead the wings. The first two have been selected. 'Sailor' Malan is going to Biggin and Douglas Bader is coming here. He has just been on the blower and will fly with us. We shall be in the thick of all the scrapping. He arrives tomorrow."

Bader turned up at Tangmere on the following day and was in the air soon afterwards, throwing his Spitfire about the sky. Despite his terrible crash in 1931, when he lost his legs, he was still very keen on aerobatics and contended that no man was master of his aircraft until he could control it in all attitudes. He was careful to point out that precise aerobatics were not of the slightest use in a dog-fight but rather served to give the pilot complete confidence in his Spitfire. Bader's frequent, almost daily displays were the delight of the ground crews, and we all strolled on to the tarmac to watch the wing commander.

His favourite manoeuvre was to climb swiftly to a height of about 3,000 feet over the centre of the airfield. Then he would aileron-turn into a steep dive and, just above our heads, reef the Spitfire into a series of upward rolls before regaining level flight with a roll off the top of the loop. The display was faultless whenever he carried out two upward Charlies[1], but after a few days at Tangmere he attempted to introduce a third roll into the drill. The evolution was now seldom achieved with its former polish and often our wing commander stalled his Spitfire and spun ignominiously before the assembly. But his acrobatics revealed the pattern of his approach to life, he would not give up and tried, without marked success, to perfect the manoeuvre.

Some time later there was posted to the squadron a somewhat elderly, pedantic and heavily mustachioed flight lieutenant who, although possessing no combat experience, proved to be an acrobatic pilot of exceptional ability.

One hot day in the early summer Bader had given the troops his usual breezy performance and was now lounging in his undershirt, cooling off after his exertions in the warm cockpit and chatting to Billy Burton and Ken Holden.

"Y'know, Billy, the Spit's not built to do more than two upward Charlies before the roll-off the top. It's just not got the speed. I've pulled it off once or twice, but she's very slow at the top. Uncomfortable." And the wing commander sucked his pipe reflectively. He continued:

"We ought to start some formation acrobatics here. The ground troops would love it. Ken could lead. I'll fly on the starboard and Billy on the port. And if the Huns won't come up, we'll put on a show over St Omer!"[2]

But any further conversation was interrupted by the shattering roar of a Spitfire that retracted its wheels a few feet above our heads. It was our new flight lieutenant. Bader looked displeased and grunted:

"I say, Billy! Who's that chap? Can't have that sort of thing. Bad

[1] Pilot's jargon for rolls.
[2] Well-known enemy fighter airfield in France.

flying discipline." We turned away to hide our grins.

All eyes were now glued on the newcomer, who stall-turned and streaked down towards our little group. Overhead he pulled the Spitfire into a steep climb and straight as an arrow he commenced a series of beautiful climbing rolls. It was as if he had thrown the gauntlet at the wing commander's feet. Fascinated we watched and counted the evolutions.

"One."

"Two," we chanted Out aloud.

"He'll never do the roll-off," said Bader.

"Three," we chorused and the Spitfire, now quite vertical, arced directly above.

"He'll never make it. No speed. I could've told him," commented Bader.

Very slowly but with perfect timing the Spitfire half-rolled off the top of the loop and resumed level flight. The whole manoeuvre was carried out with exquisite skill, and to demonstrate that it was no fluke the pilot repeated the performance and then side-slipped his Spitfire to a perfect three-point landing. And so he became the aerobatic king of Tangmere.

Soon after Bader's arrival we flew on a two-squadron sweep. We were to climb across the Channel, poke our noses over Boulogne, skirt down the Somme estuary and withdraw. Although the Luftwaffe had withdrawn some of its fighter units from northern France to Rumania, to support the campaign in the Balkans, a considerable number of fighters and bombers remained to oppose us. During these early spring days of 1941 both sides regarded the Channel as neutral territory and Spitfires and Messerschmitts often clashed in bitter air battles.

There had been no time for Bader to teach us his own theories of combat formations and tactics. For this show we would fly in the old, tight, line-astern style and he would lead our squadron.

Climbing and still holding a close formation, we curved across the Channel. I was in the number three position in Bader's section and ahead of me were Cocky and the wing commander. Behind me, in the unenviable tail-end Charlie position, was an apprehensive Nip. Suddenly I spotted three lean 109s only a few hundred feet higher than our formation and travelling in the same direction. Obviously they hadn't seen us and would make an ideal target for a section of 145 Squadron who were still higher than the 109s. I should have calmly reported the number, type and position of the 109s to our leader, but I was excited and shouted, "Look out, Dogsbody[1]." But the other pilots of the wing weren't waiting for further advice from me. To them 'look out' was a warning of the utmost danger – of the dreaded bounce by a strong force of 109s. Now they took swift evasive action and half-rolled, dived, aileron-turned and swung out in all directions, like a wedge of fast-moving teal avoiding a wild-fowler on the coast. In far less time than it takes to tell, a highly organised wing was reduced to a shambles and the scattered sections could never be re-formed in time to continue the planned flight. I was the last to land, for I had realised the error and knew the consequences would be unpleasant. They were all waiting in the dispersal hut.

"Close the door, Billy," ordered Bader. And then:

"Now who's the clot who shouted 'look-out?'"

I admitted that I was the guilty party.

"Very well. Now tell us what we had to 'look-out' for?" demanded the angry wing commander.

"Well, sir, there were three 109s a few hundred feet above.—."

"Three 109s!" interrupted Bader. "We could have clobbered the lot. But your girlish scream made us think there were fifty of the brutes behind."

This public rebuke hurt deeply, but it was well justified, for our first operation together had been a complete failure, thanks to my error. Bader went on to deliver an impromptu lecture on tactics. We were utterly dependent upon each other for cross-cover and accurate reporting. In future the words 'look-out' would not be used. In dire emergencies we would cry 'break port, blue section' or even 'break port, Ken', for Bader preferred the use of Christian names. The pilot who called the break would then be responsible for controlling the safety of the formation until it was out of danger. In all other instances enemy aircraft would be reported according to the clock code, with full details, thus: "Dogsbody from red two.

[1] Call sign of the wing leader, derived from his initials-D.B.

Six 109s at two o'clock, high. About 2,000 yards."

Bader concluded his lecture, and since he was always quick to forgive, he gave me an encouraging grin when he stumped out of the dispersal hut. I never forgot this lesson.

One morning shortly afterwards we were released until noon after some night patrols. I had not flown during the night and Ken had left instructions that I was to check the Spitfires of our flight and carry out any air tests that were necessary. I was discussing the aircraft with our flight sergeant when the wing commander swaggered in. We sprang to attention.

"Sit down, old boy. Where's the chaps?"

"In bed, sir" I answered. "They were all up late on a fighter-night and we don't come to readiness until 1 o'clock."

"Any luck?" he enquired.

"No sir. None of them had a squirt," I replied.

Bader grunted. "The Spitfire's not as good as the Hurricane at night. More room in the cockpit and a better view. And the Spit's much trickier to land at night on that little narrow undercarriage." He paused to light his pipe and continued. "I'm having a Hurricane sent down which I'll fly at night. Sailor got a couple of Heinkels one night last year, and there's no reason why we shouldn't hack down a few more." And after a further pause. "What are you doing now?"

"Flight Lieutenant Holden sent me down to check our aircraft, sir. I've got a couple of air tests," I answered. "Good show," grinned Bader. "You and I will slide up through this bit of cloud, nip across the Channel and see if we can bag a couple of Huns before lunch. It will be a pleasant surprise for Flight Lieutenant Holden, eh?"

I said there would be little doubt on this score!

We took off together and climbed through several layers of cloud. When we finally broke out into the warm sunshine, Bader grinned and waved his hand before his face, the signal for me to take up a wide abreast position.

I could hardly believe that I was flying as wingman to the legendary pilot. But there he was only a few yards away with his initials and wing commander's pennant painted on the fuselage of his Spitfire. There would be no reporting mistakes this time.

The radio buzzed with static, and the Tangmere controller broke the silence.

"Dogsbody, from Beetle[1]. You receiving?"

Bader was equally abrupt. "Loud and clear, out."

And soon afterwards the controller again: "Dogsbody, what are your intentions?"

Silence from Dogsbody. Now Bader was curving our Spitfires to the south. Beachy Head should be below and in ten minutes we would be crossing the French coast.

"Dogsbody. I say again, what are your intentions? The station commander would like to know." This, of course, was an order that could not be ignored.

"Tell him that Dogsbody section, two aircraft, are going on a little snoop over the Channel. Nothing exciting, just a little routine snoop. Out."

The controller acknowledged this information, but he was on the air again within a few seconds.

"Dogsbody, you are not to proceed with your flight. You are to return immediately. I say again, return immediately. Is this understood?"

Bader said that it was fully understood and uttered a strong oath that stung the ears of the controller and startled the Waaf plotters in the ops. room, for all our conversations were broadcast by loud-speakers. But we turned about and dropped through the cloud to pick up the Sussex coastline.

"Line-astern, Johnnie. And I'll show you how to get on the tail of a 109. A steep climb, a tight turn. Tighter yet. We can always turn inside the brutes and" – (a rude noise meant to imitate machine-gun fire) – "Nothing to it. A piece of cake, isn't it? Once more."

[1] Code name for Tangmere.

Chapter Six

TANGMERE WING

We began to carry out low-level flights over France. These operations were known by the code name *Rhubarb*. The idea was to take full advantage of low cloud and poor visibility and slip sections of Spitfires across the coast and then let-down below the cloud to search for opportunity targets, rolling-stock, locomotives, aircraft on the ground, staff cars, enemy troops and the like. They were usually arranged on a voluntary basis and a few pilots seemed to prefer this type of individual, low-level work to the clean, exhilarating team work of the dog-fight. But the great majority of fighter pilots thought privately that the dividends yielded by the numerous *Rhubarb* operations fell far short of the cost in valuable aircraft and trained pilots.

First of all we had to contend with the weather. Usually the cloud base was less than 1,000 feet when we slipped our two Spitfires into its concealing vapour. During the next few minutes all our thoughts were concentrated on the likely height of the cloud base over France. Our let-downs from the cloud were usually made over reasonably flat countryside, but here and there small hills rose a few hundred feet and presented serious hazards. If we weren't in the clear when the altimeter recorded 500 feet, then we climbed back into the cloud and called the show off.

So it was difficult to be cool and calculating when making our let-downs on *Rhubarb* flights. Perhaps two of us had flown in cloud, in tight formation, for a distance of fifty miles at 2,000 feet. Time to descend, for we are over the target area – or should be if we have steered an accurate course and the wind hasn't changed. We ease the throttle back and put the Spitfires into a gentle dive. The engine note changes, but it seems strangely loud in the cloud and the stick trembles in your hand. You flash a grin of encouragement at your wingman who is only a few feet away, his eyes and hands attuned to every movement of your Spitfire, for if he loses you in this bumpy, swirling greyness there is not enough height for him to make the difficult transition to instrument flight. You ease her down slowly. Are we slightly off course? Will the ground be higher than where we planned to break out? And the flak? 600 feet on the altimeter and you catch a sudden glimpse of a wet, sombre landscape of hedged fields and copses. Then you are at the bottom of a sort of inverted bowl, whose translucent sides of falling rain seem dangerously confining.

Then there was the light flak. Gibbs told us that, once beyond the heavily defended coastal belt, we should be lightly opposed from the ground, but it always seemed as if the enemy gunners were ready and waiting. Airfields were always extremely well defended and it was a dangerous business to try and make more than one fast, low-level attack. Straight in and out was the only method on these occasions.

The Germans prepared unpleasant counter-measures against these low-level attacks. Here and there decoy targets were established and these sometimes took the form of stationary locomotives, heavily armoured and surrounded by numerous, well-camouflaged light flak guns, arranged to provide a deadly concentration of fire against air attack. Many pilots received the shock of their lives when they streaked down upon what they imagined to be a sitting duck.

Usually our *Rhubarb* efforts yielded little more than a staff car (or was it a French civilian vehicle?) or some target ineffectively sprayed with the puny bullets of our machine guns. Whenever we went after bigger game on the airfields we took some bad knocks, and our first losses were from such operations. The engines of our Spitfires were cooled by a liquid called glycol, which was held in a small tank just below the spinner. This glycol tank and radiator were always exposed to ground fire, and one machine-gun bullet through either meant that the engine caught fire or seized up within a matter of minutes.

I loathed those *Rhubarbs* with a deep, dark hatred. Apart from the flak, the hazards of making a let-down over unknown territory and with no accurate knowledge of the cloud base seemed far too great a risk for the damage we inflicted. During the following three summers, hundreds of fighter pilots were lost on either small or mass *Rhubarb* operations. Towards the end of 1943, when I finished this tour of ops. and held an appointment of some authority at 11 Group, my strong views on this subject were given a sympathetic hearing and *Rhubarbs* were discontinued over France, except on very special occasions.

The command of Tangmere changed hands and Group Captain Woodhall arrived soon after Bader. Both had served together at Duxford, where the Woodhall-Bader team had gained an enviable reputation. Although the group captain was a dapper veteran with First World War ribbons, he was fully conversant with the modern science of controlling. In fact, throughout the war years, now at Tangmere and later at Malta, Woodhall proved to be the best controller produced by the Service.

Some controllers possessed the ability and temperament to establish the right bond of understanding between themselves and the leaders in the air, and others didn't. We were often irritated by one pompous individual (not at Tangmere) who directed our activities with flamboyant showmanship. They were his interceptions. He had shot down three enemy aircraft during his watch and when we shouted 'tallyho'[1] he dropped back into his chair with an exaggerated gesture. All that remained was for the pilot to press the firing button! Over the radio his voice portrayed his personality, and you felt that had the size of the cockpit permitted you should have stood to attention to acknowledge his commands.

At the other end of the scale was the wealthy, foppish Auxiliary officer, whom I shall call David. He drove a very expensive car, wore monogrammed ties, and his uniforms were lined with the inevitable red silk. In the small hours of a certain dull morning he handed over the reins to his subordinate and retired to his bed in the operations block. He was only to be called if a plot appeared on the board. Some time later the phone rang by his bedside. David reached for the instrument. "One bogey off Cherbourg, sir," announced the deputy controller.

"Height?" demanded David.

[1] Tallyho meant enemy aircraft sighted and about to attack.

"About 20,000 feet, sir."

"Be a good thing to scramble a section. Steer 190, angels 23," ordered David. And a running commentary was maintained between the deputy and the recumbent controller.

"Red section is about five miles from the bandit, sir."

"Good," answered David.

"They have tallyhoed, sir." And later, "They have shot down the 88 in flames, sir."

"Splendid," replied David. "Send down some tea, will you."

Over the radio Woodhall's deep resonant voice seemed to fill our earphones with confidence and assurance. When we were far out over France and he spoke into his microphone it was as if the man was in the air with you, not issuing orders but giving encouragement and advice and always watching the precious minutes, and the headwind which would delay our withdrawal, and the low cloud creeping up from the west which might cover Tangmere when we returned, tired and short of petrol. Then he was always on the ground to meet us after the big shows, to compare notes with Bader and the other leaders. Always he had time for a cheerful word with the novices. And whenever a spontaneous party sprang up in the mess, after a stiff fight or someone collecting a gong or for no valid reason whatsoever, Woodhall was always in the centre of the crowd, leading the jousting with his expensive accordion, which he played with surprising skill, his monocle still held firmly in place. We were a very happy family at Tangmere in that spring and summer of 1941.

As vacancies occurred in the three squadrons, the wing leader drew upon personnel from his old squadron and the Canadian, Stan Turner, took over the command of 145 Squadron. Fearless, and a great leader, he was given the most difficult job of all, that of top cover to ourselves and 610 Squadron. The Messerschmitt 109F possessed a higher ceiling than our Spitfire 2s so that they still swarmed above our formations, and Stan's task was to hold his squadron together in their high, down-sun position and ward off the highest 109s. He was always there with his boys. Always fanning across the sky in the right position and always ready to chortle some ribald comment over the radio. Another Bader import was

Denis Crowley-Milling, a slight, fair boy who had already won his spurs in the Battle of Britain. 'Crow' was promoted and given a flight in 610 Squadron.

Bader was always searching for the perfect formation and eventually he and Cocky devised the finger-four style which was already flown by the Luftwaffe. On most of our training flights we flew in the evenly spaced fours, and our flight commander or Billy Burton would hide in the sun and try to bounce us without being reported. Whenever we kept a good look-out we were seldom surprised, but the danger lay when we relaxed and failed to keep our necks twisting. Then some wit, waiting for such an opportunity, would close to a few yards and make rude noises over the radio to imitate cannon fire. Surprised and shaken, we broke up in all directions, but it was excellent training.

During these relatively quiet days the wing leader often slipped a section of four Spitfires over the Channel, for this was before we had secured air domination of this area and a few prowling 109s could often be found. On one occasion the four Spitfire pilots saw some 109s diving from behind, but our tactics were faulty and the cannon shells slammed into the two wingmen. Pouring white smoke, Cocky headed for the nearest coastal airfield at Hawkinge, while Bader covered him from further attack. He drove his Spitfire on to the airfield in a fast, dangerous wheels-up landing and narrowly missed several brand-new Spitfires. The C.O. of the Hawkinge squadron was also an Auxiliary officer of some repute, but the bonds of the week-end fliers were severely tested on this occasion.

Bader was quick to detect the flaw in our breaking procedure, and new tactics were immediately devised. Until now the two pairs of Spitfires had broken in opposite directions and for a few precious seconds lost sight of each other. Now the wingman would fly sufficiently far back for the leader to turn steeply towards him without danger of a collision. If the wingman was on the inside of the turn he would remain low while the outside pair of Spitfires swung to the top. But should the wingman be on the outside of the turn, then his would be the highest Spitfire in the manoeuvre and the other pair of aircraft would slide inside the leader. In this way we would never lose sight of each other and should be able to keep our cross-cover even in the steepest turns.

In early May we moved from the main airfield at Tangmere to the satellite airfield at Westhampnett which was little more than a fair-sized grass meadow.[1] The night bombers of the Luftwaffe were still very active and it was essential that we dispersed the Spitfires and ourselves as much as possible. Although we still slept at Rushmans, we took our meals in a stately old country mansion, Shopwhyke House, a few miles from Chichester. When the flying was over we drank pints of beer in the 'Unicorn' at Chichester and formed warm ties with the affable host, Arthur King, who was such a good friend to countless fighter pilots based at Tangmere during the war. Sometimes, when funds permitted, we dined under the cool rafters of the Old Ship Club at Bosham, but these were special occasions, for the daily few shillings we collected as pilot officers would not permit many such luxuries.

The doors of the Bay House, some five miles from Tangmere, were always open to us, for here lived our wing leader, his attractive wife, Thelma, and her sister, Jill. About once or twice a week we drove to the Bay House to find the hard core of the wing grouped about its leader. Stan was invariably there, listening and not saying a great deal, always sucking his pipe with a pint mug of beer in his hand. The conversation never strayed far beyond our limited world of fighters and fighting. Sipping his lemonade, Bader analysed our recent fights, discoursed on the importance of straight shooting, on the relative merits of guns and cannon, on the ability of our opponents (whom he always held in contempt), on the probable destiny of the pilot who flew with his head in the office and of our own dreadful fate should we ever lose sight of him in combat. He was dogmatic and final in his pronouncements—I can't call them arguments, because no one argued with him. There were no half measures, no ifs and buts, for everything was viewed with great clarity. It was a great privilege for us junior officers to be taken into the confidence of a wing commander, and in this fashion the separate identities of the three squadrons were blended together to form Bader's wing.

[1] Today, the perimeter track at Westhampnett is the Goodwood motor racing circuit.

Sergeant Smith, a dark, sallow-complexioned youth, always flew wingman to Bader. He was a perfect number two who never lost sight of his leader, and however violent the air battle I never knew of a single occasion when Smith failed to return with Bader. Cocky led the section of two Spitfires which accompanied the leading pair and I generally flew wingman to Cocky. We were told to fly, play and relax with our leader, to swim with him, to play golf and to know his every mood and whim so that we were the better able to serve him in the air.

Sometimes when the wing was released to one hour's availability, Bader, the C.O., Ken and one of the other squadron commanders made up a foursome and played golf on the rolling Goodwood course. Occasionally I caddied for him and was astonished to see the accuracy and strength with which he smacked them down the fairway. When he addressed the ball on the tee, his powerful arms flexed and a look of grim determination appeared on his face, it was as if he could see a little 109 perching on the peg instead of the inoffensive white ball.

Back at Westhampnett a pilot stood by the ops. telephone and outside the hut was our little Maggie.[1] Should the wing be called to readiness, the pilot would jump into the cockpit, fly low over the golf course, which was but a mile or two away, and fire off a red Very light. One of our party (Pilot Officer Johnson) would then race to the clubhouse, start the wing commander's car and drive across the course to collect the rest of the party. We estimated that we could be back at Westhampnett within half an hour of the recall message.

June opened quietly enough, for we had not yet begun the long bout of intensive operations which was a feature of the high summer. Several of us who had joined the squadron at the same time were no longer novices; we averaged between 400 and 500 flying hours and thought we knew it all. We were going through the most difficult stage of a pilot's career. We were grossly over-confident and zoomed into our loops at too low an altitude. We cut our throttles and side-slipped away any surplus height when we made our approach to land and straightened our wings at the last moment to touch down too close to the dispersal hut. A fighter pilot wants plenty of dash and

[1] Miles Magister, a slow two seater communications monoplane.

initiative in his make-up. We had this, and all we lacked was a spell of ops. to tone us down, and this was soon to come. Our over-confidence was well illustrated by the following incident.

Nip had recently become operational at night, and after a patrol he returned to Westhampnett to wait his turn to land. Ken was the officer in charge of night flying and he operated the portable radio on the flare path. Our ace was told to switch on his navigation lights and to orbit the airfield at 2,000 feet whilst Ken talked down some other Spitfires on the circuit. Eventually Nip was the only pilot remaining aloft. Ken turned his attention to the solitary Spitfire and was horrified to see the red and green navigation lights on each wing tip slowly changing position. Nip was practising his slow rolls, but had forgotten that his bright navigation lights would give the game away. The etiquette of radio-telephone procedure was forgotten:

"Nip," thundered an angry Ken.

"Sir," replied a startled Nip.

"Cut it out and come down," ordered Ken.

Flustered, Nip brought his Spitfire in for a perfect approach just to the left of the flare path. Ken watched its angle of descent, which was absolutely correct, saw the flare-out some twenty feet above the ground and the black silhouette of the Spitfire roar past him – with the undercarriage still up! Ken shouted into his hand microphone but it was too late, for the belly of the Spitfire was already tearing up the grass surface.

Shortly after this incident Ken left us, having been promoted to squadron leader and given the command of 610 Squadron on the other side of the airfield. We were sorry to lose him and missed his side-splitting mimicry and his shrewd north-country wisdom. But all that mattered was that he would still be in the wing and that his squadron would be echeloned up-sun, between ourselves and Stan's top cover Spitfires.

Soon after this we began to reach out over the Channel and into France. At first the Luftwaffe ignored our high-flying fighter sweeps, and rightly so, for we presented little threat when we patrolled the Pas de Calais at a high altitude. So *Circus* operations were introduced, in which we escorted a dozen Blenheim bombers to short-range targets in France in the hope that the Luftwaffe would oppose this daylight effrontery.

Our tactical arrangements for fighter escort to the bombers followed closely the pattern adopted by the enemy during the previous autumn, and we fell into the same trap by allocating far too many fighters to the bombers. The handful of Blenheims were often escorted by twelve squadrons, in the various rôles of close-escort, escort-cover, high-cover and top-cover wings. Usually we picked up the bombers over our own coast and later on the assemblies were made below 500 feet to avoid the enemy's radar coverage.

No fighter pilot who took part in these hair-raising and often dangerous rendezvous between bomber and fighter forces over Beachy Head, Pevensey Bay or Selsey Bill will easily forget them, especially when the early morning mists reduced forward visibility. Some squadrons circled to port while waiting for the bombers and others orbited to starboard and occasionally they met, head-on, half-way round the circuit. Sometimes the only avenue of escape was to slide underneath an oncoming formation and then the bellies of the tail-end Charlies literally scraped the tree-tops. The Polish wing from Northolt would arrive in a rigid, impeccable formation as if their leader expected the rest of us to scamper out of his dignified path. Then, if the Blenheims were a few minutes late, or slightly off course, it merely added to the turmoil. In these days of strict flying discipline and accident prevention I still shudder when I think of those erupting, low-level assemblies over the rendezvous point. We were all relieved when the bomber leader headed towards the sea and we could take up a safe position on a flank.

Sometimes we remained at low-level until the Blenheims began to climb to their bombing height a few miles off the French coast. That outstanding gun of the war, the deadly 88 mm., hampered the progress of the bombers when they crossed the coast and stained the clearness of the high sky with innumerable bursts of flak, like foul, bursting sacks of black soot. When this stuff came up the lowest fighters, those of the close-escort wing, discreetly swung to one side and gained a thousand feet, for there was little point in exposing our delicate fighters unnecessarily, but this action aroused some bitter comment from the bomber boys, who ploughed on regardless at their appointed height.

After the flak belt we settled down for the penetration into France, and since our forward speed was much faster than the bombers, we weaved and twisted round the Blenheims in pairs and fours, for this was the only means by which we could stay in position. Someone with a sense of humour aptly named this mass of aircraft the 'beehive'.

Other fighter wings provided support by carrying out diversionary, forward support, target support, withdrawal cover and flanking sweeps for the beehive. The strategy of employing daylight bombers in this rôle had the desired effect; it stung the Luftwaffe into action, and they came up in strength to oppose the daylight raids. Our longer penetrations to Lille, Roubaix and Tournai were bitterly opposed, and as far as I was concerned the air fighting was more ferocious than at any other time of the war.

We infinitely preferred flying on the freelance roving fighter sweeps to the escort rôle when we were more strictly tied to the bombers. The primary task of our escort wings was to protect our own bombers from attack by the 109s, and this was not always easy, for when you flew close to the bombers, in either the close-escort or escort-cover wing, there were so many pairs and sections of fighters that when the 109s came in it was difficult to distinguish friend from foe.

When the 109s came in! They could see the beehive from a great distance, and the heavy flak bursts here and there accurately traced the pattern of our flight over France. So that the advantage of surprise usually lay with the enemy and the first thing we knew of their presence was when they bored in with a fast, slanting attack from six o'clock high. Sometimes they were seen by the top-cover boys, who gave chase and were joined by half a dozen Spitfires from the high-cover squadrons. Down below, alongside the bombers someone would shout a warning or you would catch a glimpse of the glinting activity high above. Now was the time to move quickly, not to intercept the four diving 109s but to get out of the way of the highly disorganised pack of Spitfires who streamed, funnel shaped, behind the enemy. It seemed to us that the risk of a collision was far greater than the threat from a handful of

Messerschmitts.

One of the enemy units opposing these daylight excursions was the famous J.G. 26, 'Schlageter' Geschwader, with its nine squadrons of Messerschmitts based at various airfields in the Abbeville area. J.G. 26 was still led by the successful Adolf Galland, who claimed no less than seventy victories and was now at the very peak of his fighting career. After the war, when we interrogated him at Tangmere, we were greatly impressed by the man's quiet dignity and his unshakeable confidence in his own tactics and theories. He told us that he was a chain smoker of cigars and how he had given himself permission to smoke on operations. He claimed to have flown the only German fighter equipped with an electric cigar-lighter, and when he was promoted to high rank, five tobacco firms requested the exclusive privilege of providing his cigars for the duration of the war. He very decently accepted all these offers and enjoyed twenty cigars a day until captured by the Americans at the end of the war, when he still had a modest stock of sixty boxes. He related how Hitler objected to his incessant smoking on the grounds that it was a poor example to the youth of the master race and forbade him to be photographed with a cigar clenched in his teeth. Obviously Galland was a man after our own hearts, but at the time we only knew him as a cunning and highly dangerous opponent.

The enemy pilots surprised us with a skilful and brave ruse. In addition to their steep, fast dives they eased their way into the beehive, sometimes assisted by clever use of cloud cover, just as if they were four Spitfires protecting the bombers. The silhouette of the 109 was not unlike the Spitfire, and in any case we were not looking for four cool-headed pilots who slowly worked their way into our midst. Often this type of stealthy attack was timed to coincide with others from the flanks and high astern and we were taken unawares.

Sometimes individual Messerschmitt pilots took advantage of any cloud formations below the bombers. They would shadow the Blenheims or Bostons, hiding themselves in the cloud as much as possible. Then in an opportune moment when other attacks developed from above and behind, they would dart out of the cloud immediately below the bombers, pull their fighters into a near-stall attitude to fire a long burst before they half-rolled back to the sanctuary of the cloud. This tactic achieved some success – and deservedly, for it took a brave man to fly alone into the beehive. But Galland and his colleagues probably realised the confusion caused by far too many escort fighters, and took full advantage of our dilemma.

About this time we heard that some of the 11 Group squadrons were re-equipping with Spitfires 5As and 5Bs. The engine of the Spitfire 5 was only slightly bigger than that of our 2s, and consequently there was little difference in performance. The 5A still carried eight machine guns, but the 5B had two 20-mm. cannon and only four machine guns. Cannons would be useful to smash through the armour plate of the enemy's bombers and would also improve our chance against the 109s.

We thought that the most important difference between the Spitfire 2 and the 5 was that the former was fitted with fabric ailerons whilst the latter had an improved metal type. In the air the difference in performance was quite remarkable, for the previous heavy stick-pressures were greatly reduced and the rate of roll, at high speeds, was more than doubled. In other words, the lateral manoeuvrability of the Spitfire was improved tremendously with the introduction of metal ailerons. The new ailerons were exactly the same size and shape as their fabric counterparts and there was no technical reason why they should not be fitted to our present Spitfires, provided we could get hold of them.

Our intelligence system went into action and we found that the new ailerons were being manufactured at the Air Service Training factory at Hamble, near Southampton. We flew to the airfield and met the test pilots and the managerial staff. Everyone was flat out to help and it was arranged that the squadron's aircraft should be flown in one by one for the modification to be carried out at Hamble. Test pilots would put each Spitfire through its paces after the new ailerons were fitted, and test them for trim and balance. Various pieces of paper would have to be signed by the pilots when they collected their Spitfires. We would have signed anything to get our hands on those new ailerons.

Bader was the first to fly his Spitfire to Hamble and an hour later I landed in the Maggie to collect him. We flew back together, highly pleased with the result of our negotiations and the fact that it had all been achieved in a matter of days simply because we dealt directly with the factory. But about a year later I received an official letter requiring an explanation as to why 616 Squadron had decided to fit metal ailerons to its Spitfire 2s. Who had authorised the work at Hamble and to what department should it be charged? In my reply I said that as a pilot officer at the time I had little voice in policy matters, but perhaps Bader, who was a prisoner of war, or Burton, who was fighting in the Desert, could throw further light on the affair. We heard nothing more about this incident.

The squadron's total of kills and the scores of individual pilots began to mount now that the 109s opposed our daily escorts and sweeps. Cocky had already opened his 1941 account against the Luftwaffe and both Bader and Burton had confirmed kills. Some of the sergeant-pilots who joined the squadron after me scored against the 109s, and although I tangled with the Messerschmitts on numerous occasions it seemed as if there just wasn't time to select my own opponent from the maelstrom of fighters when we jockeyed and twisted for an opening.

For me it was a period of acute frustration. My job as one of the two wingmen in Bader's finger-four was to guard the remainder of the section from a flank or stern attack, whilst Smith did likewise from his position on the port side. So my head was usually turned to the left or strained right round so that I could watch our rear. We had little idea of what lay ahead, but knew from the radio chatter and our own manoeuvres when Bader was working his way into a bunch of 109s. Then suddenly we were in the middle of a fight. Watching the spurts of white smoke from Bader's guns. Darting a glance ahead to see a couple of 109s, surprisingly near and half-rolling away. Calling a break as other enemy formations streaked out of the sun. Bunching up in the cockpit the better to take the 'g' as we turned to meet the attack. Always watching our leader. Fighting down the natural instinct to fasten on to a 109 and follow him down. Kicking our top rudder to hold the outside position on top of a turn. Falling too far behind Bader and almost laughing out loud when in the midst of all the turning and cavorting and sweating, Flying Officer Dundas admonished Wing Commander Bader:

"I say, Dogsbody, we haven't all got metal ailerons," and the reply, straight back:

"OK, Cocky. Don't panic. Re-form."

And then there is not a Hun to be seen in the sky and we cross out at Dunkirk in our wide, easy formation.

Back at Westhampnett the wing leader would sketch the complete pattern of our skirmish. A dozen 109s had been sighted below us. But Stan had warned of two more gaggles above his own squadron. One of these enemy formations had come down, that was when we broke hard to the left and the 109s had stayed to fight. Bader had fired at one and it had poured black smoke. Cocky and Smith nod their heads and Smith says that he saw large pieces fly off. I had not even seen this particular 109, so swift moving was the engagement. Bader concludes his summary of the fight. Ken drives over from the other side of the airfield with his story and Stan phones his account from his airfield on the other side of Chichester. The group captain has listened attentively to all this and now he speaks. Yes, the two high formations climbed up from the Abbeville area and the bottom gaggle came from Rouen. All the jigsaw pieces of information lock together and the picture is complete. The wing has knocked down a few 109s and we have no losses. We drive back to Shopwhyke House for lunch and I feel as if I am being carried on a surging tide of events over which I have little control.

The trouble was that the rigid duties of a wingman were a basic contradiction of one's natural instinct to seize on a 109, follow him down to ground level if necessary, fasten one's teeth into him and not let go until he hit the deck and burst open like a rotten egg. Had we obeyed these instincts and broken formation to chase our own opponents we should have been thrown out of the Tangmere Wing within a few minutes of landing. Although we didn't fully realise it at the time, we were serving a valuable apprenticeship to a skilled master and our turn would come if we had the patience and the luck to wait for the right opportunity. For the main task of a wingman was not to shoot down Huns but to guard his leader from attack.

We flew hard during these weeks, and with this added

experience we were able to grasp a firmer picture of our air battles. We learnt to clear our flanks and rear just as our leader launched his attack, and then for a few seconds to concentrate on what lay ahead. We found that if we flew almost abreast of the wing leader we could fasten on to our own 109 once Bader had selected his opponent. Sometimes I led a pair of Spitfires in either the wing leader's or the C.O.'s section and there seemed to be more time to think and act than when I sweated out the operation as a wingman.

Over Gravelines one day the 109s angled in from the sun and were almost within firing range before they were spotted. A voice shrieked over the radio. "Break, Dogsbody, break," and without waiting for further advice I reefed the Spitfire into a tight spiral. After two turns I was satisfied that no 109 clung to my tail and I eased out of the turn. Immediately ahead of me, not more than 300 yards away, three Messerschmitts climbed steeply as if they were being hauled up three sides of a pyramid. Their prey at the apex of the pyramid was a solitary Spitfire flying straight and level, and although I didn't know his call sign I shouted to him: "For Christ's sake, break." But it was too late, for the combined fire of the 109s smashed into his belly and the exploding cannon shells ripped over his port wing like a cross-cut saw slicing through a wooden plank. The wing drifted down, lazy as an autumn leaf, but the crippled Spitfire fell into a vicious spin.

The Messerschmitts stayed to fight and the sky was full of aircraft. It was a dangerous place for a lone pilot, and I looked round, always turning, for the nearest section of Spitfires so that I could join forces. Suddenly a 109 arced up in front of me at two o'clock and the enemy pilot put his aircraft into a gentle dive. I was very close to him and could see the square wing-tips and the tail struts of a 109E. A large black arrow head together with the number '4' were painted on the dirty grey-black camouflage and there were orange markings on the rudder. I swung my Spitfire to get behind him and thought: This is it. Nail him, and get out. Clear your tail first.

I was dead line astern of the Messerschmitt and hit him behind the cockpit with the eight machine guns. As the range closed I contrived to spray the 109 with bullets and the pilot half-rolled on to his back and jettisoned his hood. I remembered Billy Burton's precise instructions concerning enemy pilots who baled out – "I'll court-martial any member of this squadron who fires at a parachute" – but this chap was still inside the cockpit and I hammered him once more. A shapeless bundle broke away from the Messerschmitt and when I circled to watch it I saw the parachute break open. Feeling a deep exultation at this sight I drove the Spitfire round in a steep, tail-clearing turn, since the combat had perhaps lasted several seconds and much could happen in this time. But the sky seemed empty of all aircraft and I sped across the Channel and landed at Hawkinge to refuel. Several pilots of the Tangmere Wing were already there and some had seen the parachute, so that my first kill was easily confirmed.

The bombers flew over France on every suitable day, and as the high summer wore on, so the resistance of the 109s seemed to increase and sometimes we had to fight our way to the target from the coast. One day in July we shot down Tangmere's five hundredth Hun, and the same fight witnessed the squadron's fiftieth victory. This was not a large squadron score since some units, including 610 Squadron, already claimed more than a hundred kills, but we had got off to a poor start last autumn and our present masters seemed satisfied with our progress. For his leadership of the wing, Bader received a bar to his D.S.O., whilst Burton, Ken and Cocky were each awarded the D.F.C.

These victories and honours were not achieved without loss and casualties. One of our most experienced sergeant-pilots, McCairns,[1] failed to return from a sweep to Lille, but two days later Roy Marples, streaking back low over the French coast, saw the missing pilot's Spitfire intact on a stretch of beach where he had crashed after being badly shot up.

[1] McCairns, was shot down when making his way home across France at ground-level. He crash landed near Dunkirk, and since his sliding hood jammed tight he had to be assisted out of his Spitfire by two German soldiers. He was sent to a prison camp in Germany, escaped, was recaptured and punished. He escaped a second time during the severe winter of 1941-42. After some adventures he crossed the Rhine into Holland during a raging blizzard and only survived by bedding down in a pigsty with the usual occupants. Eventually he returned via France and Spain, and for his epic escape was awarded the Military Medal.

Leading a section of two Spitfires, I lost my wingman on a late evening show over France. We were badly bounced and didn't see the 109s until they had opened fire. The wingman was a sergeant-pilot, a kindly farmer's son from Gloucestershire, and the next thing we heard of Mabbett was that the Germans had buried him with military honours at St Omer. A few days later we lost the flight commander of B Flight when the handsome Collin McFie was brought down, to be a prisoner for the remainder of the war.

Our mustachioed aerobatic king only saved his neck by his remarkable aerobatic skill. During a dog-fight he was cut off from the rest of us, and the Messerschmitts settled down to hack him to pieces. His Spitfire was badly hit, but it was still flying, and he stayed with it because a pilot only takes to his parachute as a last resort. He deliberately put his aircraft into a wicked-looking spin, but the 109s still harried him and at ground-level they came in for the kill. This time he foxed them by half-rolling his Spitfire and holding it, inverted, in a shallow dive. The 109s drew off to watch the end, but our pilot had seen a reasonable field and as he crossed the boundary hedge he rolled back to a normal attitude and smacked the Spitfire into an excellent wheels-up landing. He stepped out of the wreck unscathed, with the 109s still milling overhead. This remarkable character also returned on foot via Spain and Gibraltar.

Roy, making another low-level return flight across the Channel, flew low over the water. It was one of those calm days when the smooth, glassy surface of the sea made it impossible to judge one's height accurately and Roy churned up the water with the three blades of his wooden propeller. He staggered back to Hawkinge less about nine inches from each of the blades, and had to do some fast talking to mitigate his error.

Running short of petrol after another sweep, one of our sergeant-pilots, Derek Beedham, eased his Spitfire out to sea near Brighton and then baled out. The aircraft fell harmlessly into the sea and Beedham was soon picked up by a lifeboat. He had a hero's reception from the local townsfolk, who were grateful that his Spitfire had not crashed on their rooftops; but his return to the squadron was a much cooler affair, for he should have landed on one of the many coastal airfields and saved his valuable aircraft.

But he atoned for his mistake a few days later when only one leg of his undercarriage would come down and he carried out a most skilful landing with little damage to the aircraft.

Ken had a close shave when his squadron was set upon by a determined bunch of 109s and his escape was largely due to the brilliant ability of his wingman, Tony Gaze, a young Australian, who smacked down two Messerschmitts from Ken's tail. They were split up and Ken eventually crossed the French coast alone near Calais at ground-level and, as usual, the light flak gunners were ready and waiting. Ken's Spitfire was hit and he opened the sliding hood in case he had to bale out. The flak still bracketed his Spitfire and a small piece of shrapnel tore through the open cockpit and severed the bridge of his goggles, which were pushed up on the front of his leather helmet. The goggles fell across his face, struck his knees and were later found on the floor of the cockpit. Ken's usual urbane demeanour was considerably ruffled on this occasion.

Sometimes we escorted a few of the new four-engined bombers on these daylight operations, and early one morning we witnessed the death of a Stirling. The six bombers were flying in two vics of three and we were close to them in the beehive. Although the sun was dangerously low behind us on our withdrawal, we were not altogether unaware of the ever changing tones of light and shade in earth and sky.

The Messerschmitts had not attacked since we left the target and for once the beehive simmered quietly as we winged our way to the coast, but a high astern attack by a brace of 109s would transform it to a swarming, twisting rabble. The only sound to break the muted drone of our engines was an occasional muttered command and Woodhall's reassuring comments from Tangmere. I thought of the tremendous breakfast I should devour after we landed and that in another few weeks there would be an abundance of mushrooms on our grass airfield.

A few isolated bursts of heavy flak harassed the bombers. The nearest fighters sheered off and zoomed up a few hundred feet to clear the danger zone, but the six Stirlings held their level, evenly spaced pattern. Then one of the large bombers fell slowly behind and its port wing dropped so that it went into a gentle turn to the left. At first there seemed to be no danger, but suddenly an engine fell out, red flames flickered near the cockpit and our thoughts were for the crew inside. The bomber took a long time to reach the ground in a series of slow, curving turns and only two parachutes blossomed out. We were silent, helpless and yet fascinated by these death agonies of the Stirling. When quite near to the ground she plunged into a vertical dive and then exploded with a great sheet of orange flame, which was followed by a swiftly rising pall of white smoke and thin plumes of exploding ammunition.

One of our own squadron pilots had also seen the crash from the ground. He was Sergeant Crabtree, who had been shot down a week previously and saw the incident from his hiding-place in a nearby farmhouse. Soon afterwards he returned to the squadron with the full story.

Our dead comrades from the Stirling were buried by the Germans in a village near the crash. Hundreds of French country-folk made their way to the grave and brought floral tributes to the British airmen. Crabtree told us these journeyings reached such proportions that the local German commandant ordered them to cease and ruled that no more flowers would be brought to the grave. So for a few days none visited the place, the flowers faded and it seemed as if the airmen were forgotten. And then one morning the graves were resplendent with wild flowers for all to see: they had been put there during the night, and were replaced at frequent intervals.

We were greatly encouraged by this moving little story, for sometimes when we fought our way out of France single-handed the sky itself seemed alien. If the worst happened and we were brought down and still lived, it was heartening to know that on the ground we might find warmth and humanity.

Chapter Seven

'DOGSBODY'

High summer at Tangmere. I shall never forget those stirring days, when it seemed that the sky was always blue and the rays of the fierce sun hid the glinting Messerschmitts; or when there was a high layer of thin cirrus cloud (although this filtered the sun and lessened the glare, it was dangerous to climb through it, for your grey-green Spitfire stood out against the white backcloth); when the grass was burnt to a light brown colour and discoloured with dark oil-stains where we parked our Spitfires, and when the waters of the Channel looked utterly serene and inviting as we raced out of France at ground level, hot and sweating in that tiny greenhouse of a cockpit.

High summer, and the air is heavy with the scent of white clover as we lounge in our deck-chairs watching a small tractor cut down the long clover and grass on our airfield. In some places it is almost a foot high, but it is not dangerous and we know that if we are skilful enough to stall our Spitfires just when the tips of the grasses caress the wheels then we shall pull off a perfect landing.

It is Sunday, and although it is not yet time for lunch we have already escorted some Stirlings to bomb an inland target. For some obscure reason the Luftwaffe seem to oppose our week-end penetrations with more than their usual ferocity, and now we are waiting for the second call which will surely come on this perfect day.

For once our chatter is not confined to Messerschmitts and guns and tactics. Yesterday afternoon Nip and I borrowed the Padre's car, a small family saloon, and drove to Brighton for dinner. Before the return journey we collected two pilots from 145 Squadron, and in the small hours, wedged together, began the journey back to Tangmere. Nip was driving, the rest of us asleep, and along the front at Hove he had a vague recollection of some confusion and shouting and a half-hearted barrier stretched across part of the road.

He pressed on and thought little of the incident, but soon after the engine ran unevenly and became very hot. Somehow we coaxed the car home. Next morning a close inspection revealed a sinister hole just below the rear window. Shocked, we traced the path of the bullet, for it turned out that a sentry at Hove had challenged us and, not receiving a suitable reply, had opened fire. The bullet had passed between the two pilots on the back seat, had continued between Nip and me at shoulder height, drilled a neat hole through the dashboard, grazed the cylinder head and ploughed out through the radiator. Small wonder that the little car had barely struggled back to Tangmere. The Padre is more concerned with our lucky escape than the damage to his car, but Billy Burton is incensed that his pilots should have to run a gauntlet of fire at Hove. He is busy penning a letter to the military, but we keep out of his way, for we think that he is opening his attack from a very insecure base.

There is a fine haze and the soft bulk of the South Downs is barely discernible. We can just see the spire of Chichester cathedral, but above the haze the visibility is excellent and you can see Lille from fifty miles.

Lille! It lies seventy miles inland from Le Touquet and marks the absolute limit of our daylight penetrations over France. We often escort bombers to Lille, for it is a vital communications centre and contains important heavy industries. Not unnaturally the Luftwaffe are very sensitive about it. Their ground-control organisation has time to assess our intentions and bring up fighter reinforcements, and the run-up to the target is always strongly contested. We can be sure of a stiff fight when Lille is the target for the bombers.

The ops. phone rings and the airman who answers it calls out to the C.O.; Billy Burton listens and replaces the receiver.

"That was the wing commander. Take-off at 1325 with 610 and 145. We shall be target-support wing to the bombers. It's Lille again."

Suddenly the dispersal hut is full of chatter and activity. We shall be the last Spitfires in the target area, for our job is to see that the beehive leaves the area without interference. The sun will be almost directly overhead, and the Messerschmitts will be there, lurking and waiting in its strong glare. We shall fight today.

Highly coloured ribbons are pinned across the large map on the wall to represent the tracks of the beehive and the six supporting fighter wings, so that the map looks like one of those bold diagrams of London's Underground system. The two flight sergeants talk with their respective flight commanders about the serviceability of our Spitfires, and our names and the letters of our aircraft are chalked up on a blackboard which shows three sections of finger-fours.

It is fascinating to watch the reactions of the various pilots. They fall into two broad categories; those who are going out to shoot and those who secretly and desperately know they will be shot at, the hunters and the hunted. The majority of the pilots, once they have seen their names on the board, walk out to their Spitfires for a pre-flight check and for a word or two with their ground crews. They tie on their mae-wests, check their maps, study the weather forecast and have a last-minute chat with their leaders or wingmen. These are the hunters.

The hunted, that very small minority (although every squadron usually possessed at least one), turned to their escape kits and made quite sure that they were wearing the tunic with the silk maps sewn into a secret hiding-place; that they had at least one oilskin-covered packet of French francs, and two if possible; that they had a compass and a revolver and sometimes specially made clothes to assist their activities once they were shot down. When they went through these agonised preparations they reminded me of aged country-women meticulously checking their shopping-lists before catching the bus for the market town.

A car pulls up outside and our leader stumps into the dispersal hut, breezy and full of confidence. "They'll be about today, Billy. We'll run into them over the target, if not before. Our job is to see the Stirlings get clear and cover any stragglers. Stick together. Who's flying in my section?"

"Smith, Cocky and Johnnie, sir," answers Billy Burton.

"Good," Bader grins at us. "Hang on and get back into the

abreast formation when I straighten out. O.K.?"

"O.K., sir," we chorus together.

The wing commander makes phone calls to Stan Turner and Ken Holden. Brief orders followed by a time check. Ten minutes before we start engines, and we slip unobtrusively to our Spitfires, busy with our own private thoughts. I think of other Sunday afternoons not so very long ago when I was at school and walked the gentle slopes of Charnwood Forest clad in a stiff black suit. Our housemaster's greatest ambition was to catch us seniors red-handed smoking an illicit cigarette. And I think of my own father's deep-rooted objections to any form of strenuous activity on the Sabbath during the holidays at Melton Mowbray.

My ground crew have been with the squadron since it was formed and have seen its changing fortunes and many pilots come and go. They know that for me these last few moments on the ground are full of tension, and as they strap me in the cockpit they maintain an even pressure of chatter. Vaguely I hear that the engine is perfect, the guns oiled and checked and the faulty radio set changed and tested since the last flight. The usual cockpit smell, that strange mixture of dope, fine mineral oil, and high-grade fuel, assails the nostrils and is somehow vaguely comforting. I tighten my helmet strap, swing the rudder with my feet on the pedals, watch the movement of the ailerons when I waggle the stick and look at the instruments without seeing them, for my mind is racing on to Lille and the 109s.

Ken starts his engine on the other side of the field and the twelve Spitfires from 610 trundle awkwardly over the grass. Bader's propeller begins to turn, I nod to the ground crew and the engine coughs once or twice and I catch her with a flick of the throttle and she booms into a powerful bass until I cut her back to a fast tick-over. We taxi out to the take-off position, always swinging our high noses so that we can see the aircraft ahead. The solid rubber tail-wheels bump and jolt on the unyielding ground and we bounce up and down with our own backbones acting as shock absorbers.

We line our twelve Spitfires diagonally across one corner of the meadow. We wait until Ken's squadron is more than half-way across the airfield and then Bader nods his head and we open out throttles together and the deep-throated roar of the engines thunders through the leather helmets and slams against our eardrums. Airborne, and the usual automatic drill. We take up a tight formation and I drop my seat a couple of notches and trim the Spitfire so that it flies with the least pressure from hands and feet.

One slow, easy turn on to the course which sends us climbing parallel to the coast. Ken drops his squadron neatly into position about half a mile away and Stan flanks us on the other side. Woodhall calls from the ops. room to his wing leader to check radio contact:

"Dogsbody?"

"O.K., O.K."

And that's all.

We slant into the clean sky. No movement in the cockpit except the slight trembling of the stick as though it is alive and not merely the focal point of a superb mechanical machine. Gone are the ugly tremors of apprehension which plagued us just before the take-off. Although we are sealed in our tiny cockpits and separated from each other, the static from our radios pours through the earphones of our tightly fitting helmets and fills our ears with reassuring crackles. When the leader speaks, his voice is warm and vital, and we know full well that once in the air like this we are bound together by a deeper intimacy than we can ever feel on the ground. Invisible threads of trust and comradeship hold us together and the mantle of Bader's leadership will sustain and protect us throughout the fight ahead. The Tangmere Wing is together.

We climb across Beachy Head, and over Pevensey Bay we swing to the starboard to cross the Channel and head towards the French coast. Some pilot has accidentally knocked on his radio transmitter and croons quietly to himself. He sounds happy and must be a Canadian, for he sings of 'The Chandler's Wife' and the 'North Atlantic Squadron'. He realises his error and we hear the sudden click of his transmitter, and again the only sound is the muted song of the engine.

Now Bader rocks his wings and we level out from the climb and slide out of our tight formation. We take up our finger-four positions with ourselves at 25,000 feet and Ken and Stan stacked up behind us. It is time to switch the gun button from 'safe' to 'fire' and to turn on the reflector sight, for we might want them both in a hurry.

"O.K., Ken?" from Bader.

"O.K., Dogsbody."

"Stan?" from Bader again. "You bet."

The yellow sands of the coast are now plainly visible, and behind is a barren waste of sandhills and scrub. Well hidden in these sandhills are the highly trained gunners who serve the 88 mm. batteries. We breast the flak over Le Touquet. The black, evil flowers foul the sky and more than the usual amount of ironmongery is hurled up at us. Here and there are red marker bursts intended to reveal our position to the Messerschmitts. We twist and pirouette to climb above the bed of flak, and from his relatively safe position, high above, Stan sees our plight and utters a rude comment in the high-pitched voice he reserves for such occasions. The tension eases.

On across the Pas de Calais and over the battlefields of a half-forgotten war against the same foe. From the Tangmere ops. room Woodhall breaks the silence:

"Dogsbody, from Beetle. The beehive is on time and is engaged."

"Fifty-plus about twenty miles ahead of you," from Woodhall.

"Understood," replies Bader.

"Thirty-plus climbing up from the south and another bunch behind them. Keep a sharp look-out," advises the group captain.

"O.K., Woodie. That's enough," answers the wing leader, and we twist our necks to search the boundless horizons.

"Look's like a pincer movement to me," comments some wag. I suspect it is Roy Marple's voice, and again the tension slackens as we grin behind our oxygen masks. Woodhall speaks into his microphone with his last item of information.

"Dogsbody. The rear support wing is just leaving the English coast." (This means we can count on some help should we have to fight our way out.) "Course for Dover – 310 degrees." (This was a last-minute reminder of the course to steer for home.) Woodhall fades out, for he has done his utmost to paint a broad picture of the air situation. Now it is up to our leader.

"Dogsbody from blue one. Beehive at twelve o'clock below. About seven miles."

"O.K. I see them," and the wing leader eases his force to starboard and a better up-sun position.

The high-flying Messerschmitts have seen our wing and stab at Stan's top-cover squadron with savage attacks from either flank.

"Break port, Ken." (From a pilot of 610.)

"Keep turning."

"Tell me when to stop turning."

"Keep turning. There's four behind!"

"Get in, red section."

"We're stuck into some 109s behind you, Douglas." (This quietly from Stan.)

"O.K. Stan."

"Baling out."

"Try and make it, Mac. Not far to the coast." (This urgently from a squadron commander.)

"No use. Temperatures off the clock. She'll burn any time. Look after my dog."

"Keep turning, yellow section."

So far the fight has remained well above us. We catch fleeting glimpses of high vapour trails and ducking, twisting fighters. Two-thirds of the wing are behind us holding off the 109s and we force on to the target area to carry out our assigned task. We can never reform into a wing again, and the pilots of 145 and 610 will make their way home in twos and fours. We head towards the distant beehive, well aware that there is now no covering force of Spitfires above us.

The Stirlings have dropped their heavy load of bombs and begin their return journey. We curve slowly over the outskirts of Lille to make sure the beehive is not harried from the rear. I look down at a pall of debris and black smoke rising from the target five miles below, and absurdly my memory flashes back to contrast the scene with those other schoolboy Sunday afternoons.

"Dogsbody from Smith. 109s above. Six o'clock. About twenty-five or thirty."

"Well done. Watch 'em and tell me when to break."

I can see them. High in the sun, and their presence only betrayed by the reflected sparkle from highly polished wind-screens and cockpit covers.

"They're coming down, Dogsbody. Break left." And round to port we go, with Smith sliding below Bader and Cocky and me above so that we cover each other in this steep turn. We curve round and catch a glimpse of four baffled 109s climbing back to join their companions, for they can't stay with us in a turn. The keen eyes of Smith saved us from a nasty smack that time.

"Keep turning, Dogsbody. More coming down," from Cocky.

"O.K. We might get a squirt this time," rejoins Bader. What a man, I think, what a man!

The turn tightens and in my extreme position on the starboard side I'm driving my Spitfire through a greater radius of curve than the others and falling behind. I kick on hard bottom rudder and skid inwards, down and behind the leader. More 109s hurtle down from above and a section of four angle in from the starboard flank. I look round for other Spitfires but there are none in sight. The four of us are alone over Lille.

"Keep turning. Keep turning." (From Bader.) "They can't stay with us." And we keep turning, hot and frightened and a long way from home. We can't keep turning all bloody day, I think bitterly.

Cocky has not re-formed after one of our violent breaks. I take his place next to Bader and the three of us watch the Messerschmitts, time their dives and call the break into their attacks. The odds are heavily against us.

We turn across the sun and I am on the inside. The blinding light seems only two feet above Bader's cockpit and if I drop further below or he gains a little more height, I shall lose him. Already his Spitfire has lost its colour and is only a sharp, black silhouette, and now it has disappeared completely, swallowed up by the sun's fierce light. I come out of the turn and am stunned to find myself alone in the Lille sky.

The Messerschmitts come in close for the kill. At this range their camouflage looks dirty and oil-stained, and one brute has a startling black-and-white spinner. In a hot sweat of fear I keep turning and turning, and the fear is mingled with an abject humiliation that these bastards should single me out and chop me at their leisure. The radio is silent, or probably I don't hear it in the stress of trying to stay alive. I can't turn all day. Le Touquet is seventy hostile miles away; far better to fight back and take one with me.

Four Messerschmitts roar down from six o'clock. I see them in time and curve the shuddering, protesting Spitfire to meet them, for she is on the brink of a high-speed stall. They are so certain of my destruction that they are flying badly and I fasten on to tail-end Charlie and give him a long burst of fire. He is at the maximum range, and although my shooting has no apparent effect some of my despair and fear on this fateful afternoon seems to evaporate at the faint sound of the chattering machine guns. But perhaps my attack has its just reward, for Smith's voice comes loud and clear over the radio

"One Spit behind, Dogsbody. A thousand yards. Looks like he's in trouble."

Then I see them. Two aircraft with the lovely curving wings that can only belong to Spitfires. I take a long breath and in a deliberately calm voice:

"It's me Dogsbody – Johnnie."

"O.K. Johnnie. We'll orbit here for you. Drop in on my starboard. We'll get a couple of these — "

There is no longer any question of not getting home now that I am with Bader again. He will bring us safely back to Tangmere and I know he is enjoying this, for he sounds full of confidence over the radio. A dozen Messerschmitts still shadow our small formation. They are well up-sun and waiting to strike. Smith and I fly with our necks twisted right round, like the resting mallard ducks one sees in the London parks, and all our concentration focussed on the glinting shoal of 109s.

"Two coming down from five o'clock, Dogsbody. Break right," from me. And this time mine is the smallest turn so that I am the first to meet the attack. A 109 is very close and climbing away to port. Here is a chance. Time for a quick shot and no danger of losing the other two Spitfires if I don't get involved in a long tail chase. I line up my Spitfire behind the 109, clench the spade-grip handle of the stick with both hands and send short bursts into his belly at less than a hundred yards. The 109 bursts apart and the explosion looks exactly the same as a near burst of heavy flak, a vicious flower with a poisonous glowing centre and black swirling edges.

I re-form and the Messerschmitts come in again, and this time Bader calls the break. It is well judged and the wing leader fastens on to the last 109 and I cover his Spitfire as it appears to stand on its tail with wisps of smoke plummeting from the gun ports. The enemy aircraft starts to pour white smoke from its belly and thick black smoke from the engine. They merge together and look like a long, dirty banner against the faded blue of some high cirrus cloud.

"Bloody good shooting, sir."

"We'll get some more."

Woodhall – it seems an eternity since we last heard him – calls up to say that the rear support wing is over Abbeville. Unbelievably, the Messerschmitts which have tailed us so long vanish and we are alone in the high spaces.

We pick up the English coast near Dover and turn to port for Sussex and Tangmere. We circle our airfield and land without any fuss or aerobatics, for we never know until we are on the ground whether or not a stray bullet has partially severed a control cable.

Woodhall meets us and listens to his wing leader's account of the fight. Bader has a tremendous ability to remember all the details and gives a graphic résumé of the show. The group captain listens carefully and says that he knew we were having a hard time because of the numerous plots of enemy formations on his operations table and our continuous radio chatter. So he had asked 11 Group to get the rear support wing over France earlier than planned, to lend a hand. Perhaps the shadowing Messerschmitts which sheered off so suddenly had seen the approach of this Spitfire wing.

Bader phones Ken and Stan while the solemn Gibbs pleads with us to sit down and write out our combat reports.

"Please do it now. It will only take two minutes."

"Not likely Gibbs. We want some tea and a shower and..."

"You write them and we'll sign them," suggests a pilot.

Cocky walks in. He came back on the deck after losing us over Lille and landed at Hawkinge short of petrol.

"Dinner and a bottle at Bosham tonight, Johnnie?"

"Right," I answer at once.

"Count me in, too," says Nip.

The group captain is trying to make himself heard above the din.

"You chaps must watch your language. It's frightful. And the Waafs seem to be getting quite used to it. They don't bat an eyelid any more. But I'm sure you don't know how bad it sounds. I had it logged this afternoon." And he waves a piece of paper in his hand.

Someone begins to read out from the record. We roar with laughter, slap each other on the back and collapse weakly into chairs, but this reaction is not all due to the slip of paper. Woodhall watches us and walks to the door hoping that we don't see the grin which is creasing his leathery countenance.

We clamber into our meagre transports, one small van per flight, and drive to Shopwhyke. We sit on the lawn and drink tea served by Waafs. These young girls wear overalls of flowered print and look far more attractive and feminine than in their usual masculine garb of collar and tie. One of our officers is a well-known concert pianist and he plays a movement from a Beethoven concerto, and the lovely melody fills the stately house and overflows into the garden. The sweat from the combats of but an hour ago is barely dry on our young bodies.

Shortly afterwards we were staggered to hear that Stan's 145 Squadron was to be withdrawn from the front line. They were to be transferred to Yorkshire and would be replaced with a relatively inexperienced squadron, right in the middle of the shooting season.

Stan remained indifferent and simply said that he wasn't leaving Bader; there were hot debates and long telephone calls, during which it was hinted darkly that Bader was one of the very few people who commanded Stan's respect. But the protests had little effect and, after the usual party, we saw them off to the north.

In his book *Reach for the Sky*, Paul Brickhill said of Stan Turner that he had 'a penchant for firing off a large revolver in public' and we heard that a rugged thrash developed in the officers' mess on the first evening in their new home. It was said that Stan had produced his large revolver and, backed up by an assortment of arms from his pilots, various ornaments had been brought down from the walls of the ante-room. The station commander, it was further alleged, had taken a very dim view of the proceedings.

The wing was far weaker after Stan's departure, for during the last few weeks we had fought hard together and it would take a long time to work up the new squadron. In the present type of offensive air fighting we felt strongly that we should remain together until the end of the present season. When the weather closed in we could be replaced with a new wing which would have ample time for training before the resumption of sustained operations the following spring. But we were told that the present policy was to rotate squadrons at regular intervals. 610 Squadron would be next, and ourselves in 616 the last of the original wing to leave Tangmere.

During the last week of July the weather closed in with plenty of low cloud and rain. These conditions were quite unsuitable for *Circus* operations and we had to be content with local flying and the inevitable *Rhubarbs*. We lost our Spitfire 2s and were re-equipped with the cannon-firing 5Bs. Except, of course, for the wing leader, who would not countenance the cannons, claiming that they reduced manoeuvrability and encouraged pilots to open fire from too great a range.

July gave way to August, but even when the clouds lifted we were still inactive and it seemed as if 11 Group had forgotten the Tangmere Wing. Then one evening after tea we flew on a fighter sweep, and although the 109s were above us, they seemed reluctant to engage. When we got back we were surprised to find that one of the flight commanders of the new squadron was missing.

That evening a party developed in the mess and eventually we repaired to Woodhall's suite of rooms, where the accordion was produced. Towards midnight the conversation turned to shop, and we complained to the group captain about our lack of operations.

"Don't beef at me, Douglas," said Woodhall. "I don't lay on the shows. You should complain to the A.O.C."

"Well, let's ring him up," replied Bader. "Where's the blower?"

The call was put through to 11 Group. Was it important? asked some staff officer. The A.O.C. had retired, but if it was an urgent matter the call could be switched to his bedside.

"Put it through," ordered Bader. And then:

"I thought you would like to know, sir, that we have carried out exactly one wing show in the last fortnight. The new cannons are getting rusty and the boys are fed up."

Bader listened to the genial Leigh-Mallory, who seemed to be far from displeased at this late call from one of his wing leaders.

"More fighter sweeps, sir, is what we want. Thank you, sir. Good-night." And the receiver is replaced.

"They haven't forgotten us at group," Bader explained, "and the A.O.C. has just promised that he will make sure we're not left out of the big shows. It would be a good thing to get some sleep."

The following Saturday morning found us taxying over the hard surface into our take-off positions. We are again target-support wing in the Béthune area, and Cocky and I jockey our Spitfires alongside Bader's starboard wing. The leech-like Alan Smith is about to be commissioned and is in London buying his uniform. Jeff West, an ex-civil servant from New Zealand, is flying in Smith's usual position, wingman to Bader.

Ken slides his boys into their usual position over Chichester; but where is 41 Squadron, which should fill Stan's old rôle of top cover? They fail to rendezvous, and we cannot wait, otherwise we shall miss the beehive. When the flak spits at us with its customary venom we miss Stan's uncouth but reassuring remarks.

France unfolds before us like a map, but soon the countryside is covered with cloud up to about 12,000 feet. Here and there are large gaps and occasionally we catch glimpses of the ground. The target is only a few miles ahead and Bader puts us in a slow orbit to port. Ken's voice, calm and matter of fact, fills our earphones:

"Dogsbody, 109s below, climbing up."

Bader dips first one wing and then the other. Our formation wavers when we all try to spot the Huns.

"Where the hell are they, Ken? I can't see the bastards," testily exclaims Bader.

"Under your port wing."

"O.K., I have them. Going down!"

"Shall I come down, Dogsbody?"

"No, cover us," orders the wing leader.

We fan out alongside Bader in a steep, plunging dive. For the first time I see the enemy flying in loose abreast sections, each of four Messerschmitts. We are bouncing the centre section and Cocky is lined up on the extreme starboard Hun. There is a spare 109 on the port side, so I skid under the oil-stained bellies of Cocky, Bader and West to swing alongside the New Zealander. For the last time I see Bader in the air, closing in on his opponent.

The attack is well co-ordinated, but we have lost precious seconds. On our starboard side Burton leads his four pilots of yellow section to attack, but the 109s see the Spitfires, pull up in steep climbs, and individual dog-fights take place. A highly painted 109 with a coloured spinner and an orange tail pops up in front of Nip, who bores in to point-blank range, his cannon shells thudding into the Messerschmitt.

On our port side, blue section, led by Buck Casson, are also too late for complete surprise. The Spitfires fasten on to individual opponents and the dog-fights develop on all sides. Roy cuts inside a 109 whose pilot is trying to get up-sun and pours burst after burst into his victim.

In the centre I pull up behind a Messerschmitt, but my Spitfire is travelling very fast, and she is not a steady gun platform after the coarse, skidding manoeuvre. My first burst of fire is far wide of the mark and I try to hold the bucking aircraft steady with heavy stick and rudder. When the 109 pulls into a steep climb I hang on and knock some pieces from his starboard wing.

Twenty-three pairs of eyes had watched the wing leader launch his attack. Spitfires and Messerschmitts are spilling and scattering over a wide area. Above us Ken orbits his squadron, assessing the fight and ready to lend a hand if necessary. He decides to bring his own section down into our arena, leaving eight of his Spitfires as top cover. Suddenly, just below his own position but well above us, he sees a loose bunch of twenty 109s followed by another gaggle of ten or twelve. He dives his squadron to intercept them before the Messerschmitts attack the lower Spitfires.

"Break!" over the radio. "For Christ's sake break!" But no call sign. And for whom is this urgent compelling call intended? We all break. I swing away from my 109 into a confused, savage nightmare of twisting Spitfires and cannon-spitting Messerschmitts. Three of them are behind me, their leader not more than a hundred yards astern, and I see his cannons flashing like electric lights and two streaming vortices from his wing-tips when he tightens the turn to hold me. Below me is plenty of cloud cover and I lose height in a tight spiral and hear Billy Burton's instructions:

"Get out. Withdraw. Use the cloud if you're in trouble." Normally one enters cloud with extreme care, with the aircraft nicely trimmed, the throttle set to give the correct rate of descent and with the attitude displayed by the various instruments. But this time I plunge into the concealing vapour in a steep dive at nearly 400 m.p.h., with the throttle wide open and all the instruments toppled in the dogfight. It will be several minutes before they can be used again.

I pull back the throttle and try to centralise the controls. Don't fight the Spit. Give her a chance. The altimeter has stopped unwinding and the speed falls off to less than 100 m.p.h. We must be climbing. The altimeter is unwinding again, less than 6,000 feet, but the speed is low – too low. I have an ugly sensation of being forced into one corner of the cockpit and of being sucked down by some outsized whirlpool.

We plunge out into the clear sky below the base of the cloud.

The nose of the Spitfire is well down and is slicing wickedly across the horizon. Are we hit? Damaged control? An aileron gone? It takes a second or two to realise that we are in a normal spin and automatically I take the right action. Full opposite rudder. Count one, two, three. Stick forward, centralise the controls and she comes out like the thoroughbred she is – I could hug her!

I fly just below the base of the cloud, exercising the neck muscles and ready to slide into its friendly greyness at the drop of a hat. Better check my course for Dover.

"Dogsbody four to Swallow. Emergency homing, please."

It came straight back. Confident and reassuring. A precious link with England.

"Dogsbody four from Swallow. Steer 305 degrees. Out."

A solitary 109 flies below me. Probably one of the three who gave me such a shaking a few minutes ago. Where are the other two? Is this a decoy, a trap? Or is it my turn now? I yaw the tail of the Spitfire to cover the blind spot, kick a rudder, drop each wing and search the area below. No sign of his comrades and I drop from the cloud base well below the 109 and stalk him so that I climb towards his soft belly. For here is no armour plate but only a complicated mass of engine and petrol, oil and hydraulic lines. One more look behind. All clear. He is probably flying back to his base at Wissant, but he will never get there, for the stick shakes in my hand as the Spitfire spews the cannon shells into the thin fuselage, and soon only a tell-tale plume of thick black smoke marks his fall to the earth below.

The smoke may attract unwelcome attention, and since I have reached the edge of the cloud I dive for the ground and come out of France on the deck. Low and fast. Below the tree-tops, hugging the contours of the high ground at the back of Calais and Boulogne. Over the waving peasants. A few feet above the stubble. Might be a good partridge country. Swerving to avoid a flock of wood pigeon which flutter from a thicket, for two or three smashing into the leading edge of the Spit at this speed could bring me down. Streaking over the sand dunes to see German soldiers running to their guns. Give them a ripple of cannon fire. Can't possibly hit them, but it will keep their square heads down. Over the beaches. More Huns – sunbathing. Another burst of fire and I am out of France, hot and sticky in the cockpit but supremely happy, for Dover is only a few miles through the haze.

I climb to cross the English coast. Our own gunners are always alert and we must cross in at certain points and never below 2,000 feet. Woodhall calls:

"Douglas, are you receiving?"

There is no answer, so I call the group captain.

"We've had a stiff fight, sir. I last saw the wing commander on the tail of a 109."

"Thank you, Johnnie," courteously replies the group captain.

We land at Westhampnett, singly and in pairs. Our C.O., Ken, Cocky, Roy, Nip, West and the rest of us, except Bader and Buck Casson. Woodhall is there to meet us, and with Ken's help we reconstruct the fight. We feel guilty because we lost sight of our leader and cannot say what happened to him. We look at our watches. There is still time for him to arrive and for Cocky, West and me to receive a good wigging for losing him.

Woodhall calls his ops. room in Chichester. There is no news of either pilot. The controller has checked with all the coastal airfields and has alerted the air-sea rescue boats. Woodhall telephones Leigh-Mallory and our numbers thin out, for it is time for lunch and we are hungry.

Cocky studies the large map and with his fore-finger traces a rough arc from Calais, through Cap Gris Nez down to Boulogne.

"Come here, Johnnie." I stand beside him. "Our fight was about here," and he stubs Béthune with his finger. "If they were shot down then that's that, but if they weren't too badly hit, both Douglas and Buck would make for the coast. Right?"

"O.K.," I answer.

"Good. Then there may be a chance that either of them may be in their dinghies somewhere in this area. If they are in mid-channel the air-sea rescue boys will find them. But if they're near the French coast then they'll be picked up by the Huns unless we find them first," pronounced Cocky.

"When do we take-off?" demands Nip, who, together with West, has listened intently to the conversation.

Cocky obtains permission from both the controller and Billy Burton and we are soon heading for the French coast again. But this time we are only a few feet above the Channel and although it is only a quietly lifting sea, we watch our height carefully.

When he sees the small waves breaking against the yellow sands Cocky swings us to the north and we fly parallel to the coast towards Cap Gris Nez. The enemy gunners are soon on to us and the shells from the big coastal batteries bracket the four Spitfires; but Cocky ignores the flak and holds his search line.

Round the cliffs to Gris Nez to see a small shore-hugging convoy of five or six tankers escorted by a heavily armed E-Boat which turns broadside on when we approach. On to Calais. More flak and the sea seems to boil where a flurry of shells strikes the water. A steep turn with eyes focused on the sea at this low level and back to Le Touquet. Suddenly Nip peels away and we see him diving to attack something on the water.

"What's the form, Nip?" demands Cocky.

"I think it was a small submarine. I thought I'd give it a squirt," answers Nip.

"Re-form," orders Cocky. "We're not after submarines this trip."

Jeff West sights a dinghy bobbing up and down, but it is empty, and perhaps symbolic of our search. We see a large enemy rescue-float, but it, too, is deserted and we turn to the north again. Cocky keeps us out until our petrol is getting very low, and we barely have enough to trickle back to Hawkinge at low revs.

We are met by a sympathetic intelligence officer, who tells us that there is still no news of either pilot. He is very interested in Nip's account of the small submarine, but we only half listen to his queries, for we are watching the ground crews refuel our Spitfires. After this task is finished we shall be in the air again and Cocky is plotting his new search lines.

But immediately we are airborne Woodhall calls from Tangmere and cancels our trip. We are to return to Westhampnett and land, for other squadrons will take up the search.

Woodhall had already broken the news to Thelma, and Cocky went to the Bay House to tell her what little he could of our last flight together. Cocky was now in charge of A Flight and he asked me to stay at our dispersal and check the Spitfires for tomorrow's sweeps. We made out our combat reports, for between us, Nip, West and I had destroyed four Messerschmitts and Gibbs was clamouring for the paper work. After ten minutes with our hard-working Flight Sergeant Dale, we climbed into our little van and drove towards the mess.

It was one of those August evenings which mark the end of high summer. Although it was barely nine o'clock the sun had disappeared below the Downs and the tall beeches on the other side of the meadow were barely visible in the fading light. It was the quiet time, when all the Spitfires were down and the Beaufighters had not clawed into the air for the night patrols.

Our ground crews were bedding the Spitfires down for the night. Placing chocks under the wheels, tying on the cockpit covers and carrying out last-minute tasks so that they would be ready at dawn. All except the crews of the two missing Spitfires, who stood apart in a restless, disconsolate little group and who occasionally fell silent and strained their eyes to the east, as if peering hard enough they would see their two Spitfires swinging in to land.

We, too, were silent when we drove to the mess, for we knew that even if our wing leader was still alive he would have little chance of evading capture with his tin legs. Before this we had rarely thought of his artificial limbs, and it was only when we swam together and saw his stumps and how he thrashed his way out of the deep water with his powerful arms that we remembered his infirmity. At Tangmere we had simply judged him on his ability as a leader and a fighter pilot, and for us the high sky would never be the same. Gone was the confident, eager, often scornful voice. Exhorting us, sometimes cursing us, but always holding us together in the fight. Gone was the greatest tactician of them all. Today marked the end of an era that was rapidly becoming a legend.

The elusive, intangible qualities of leadership can never be taught, for a man either has them or he hasn't. Bader had them in full measure and on every flight had shown us how to apply them. He had taught us the true meaning of courage, spirit, determination, guts – call it what you will. Now that he was gone, it was our task to follow his signposts which pointed the way ahead.

Chapter Eight

NO ROSE WITHOUT A THORN[1]

"ATTENTION, all ranks. This is the station commander speaking. You will all be pleased to know that Wing Commander Bader is alive and well on the other side of the Channel. He is a prisoner of war."

So a day or two later Woodhall broadcast the welcome news on the Tannoy system; a few minutes later he walked into our dispersal hut. For once this splendid controller showed signs of intense excitement.

"We've heard from the International Red Cross that Douglas is in hospital at St Omer. One of his legs was badly damaged when he baled out. The Germans have offered safe conduct for a small aircraft to fly across to France and take a spare set of legs." Woodhall paused and looked out of the window at our small Magister. He continued:

"We could paint the Maggie white and stuff the legs into the back seat. I'm just the chap to fly it. I'd probably land at St Omer and," he concluded wistfully, "I might even see Douglas again."

"We'll give you a close escort, sir," we suggested. "Just in case the 109s try any funny business."

"Not damned likely," rejoined the group captain. "This must be played as a solo hand, or else it will get out of control. I'll get on to group right away."

But we didn't accept the Luftwaffe's sporting and even chivalrous offer. Perhaps the blitzing of our cities and the reverses in the Western Desert had not left us in a chivalrous mood. At Tangmere we were almost brusquely informed that the legs would be dropped on a normal daylight bombing raid. The leading

[1] Extract from the squadron diary, dated 26th August 1941: "A.V.M. Leigh-Mallory paid us a visit in the afternoon and presented us with our crest, approved by H.M. the King. It depicts a white rose of Yorkshire with an arrow through it, denoting speed and death. 'Nulla Rosa Sine Spina' – 'No Rose without a Thorn' – is the motto.

Blenheim would drop the package in the St Omer area before the bombers went on to their target. At the time this high-level decision seemed right and proper, and there was no doubt that it reflected our own mood.

We provided close escort to the Blenheims. Heavy flak bracketed the bombers when the parcel dropped out and our new wing leader spoke distinctly over the radio so that the enemy would intercept and understand his message: "We have dropped Wing Commander Bader's spare legs. I say again, we have dropped Wing Commander Bader's spare legs ten miles south-west of St Omer."

Two days later we had a stern fight when the wing again provided high cover to the Blenheims. It was one of those hazy autumn days when you could see the ground below but the forward visibility was very poor. To make matters worse there was a thick layer of cloud at 19,000 feet and the four escort wings were sandwiched into a tight space between the Blenheims and the cloud.

The enemy pilots were quick to turn the weather conditions to tactical advantage and, operating in twos and fours, they bounced our cramped Spitfires all the way to the target at Choques. I saw one of our Spitfires streaming glycol but going down under control for a crash landing. Subsequently I found out that this was Crow, who, fighting a running battle along with Ken and Tony Gaze, had been badly hit.[1]

610 Squadron left us soon after this fight, for, apart from Crow, three other pilots were shot down during this engagement. The pilots of the two Auxiliary squadrons, 610 and ourselves, had developed a perfect understanding in the air and we should miss the wise, utterly dependable Ken Holden. After they had gone, we found that throughout the season we in 616 had enjoyed the easiest

[1] Crowley-Milling crash landed his Spitfire and evaded capture. Soon he was in the hands of the Resistance movement and was hiding in St Omer. There he learnt of a plan to rescue Bader from the nearby hospital, but unfortunately the wing commander had already made an unsuccessful bid to escape and was on his way to Germany. Crow began his long journey home, which was to lead him over the Pyrenees, into Spain and a concentration camp, and ultimately back to 610 Squadron to continue the fight.

task in the Tangmere Wing. For we had always flown, with the wing leader, in front and below the other two squadrons, and when we manoeuvred for an opening against the Messerschmitts we knew that twenty-four Spitfires were above us guarding us from a bad bounce. Now, as the senior squadron, it fell to our lot to provide top cover to the wing while the new wing leader led one of the other squadrons one mile below. We soon learnt that it was far easier to fly next to the wing leader in the spearhead of the formation, guarded by two squadrons, than to hold a high, steady down-sun position and keep a constant look-out at the same time.

For the past month or so I had worn the single, medium stripe of a flying officer and for some time had been deputy flight commander to Cocky. One day in mid-September the C.O. met me when I climbed out of the cockpit, held out his hand and said: "Congratulations, Johnnie. You're to put up your second stripe and take over B Flight."

There were more congratulations on the following day when it was announced that Nip and I were each awarded the D.F.C. and Jeff West the D.F.M. The promotion meant that my days as a wingman were over. From this day I should always lead my own section of four Spitfires, and on the ground would be responsible for nine or ten pilots and the well-being of half a hundred airmen. And when Burton was away I would get an opportunity to lead the squadron. The silver-and-mauve ribbon which we wore meant a great deal, for it seemed to stamp us with the coveted hall-mark of veteran fighter pilots and leaders.

Soon after this Cocky left us. He was fatigued from a long tour of operational flying during which he had suffered two shattering experiences: once when he was shot down in the Battle of Britain and again early in 1941 when he crash landed his crippled Spitfire at Hawkinge. He was the last of the original Auxiliaries and loathe to leave the squadron to which he owed great allegiance. He was undoubtedly ready for a rest from ops., but at this time the word 'rest' was something of a misnomer, since it usually consisted of six months at a training school, where you flew hard to try and teach the newcomers the elements of the game. The environment was quite different from the vital comradeship of squadron life, and your rest seemed to resolve itself into a frustrating search to escape. Eventually your stint was over and you went back on ops., far more tired than when you were taken off six months earlier.

The Luftwaffe approached their problem from a different angle, and Galland himself relates how after a strenuous bout of operations their squadrons were withdrawn, one by one, and the pilots sent off on a free skiing leave, or to the Mediterranean, where they relaxed on a sun-drenched beach. And it was said that other suitable amenities were provided. After such a complete and refreshing break from flying they returned to their units, fit and ready for the fight. In the damp, grey winter of 1944-45, when we were bogged down in Holland and Belgium, our far-sighted group commander started a similar scheme and we flew to the French Alps, where we skied hard for two weeks in the sunshine. But in 1941 such an arrangement was quite impossible.

So one Sunday morning in September it was time to say good-bye to Cocky Dundas. He was posted to a training unit in the North of England and was flying there in the tiny two-seater Maggie. A Canadian pilot, Huck Murray, would go with him and bring the Maggie back. For a few moments we clustered round the aircraft to wish him well. He was hardly dressed for the occasion. Upwards of a hundred sweeps and escorts over France had not improved the appearance of the silk-lined tunic. One of the two unbalanced 'A's was missing altogether, and a vivid yellow scarf added a sporting touch to his ensemble. His cap was mercifully already stowed away in the Maggie.

We poured him into the front, open cockpit of the aircraft, which was never intended to accommodate such a long, sparse frame. His helmeted and goggled head towered above the windscreen. I stood on the wing root, fastened the safety straps and shouted above the noise of the engine:

"All the best, Cocky. Keep in touch and don't let the training business get you down. Pity you haven't got any oxygen in this crate. You look as though you could do with a few whiffs!"

He turned a pair of pale bloodshot eyes upon me:

"Don't worry, Johnnie. I'll be back on ops. before Christmas. I've got it all worked out. Cheerio."

The Maggie chugged out and Cocky turned it into wind.

Just before he opened up for the take-off we gave him a ragged cheer. Hours later the Canadian returned and seemed pleased to get back.

"What's the form, Huck?" we demanded. "How did it go?"

"Well," replied our pilot, "we landed about noon and went to the bar for a drink. Cocky said he was thirsty." He paused to recollect a scene that he wouldn't easily forget.

"Go on, Huck," we ordered.

"Well, we walked into the bar and ordered two beers. There was some sort of inspection going on, for the place was full of brass. I think an air vice-marshal was there."

"What happened then?" we demanded.

"Nothing, if you know what I mean," answered Huck thoughtfully. "They just looked at us. Nobody said anything. But I didn't feel like any food so I took off straight away and flew back here." And he walked away with his shoulders set and the air of a man who has done his duty.

Cocky established an all-time record for the brevity of a non-operational tour. Powerful forces were enlisted to support his return to ops., and after exactly four weeks he joined Ken and 610 Squadron as a flight commander. He received a handsome Christmas present when he was promoted to squadron leader and given the command of the first Typhoon squadron. He would not be divorced from the close fraternity of the fighter squadrons, and his rapid return to the fray proved that you could always get to the squadrons – if you tried hard enough and had the guts. Cocky never looked back, and finished the war in Italy, handsomely decorated and one of the R.A.F.'s youngest and most able group captains.

Group Captain Victor Beamish, who played rugby for the Harlequins, was on the staff at 11 Group headquarters and often flew down to Tangmere to discuss current operations and tactics. He was the ideal type of staff officer, for he not only planned our fighter sweeps and escorts but also flew on a great many of them. He was experienced, wise and approachable, and spoke the same language as the fighter pilots whose destinies he so intimately controlled. He had a habit of wearing a set of blue mechanic's overalls over his uniform, without any badges of rank, and this had led to an amusing incident, for the first time he paid us a visit he parked his Spitfire outside the dispersal hut on the very spot reserved for our own C.O.

An outraged fitter looked at the bare overalls and probably took Beamish for a thoughtless sergeant-pilot. When the engine was switched off, the airman shouted his displeasure in no uncertain terms. The group captain said nothing, but climbed from the cockpit, stripped off the deceiving overalls to reveal the four stripes of a group captain and a row of decorations and handed the garment to the astonished fitter.

But this time he was on a different errand and he talked to Billy Burton and me as we paced the concrete perimeter track.

"We're taking you out of the line, Billy. You've had a good spell down here and we're sending you back to Kirton next week. 65 Squadron will replace you."

"But I thought we'd be here a bit longer," protested the C.O. "I mean, we're the most experienced squadron, the others are very new."

"I know," replied Beamish, "but the weather is clamping and there won't be a lot of action before next spring. Far better to go now and come back fresh and keen next year. Anyhow, there it is, and now I'd like a word in private with you, Billy."

Soon after, Beamish took off and I rejoined the C.O., who stood alone on the perimeter track, shoulders hunched and hands thrust into his pockets.

"What's the form, sir?" I asked.

"I've had it, Johnnie. They're taking me off ops. and I'm handing over to Colin Gray tomorrow. You'll like him. He's a New Zealander with sixteen or seventeen Huns already."

"What's happening to you, sir?" I enquired.

"They're giving me a desk job at 11 Group. It will be the next best thing to this," he replied.

I tried to cheer up this intense, straightforward regular officer who had served the squadron so well.

"Your job is really over, sir. You took over a pretty demoralised bunch of pilots a year ago. You trained them up again. Brought them down here to the fighting. We've had a good year and you've put 616 back on the map."

The C.O. remained silent.

"And I agree with Victor Beamish," I continued. "Far better for us all to go now and come back in the spring. You'll probably get a wing of your own, sir, after a few months at group."

"Perhaps you're right, Johnnie. Will you tell the chaps, please? Squadron Leader Gray will take you back to Kirton next Tuesday. I suppose there's bound to be a thrash tonight?"

"Naturally, sir," I admitted, and took my leave of him to make the necessary arrangements.

The permanent staff at Kirton Lindsey welcomed us back with lavish hospitality. They had spent a quiet summer in Lincolnshire and they had followed our exploits with great enthusiasm, for they regarded 616 as their own squadron. Our dispersal huts were freshly painted and new carpets were on the floor of our crew room. There was a liberal supply of armchairs, current magazines and good books, a radio and a gramophone. Although our daily round at Kirton would be confined to routine convoy patrols over the North Sea, air firing and training flights, with perhaps an occasional sweep from an airfield in 11 Group, we were comfortably bedded down for the winter.

Each of the Auxiliary squadrons had its own honorary air commodore, and ours, the Marquis of Tichfield, drove over from his country seat in Nottinghamshire to welcome us back at a guest night in the mess. After dinner the conversation turned to shooting. Were we interested, Tichfield enquired? Of course, there was no rearing nowadays, but the pheasants were quite good at Welbeck and there had already been some reasonable partridge drives. We were too enthusiastic, for I think he went away with the impression that we could produce several experienced game shots, whereas in actual fact only I had fired at a driven bird. And Welbeck was probably one of the best stocked and administered shoots in the country. I told Colin Gray my fears, but he had a quick answer: "Don't worry. I'm sure it will be all right. And anyhow, from today you're officer in charge of shooting!"

Two days later there was a phone call from Welbeck. Lord Tichfield would like the squadron to provide four guns next Thursday. Bring plenty of cartridges and some lunch. Yes, it would be all driven game, no walking. I had exactly a week in which to select the team and teach them something of the strict ethics of the English shooting-field.

Our new C.O. was a natural shot and would lead the expedition to Welbeck. Nip could hit a pheasant and was quite safe with a loaded gun. As the fourth member I selected Jeff West, newly commissioned and keen to see something of our country life. He had never shot game before, but he could bring down Messerschmitts, where the same basic principles of deflection shooting held good.

The majority of our fighter pilots could fly reasonably well. They were trained sufficiently to hold their own in a dogfight, but when it came to the ultimate test, judging the range and deflection angle of their opponents, the average pilot failed, and this was because we paid too little attention to the science of air gunnery. Perhaps I should qualify this statement to apply only to those of us who completed our training during the war years. The fact remains that the average pilot could knock down a 109 when he overhauled it from dead line astern and hose-piped his opponent with two cannons and four machine guns. But give him a testing deflection shot at angles of more than a few degrees and he usually failed to nail his opponent. Personally, I found my own game and wild-fowling experiences to be of the greatest value. The fighter pilot who could hit a curling, down-wind pheasant, or a jinking head-on partridge, or who could kill a widgeon cleanly in a darkening sky, had little trouble in bringing his guns to bear against the 109s. The outstanding fighter pilots were invariably excellent game-shots.

Generally acknowledged amongst fighter pilots to be the finest shot in the air was the New Zealander, 'Hawk-Eye' Wells. Before the war he had won several clay-pigeon championships in New Zealand and established himself as that country's number one marksman with a twelve bore. Aptly dubbed Hawk-Eye during the Battle of Britain because of his amazing eyesight, he shot down many enemy aircraft whenever he got within range. Today, there are few to match him on the partridge stubbles of East Anglia.

Second only to Hawk-Eye was the Canadian, 'Screwball' Beurling, who made his name in Malta, where his shooting ability became a legend. He brought down no less than twenty-seven German and Italian aircraft within a period of two weeks, and some of his combat reports described where and how many times his cannon shells struck home. On one occasion in Malta he claimed a 'probable', and stated that there would be five cannon shells in the cockpit. Shortly afterwards a report came in that an Italian aircraft had crashed on the island with five cannon holes in the cockpit. Beurling, too, was a natural shot with a shotgun, and later, when he was a pilot in my Canadian wing, he often borrowed my gun and Labrador.

We were confident that Jeff would be all right once we had given him some elementary training, so we began on the clay-pigeon range, where he proved to be an above-average shot. Then we explained how the beaters brought the birds to the guns and told him of the safety factors which applied not only to the beaters but also to the guns themselves. I fell back on the time-honoured method of placing two sticks in front of him, one on each side, so that when he swung his gun over either stick he remembered to bring it to a vertical position and didn't lower it until the birds were well clear of the line of guns.

We reported at Welbeck. It was a crisp, firm winter day which promised well for the sport. The customary draw for positions took place and for the first drive Jeff found himself between our host and a famous amateur golfer, and I was next along the line of guns. The horn sounded and the partridges swung across the sugar beet, fast, jinking and very low. The first few coveys came straight at

Jeff, and he went into action. The guns on either side fell silent and with good reason, for Jeff had his sights on the enemy and swung his gun from front to rear at shoulder height! His lordship and his retinue – loader, under keeper and dog handler – took suitable avoiding action, as did the amateur golfer.

After the first drive I had strong words with the New Zealander and suggested to our host that, since West was very inexperienced at this sort of thing, it might be wise to put him well behind the guns as a stopper. Lord Tichfield never batted an eyelid and said he was sure Mr West would soon pick up the drill and that we had better get along to the next drive. For me the day was not improved when one of our more enterprising airmen, acting in the temporary capacity of loader, decided to take a hand in the proceedings and brought down a wild duck!

We continued to shoot at Welbeck until the end of the season, and for us those days were some of the happiest of the war years. We always shot until it was nearly dark. Some very old men acted as beaters, for the youngsters were away at the war. One cold, wet afternoon when the light began to fade, we finished a drive and our host addressed the beaters, who were bunched together:

"Would you fellows mind if I asked you for another drive?"

The simple reply came straight back from an aged countryman:

"We'll beat till midnight for 616, m'lord."

12 Group always provided a duty wing of Spitfires which could be sent to the south at short notice. Early in November we refuelled at West Malling, and with two Canadian squadrons above us we patrolled just inside Dunkirk to provide withdrawal cover for the beehive returning from Lille.

The Canadians were heavily engaged, and Roy Marples, flying next to our inexperienced wing leader, quietly reported a dozen Messerschmitts well above us. When they slanted down to attack us, Roy called the break and Nip and I, leading our finger-fours on either flank, drove our Spitfires round in steep turns to meet the threat. But Roy was horrified to see the wing leader still flying straight and level, quite unaware of the danger. Roy yelled over the radio and as the cannon shells streamed at them, all except the wing leader took desperate evading action.

We were puzzled by the unfamiliar silhouettes of some of the enemy fighters, which seemed to have squarer wing-tips and more tapering fuselages than the Messerschmitts we usually encountered. Later Nip swore that one of the enemy aircraft which fastened on to him had a radial engine, and another pilot said he had distinctly seen a mixed armament of cannons and machine guns, all firing from wing positions.

Whatever these strange fighters were, they gave us a hard time of it. They seemed to be faster in a zoom climb than a 109, far more stable in a vertical dive, and they turned better than the Messerschmitt, for we had all our work cut out to shake them off. One of our Canadian sergeants, Sanderson, who was in the leading section, was set upon by two or three of these enemy fighters, was chased and harried all the way across the Channel and barely managed to crash land his Spitfire on the east coast near Southend. We never saw the wing leader again, and later we heard that he had been shot down and killed.

Our own troubles were not over, for we returned to find the south-east corner of England covered by a thin fog which persisted to a thousand feet and reduced forward visibility to less than a few hundred yards. More than two hundred Spitfires, all of which had only enough petrol for another few minutes' flying, were trying to find an airfield, and the radio homing channels were jammed with requests for assistance. I headed my section down-sun, where the visibility was a little better, and by a stroke of sheer luck found what appeared to be an abandoned airfield. It was very small and we brought our Spitfires carefully over the boundary for precautionary landings with plenty of power and the nose well up so that we should stop in the shortest possible space. We had, in fact, landed on a disused, bomb-cratered airfield near Chatham, and it was only after a long delay that we were refuelled. Even then our misfortunes were not over, for Alan Smith nosed his Spitfire into a crater when we took off at last light.

Back at Kirton, and encouraged by Gibbs, we drew up our

chairs and sketched plan and side views of the strange aircraft. Nip thought the wing-tips were very similar to those of a Miles Master and Jeff West said he thought the fuselage was slender because of the bulk of the radial engine. We were all agreed that it was superior to the Messerschmitt 109F and completely outclassed our Spitfire 5s. Our sketches disappeared into mysterious intelligence channels and we heard no more of the matter, but fighter pilots reported increasing numbers of these outstanding fighters over northern France.

Later we were given the novel explanation that the new enemy fighters were probably some of a batch of Curtis Hawk aeroplanes which the French had bought from the United States shortly before the war. It was suggested to us that the Luftwaffe had taken over the Curtis Hawks and were using them operationally. This was an absurd theory, for no pre-war aircraft had a performance to compare with these brutes, and it was not for some months that our intelligence admitted the introduction of a completely new fighter, the redoubtable Focke-Wulf 190, designed by Kurt Tank.

Soon after this the character of the squadron changed completely. Jeff West and Nip went to continue the fight from Malta. Roy was posted to non-operational duties and we missed his breezy nature and never-ending fund of spicy stories. Later he returned to ops. and had a distinguished career, which ended tragically when his wingman, climbing behind him in line astern, lost him in the sun and sliced off the tail of his Spitfire. Alan Smith, who had flown so well during the past year, also left us. Their places were taken by a keen bunch of nineteen- and twenty-year-olds from overseas; my flight of eleven pilots consisted of three Canadians (Bowen, Sanderson and Strouts), four New Zealanders (Crafts, Ware, Bolton and Davidson), one Australian (Smithson), one Rhodesian (Winter) and one Englishman (Welch), in addition to myself. We were a very mixed bag, and although the South Yorkshire Squadron had lost its original north-country flavour, the newcomers flew every bit as well as their Yorkshire predecessors.

Early in 1942 we moved to a new airfield at Kingscliffe, a satellite of the sector airfield at Wittering which lies on the Great

North Road just south of Stamford. Our quarters were bleak, wooden huts and we sorely missed the luxury of our permanent, centrally heated accommodation at Kirton. The weather was cold and cheerless and our numerous reverses in the Far East and the recent escape of the great German ships – the *Gneisenau* and *Scharnhorst* – seemed to add to the gloom.

Our station commander at Wittering was the famous Group Captain Basil Embry, who already held the D.S.O. and two bars. He had been shot down in 1940 and captured by the Germans. After many adventures, including the killing of his guards, he escaped to Spain. The Germans put a price on him, dead or alive, but until the end of the war he flew on operations under the name of a fictitious wing commander. When we served under him at Kingscliffe he was exactly forty years old, and he beat me soundly at squash on his birthday.[1]

Another strong character at Wittering was the intelligent, urbane Peter Clapham, who was a controller in the ops. room. Like many others he fell under the magnetic spell of our group captain ('Basilized', we called it) and began, in 1942, to fly in his Beaufighter as radar operator. There began a protracted struggle to have Peter transferred from administrative to flying duties. When Basil Embry became an air vice-marshal and commander of 2 Group, Peter joined him and they flew on many of the epic low-level raids together. Peter was awarded the D.F.C. and bar; four days before the end of the war he was officially informed that his transfer to flying duties had been approved.

The Wittering wing leader, Pat Jameson, was a tough, resilient New Zealander who had also proved himself to be a leader of the highest quality. As a flight commander in 46 Squadron Jamie had taken part in the ill-fated Norwegian campaign. When the end in Norway seemed inevitable, his squadron commander, 'Bing' Cross, received orders either to destroy his Hurricanes or fly them to another airfield and stow them in a cargo ship which might be in a nearby harbour. Neither of these proposals seemed satisfactory to the clear-thinking Cross, so he visited the *Glorious* and made

[1] Basil Embry's 1940 adventures are described in *Wingless Victory*, by Anthony Richardson.

arrangements with her captain to try and land his ten remaining Hurricanes on the flight-deck. For this occasion the *Glorious* would make the fastest speed since her acceptance trials.

No modern fighter of the Spitfire or Hurricane class had yet landed on a carrier. There were no arrester hooks on their fighters, so they strapped bags of sand into the rear of the fuselages to hold their tails down when they hit the deck. Jameson would have the first crack at it with three aircraft. If successful, he would send a signal to his squadron commander, who would follow with the remaining seven.

Jamie's small formation, led by a slow Swordfish from the *Glorious*, was soon lost to sight. Hours passed and there was no news. They were either safely on the carrier or in the drink. Cross and the remaining pilots took off, with another Swordfish leading, and flew a long way out to sea before they found the *Glorious*. Fighter pilots, with their single-engined aircraft, do not relish lengthy flights over the sea. But on this occasion their spirits rose as they left Norway behind. They were going home and taking their Hurricanes with them. All the fighters got down on the *Glorious* and were soon stowed away in the hangar below.

Cross soon made a tour of the *Glorious* and visited the chart room, where he found they were about two hundred miles from the Norwegian coast. The chief dangers in these waters, he was told, was from submarines, but no sub. could harm them at their present speed of seventeen knots. On their previous crossing to Norway the carrier's own Swordfish had patrolled ahead and on the flanks of the *Glorious*. Now, on the return journey, there were no such flights, but one Swordfish armed with anti-submarine bombs was at readiness on the flight-deck. (The official report on the loss of the *Glorious* stated that the carrier was an old ship whose endurance was limited; had she possessed sufficient fuel she would have accompanied a larger group of ships on the return journey. Five torpedo-spotting reconnaissance aircraft were aboard, but no reconnaissance patrols were flown on the day she went down.)

When 'action stations' was sounded, Cross made his way to the quarter-deck and saw that all eyes were focused on two distant plumes of smoke. Almost immediately three large columns of water, some twenty yards from the *Glorious*, announced the arrival of the first salvo of shells from either the *Scharnhorst* or the *Gneisenau*. Cross thought: I'm going to see a full-scale naval action. Must watch it very closely. Most useful when I get to staff college!

He walked to the flight-deck and another salvo hit the carrier on the starboard side, destroying the very stairs from which he had just stepped. A single round fell a few yards ahead of him. Fortunately it didn't explode, but merely left a large hole with a raised lip through which came a wisp of smoke. Soon the German cruisers seemed to be hitting the *Glorious* with about two salvoes out of every three they fired. The noise when the shells struck home was quite different from anything Cross had heard before. It was like the noise of tearing calico, but magnified a thousand times. Someone came up to him and said: "That last salvo set fire to your Hurricanes below. But don't worry. We'll soon have it out."

The *Glorious* was burning and listing. The discipline was magnificent. Cross saw frantic efforts by officers and men of the Fleet Air Arm to raise their Swordfish to the flight-deck and get them armed with torpedoes. These efforts were of no avail, and about half an hour after the attack began the ship's intercommunication failed. Then the 'abandon ship' order was passed from man to man, and someone said that the bridge had received a direct hit and the captain was dead. The abandon ship order was cancelled, but soon the original command was heard again. The *Glorious* was still moving and there was a trail of rafts, wreckage and bodies in the wake of the ship.

Cross said to a young lieutenant: "What's the best way to get on a raft?"

"Wait till they drop a Carley float, sir. Then jump after it bloody quickly or else you'll have a long swim!"

The squadron leader jumped overboard and swam to a Carley float which had just been dropped. Already three or four sailors were on the float and soon afterwards he saw a strong swimmer knifing through the sea with an immaculate Pacific crawl. Jamie slid on to the float but immediately plunged in again and returned with a half-drowned sailor. Finally there were about thirty-seven men aboard the raft.

The *Glorious* seemed to come to a stop about a mile from their float and one of their escort destroyers appeared to be stationary a good deal farther off towards the German cruisers. Cross and Jameson did not see the *Glorious* sink, for they were sitting with their backs to her. One moment she was there, and then the sea was empty except for the rafts and a thousand pieces of wreckage. The German cruisers came quite close to the rafts, and Cross took his squadron records from inside his Irvine jacket and threw them into the sea. But the enemy ships turned away and left.

On the third day they were picked up by a small Norwegian ship, but by then only seven of them were still alive. After his long convalescence, Cross was sent to continue the fight from North Africa. Jamie recovered in time to fight in the Battle of Britain and now served as Basil Embry's wing leader.

Such was the calibre of the men who were to lead us at Wittering during that bleak winter.

For some extraordinary reason which we never fathomed, we were suddenly re-equipped with the Mark 6 version of the Spitfire. Only a hundred of these aircraft were produced, and according to the firm's representative, who came to see us at Kingscliffe, it was the first pressurized fighter and had been hurriedly produced to counter the high-flying reconnaissance Junkers 86Ps in the Middle East, which were operating at altitudes of well over 40,000 feet and proving very difficult to intercept.

The cockpit was sealed and a great deal of hot air, which was impossible to control, was blown over our perspiring bodies. The cockpit cover was placed over the pilot before take-off and locked securely in position by four clamping-levers. We didn't like this gadget, for we were used to our sliding hoods, which remained open for take-off and which we slid back for landing: this locked hood looked like a sealed, transparent coffin. Most of our operations from Wittering were carried out at low-level, and patrolling an East Coast convoy at this height in the warm spring sunshine in a Spitfire designed to operate at well over 40,000 feet was a sheer test of stamina. It was like flying in a Turkish bath, and we lost weight despite the formidable quantities of beer that we drank. We made the best of it, for perhaps we should soon find ourselves in the Desert.

We managed to get our new Spitfires well above 40,000 feet on practice flights, but it would be a very tricky business to fight at these altitudes. We found that the nearer we got to the absolute ceiling of the fighter the more accurately we had to fly, and the Spitfire must be held as steady as possible. The controls must never be used coarsely, and all changes of attitude had to be carried out very slowly, otherwise we stalled or lost height.

One fine evening towards the end of May, I left my flight at readiness and slipped away to change into a decent uniform, for I was going to a cocktail party given by one of the Wittering officers. After changing I drove back to the dispersal hut to have a final word with the chaps, and when I walked in I was almost knocked down by two pilots, Brown and Welch, who raced to their Spitfires. Brown was a smallish, fair-headed youngster who, although he had only been with us a few weeks, shaped so well that I had made him a section leader.

"What's all the flap about?" I demanded, for we hadn't had a scramble for months.

Sergeant Smithson, a cheerful and assertive young Australian and already earmarked for a commission, answered:

"Don't know, sir. We just had the scramble over the blower. They were told to patrol over Leicester at 2,000 feet."

This sounded interesting, so I called the controller, who turned out to be Peter Clapham.

"What's the form, Peter?" I asked.

"We've got a lone bandit near Leicester. He's stooging about below a thousand feet. Your blue section is very close," he replied.

"Can I take up another section?" I said.

"Press on. Give me a call as soon as you're airborne."

I shouted to Smithson and we jumped into the two nearest Spitfires. No time to place the hood on and lock it, and a good thing too, for I didn't want to ruin my best suit.

"Green section airborne, Peter," I reported.

"Steer 270. Bandit is ten miles ahead." And a second or two later: "Steer 300. Bandit is five miles ahead."

We were only a few feet above the ground and just below the cloud base. We raced and curved over the wolds of Leicestershire and Rutland and occasionally I caught a glimpse of the squat, grey tower of a village church. I had spent my boyhood in this country and knew our exact position.

Peter called for the last time on the radio: "Steer 350 Johnnie. Buster.[1] You're very close."

We both saw him at the same time. Smithson sang out, but my thumb was on the firing button. It was a twin-engined Dornier with a blunt nose and two rudders and he was turning to port below us. We cut across his wider turn and with his wings filling and spilling over the gunsight we bored in for the kill.

Suddenly a sickening shadow of doubt stopped me jabbing the firing button, for instead of the black-and-white German crosses on the wings, the bomber bore large dark circles strangely like the roundels of our own Service. And wasn't there one of our aircraft like this with twin rudders which was manufactured in the States? I was very close, less than seventy yards, but not in a firing position, for I had automatically pulled up when I saw the roundels: there had been many instances of mistaken identity in the air. But all my fears were put aside when the gunner in the upper dorsal turret gave my Spitfire a long burst of fire and it seemed as if a hundred golf balls were hurtling past the cockpit. Furious at this intruder who wore false colours, I shouted to Smithson: "Get him, Smithy. Get the — "

I pivoted the Spitfire on her wing-tip and came round for my real attack, burning with resentment against the Hun and angry with myself for missing the first opening. I saw Smithson break away and the Dornier slide into the low cloud. We didn't see the Hun again.

The two pilots of blue section heard my bitter oath and young

[1] Increase speed.

Brown raced in to attack. Wisps of white smoke began to stream from one of the engines of the Dornier, but when Brown broke away the gunner nailed him and shattered his hood, and something struck his right eye, like the stinging slap from an open hand. He reached up to his injured eye to find his white silk glove covered with blood, and in great pain and half blinded, he put his damaged Spitfire down perfectly at North Luffenham.

The rest of us landed at Kingscliffe and were met by Basil Embry and his wing leader. They had caught a glimpse of the Dornier and heard our cannon fire. Where was it? Burning in some field, of course, and had any of the crew baled out? I told them the ugly truth and how four Spitfires had only managed to damage one engine and that I had not fired a single shot. The other pilots had also seen the dark roundels, and the two senior officers were furious at this deception.

Young Brown had lost his right eye, but nevertheless he soon reported back to the squadron as perky as ever and anxious to continue his tour. The wing leader checked him out in a dual trainer and then sent him solo in a Spitfire. Higher authority suggested that Brown should cease his flying career and should be transferred to ground duties. Then Basil Embry entered the arena. The group captain personally recommended that Brown continue on operations, for far better a brave pilot with one eye than a craven-hearted creature with two! But, said authority, how can he be expected to fly modern fighters with one eye? The group captain then played his ace and said that his pilot was already flying a Spitfire with his usual ability.

So young Brown stayed on ops. and joined the night fighter squadron at Wittering. Later he commanded a Shackleton squadron in Coastal Command, and became known throughout the Service as 'Cyclops' Brown, following his exploits with his Spitfire Squadron.

We moved again and this time back to Kenley, in 11 Group, where the squadron had taken such a mauling in the Battle of Britain. Our Spitfire 6s would be useful operating high over

France, since the Focke-Wulf had proved far superior to the Spitfire 5s, with which the bulk of Fighter Command was equipped, and they had regained most of the hard-won air superiority we had established during the previous year. But my own future did not lie with 616 Squadron: I had been recommended for the command of another fighter squadron. After two days at Kenley I was told to report to 610 Squadron in Norfolk.

There were only a few hours in which to bid the squadron a decent farewell. The whole squadron turned out and we spent our last evening together drinking pints of beer in a local pub. I was able to thank my own flight sergeant, Randerson, my fitter, Fred Burton, my rigger, Arthur Radcliffe, Fred Yarley, Gledhill, Jackman, Durham and a host of others who had laboured long hours to keep the Spitfires in the air. Early the next day Varley loaded my few possessions into a recent purchase, an aged Morris Minor, and I set out for Norfolk and 610.

Chapter Nine

COUNTY OF CHESTER SQUADRON

The following day I reported to Group Captain Ronnie Lees who commanded Coltishall, and he gave me a brief sketch of his units. Max Aitken, distinguished son of Lord Beaverbrook, led 68 Squadron and they were doing extremely well with their Beaufighters. A good thing, too, for it was high time we closed the gap at night. There were two satellite airfields: Matlask, which held a Whirlwind squadron and Ludham, hard by Hickling Broad, which was to be my new home. The group captain told me something of the recent activities of my new squadron: convoy patrols, enemy shipping reconnaissances off the Dutch coast, a few odd sweeps from 11 Group and (I knew it was coming) plenty of *Rhubarbs*.

"What's the chance of getting the squadron back to 11 Group, sir?" I enquired.

"Very good, I should think," he answered. "They've been out of the front line since last autumn. But let's see what you make of the job here to begin with. And one final piece of advice. Keep in touch with Max. His Beaus are getting a lot of radar contacts – in fact, more than they can cope with. On a moonlight night it might be worthwhile to put one of your Spits alongside and see if your boys could use some of this information. I am going to have a crack myself in a Spit the next time the Huns come across. Good luck with 610."

Crow was one of the first to greet me at Ludham. He had made his escape from France during the previous autumn and still fought on with the squadron. It was embarrassing to hear him call me 'sir', for he had been senior to me in the Tangmere Wing and was well qualified to command his own squadron. At this time it was not the policy to select squadron commanders from within the unit itself, but Crow's turn would soon come and for the present I could not have had a more able deputy.

We called the squadron pilots together and Crow introduced

me to a diverse collection of men, including Canadians, Australians, Frenchmen, a New Zealander, a Belgian, a Rhodesian and a blond Norwegian who was sometimes mistaken for a member of the Luftwaffe when he cycled round the Broads in search of a pint of beer.

I talked to them for a few minutes. I wanted to get the squadron back to 11 Group; that was my ambition. We had been out of the front line almost a year and our turn must surely come before the summer was over. I asked them for an average of 1,000 hours operational and training flying each month. To knock down as many Huns as possible and to keep the accident rate to a minimum. Accidents are inevitable and will be with us as long as we fly aeroplanes. But the accident rate can be kept down through constant supervision of training, through a profound knowledge of our own aircraft and the various flying techniques. Meet these standards for two or three months, I told them, and we'll get back to the south. It was a goal to aim at, and owing to the method of rotating squadrons it seemed that our chances of going south were high. I followed the group captain's advice and flew to Coltishall to see Max and to try and work out tactics whereby we could operate with his night fighters. He was keen to co-operate, but the group captain had already staked his claim and the wing leader was next. We would start practice flights at the first opportunity, and later, if all went well, we would try our hands at the real thing. Better stay to lunch, said Max, and meet some of the local celebrities.

I met Roger Franklin, senior controller, president of the mess committee and member of the Auxiliary Air Force. Roger ran his mess exceedingly well, was fond of his Sunday lunch-parties and generally saw to it that his mess members lived better than they were supposed to in those austere days of 1942. After all, the local lobsters were excellent, and Norfolk had always been famed for its game, war or no war. But on this occasion Roger was disgruntled. He had pranged his staff car and it was badly damaged. He had been on the mat before the group captain, and according to King's Regulations and Air Council Instructions, had been invited to pay £5 towards the cost of the damage.

Soon afterwards the enemy bombers came over Norwich at

night and there was a lot of trade for the Beaufighters. The group captain drove to his Spitfire so that he could take off with the next Beaufighter and test his theory. His Spitfire was parked near the control tower and he taxied out fast, for precious seconds had already been lost. There was a lot of noise when the propeller of his Spitfire sliced into the roof of a staff car.

The following morning the M.T. officer was optimistic. The two damaged cars were of the same make and year, and he felt sure that one serviceable vehicle could be produced from the two wrecks. The course of action was obvious. At lunch-time, station commander met senior controller.

"Morning, Roger. Have a drink," cheerfully invited the group captain.

"Thank you, sir," replied Roger, who always kept his ear close to the ground. "A pink gin, and I think you owe me two pounds ten!"

We carried out a great many *Rhubarbs* from Ludham. Fortunately, the light flak over Holland was not as deadly as over France, and we suffered no losses, although our claims against lock-gates, barges, dredgers, vehicles, locomotives, gasometers and the like were not impressive. The more experienced members of the squadron tried their hands at Intruder operations over Holland on moonlight nights. We went after enemy aircraft and tried to emulate the Mosquito pilots who stalked and shot down their victims when they came in to land. Our Spitfires had not the endurance to make long penetrations to the enemy's training areas, so our searches were confined to the airfields near Rotterdam and Amsterdam.

We had no luck on these highly specialised Intruder operations, but it was a great thrill to fly low to Holland over the silvered North Sea. Some of our sea crossings seemed a long way in our single-engined Spitfires. Sometimes the quietly heaving water looked coldly beautiful on these solitary night flights, but I always felt better when I crossed over the land. Rather than return without firing our guns, we sometimes attacked ground targets; but we found that the ground had a deceptive look, especially when the moon was low, and these attacks could be extremely dangerous. It was a task which called for high skill and steady nerves, and to be effective it required a navigator who could call out the different heights when the pilot focused all his attention on the target. Ground strafing at night from Spitfires was really beyond our capabilities, and we gave it up.

Something big was afoot. One Saturday evening in August we entertained a few guests to dinner, and Ronnie Lees called me aside. Certain modifications had to be made to our Spitfires at once to give them a little more urge: we were due to leave for West Malling at dawn. Packing off our guests, we snatched a few hours' sleep before taking off for the south.

At West Malling we found we were to form a 12 Group Wing with the New Zealand 485 Squadron and the Canadian 411 Squadron. Pat Jameson from Wittering was appointed wing leader: he told us that we would be based at West Malling until the big show was over. Jamie flew off to various conferences at 11 Group, and although we had no official news, the security of the proposed operation was exceedingly bad, for it was common knowledge that the Canadians were to assault a selected point on the French coast. We were about to take part in Operation *Jubilee*, the disastrous combined operation against Dieppe.

According to the Canadian official history[1] of the Dieppe raid, the troops were originally embarked on the 2nd and 3rd July and sealed on board their ships. High-ranking officers visited the various ships and all the troops were fully briefed. The operation was cancelled because of the weather and the troops were disembarked, but not before the Luftwaffe had attacked the ships lying in Yarmouth Roads near the west end of the Solent. The Canadian historian says: "As the troops had been fully informed of the objective of the proposed raid, and once they left the ships it would no longer be possible to maintain complete secrecy, General Montgomery recommended that the operation should now 'be off for all time'."

Now, six weeks later, the operation was on again and Jamie briefed us on the evening of 18th August. More than 6000 troops, of whom

[1] *The Canadian Army 1939-1945.*

about 5000 were Canadians, would take part in the assault, the stated objectives of which were to destroy enemy defences, airfield installations, radar stations, power stations, dock and rail facilities; to capture enemy invasion barges and prisoners and remove secret documents from an enemy headquarters.

Our first thoughts at the briefing were that we far preferred our own task in the air to that of the troops on the ground. We were pleased we were airmen and not soldiers, for some of us had flown over this part of France for almost two years and had a healthy respect for the German defences and gunners. Quite a few of our own pilots had been shot down in this area, to return with tales of bristling defences and a heavily fortified coastal belt. Our own opinion of Dieppe was hardly in accord with the official intelligence estimate, which indicated that the town was only lightly defended.

The air effort would be controlled by Leigh-Mallory from his headquarters at 11 Group. The operations would begin with bombing attacks against enemy strong-points and all ground-attack leaders would report on their outgoing flight to a fighter controller in the headquarters ship. Flying Fortresses of the Eighth Air Force would make their second daylight operation of the war when twenty-four of them attacked the airfield at Abbeville. Our own job was simple and straightforward. Spitfire wings of Fighter Command would maintain an air umbrella over Dieppe; and although Lord Tedder later said that air umbrellas are apt to leak, we can claim that we held the Luftwaffe off the backs of the troops and naval forces below.

We took off for our first patrol and for the greater part of the journey across the Channel Jamie held us just above the choppy sea. About ten miles off Dieppe we began to climb to our allotted height of 10,000 feet. We were top cover to the wing, and when I levelled out and waggled my wings the boys popped into their finger-four positions like champagne corks. A heavy pall of black smoke hung over Dieppe. We listened intently to some wing leader who instructed his pilots: "Fight your way out now. Get out. Watch those 190s above at six o'clock. All Elfin aircraft – get out!"

Ahead of us Spitfires, Messerschmitts and Focke-Wulfs milled about the sky. It was too early to search for an opening, since the 190s had the height on us, and my task was to keep the squadron together as long as possible and guard the two squadrons below. Crow called a break and we swung round together to find the 190s at our own level in pairs and fours and seemingly baffled by our move. A 190 pulled up in front of my own section and I gave him a long burst from the maximum range. Surprisingly it began to smoke, the wheels dropped and it fell away to the sea, and Crow said, "Good shooting, Johnnie."

The Messerschmitts and Focke-Wulfs came down on us from astern and the flanks. They were full of fight, and for the present we thought of nothing but evasion and staying alive. During a steep turn I caught a glimpse of a strong formation of enemy fighters heading towards Dieppe from inland and I called the wing leader: "Jamie, strong enemy reinforcements coming in. About fifty-plus. Over."

Jamie was hard at it, but he found time to call 11 Group and ask for assistance. During a lull in the attacks my own section, which had been reduced to three aircraft, fastened on to a solitary Messerschmitt and sent it spinning down. Then they came at us again and we later estimated that we saw well over a hundred enemy fighters. Three of my Spitfires were shot down and I saw my own wingman, the Australian sergeant-pilot 'South' Creagh, planing down streaming white glycol from his engine. It was impossible to protect him, for if we took our eyes off the enemy fighters they would give us the same treatment. They're bound to finish him off as he nurses his crippled Spitfire, I thought. I still had another Spitfire alongside, but I lost him when we broke in opposite directions. Then I was alone in the hostile sky.

Ranging from ground-level to 20,000 feet and having a diameter of twenty or twenty-five miles, the air battle drifted and eddied over the coast and inland. The wing had long lost its cohesion, but thirty-six Spitfires, or what was left of them, still carried out their task by fighting in pairs and fours and so achieved some concentration in the target area.

I spotted a solitary aircraft over the town. I eased towards him and recognised the enemy fighter as a Focke-Wulf 190. For once I was not harried and I yawed my Spitfire to cover the blind spot behind me. But these movements attracted the attention of the enemy pilot and he snaked towards me, almost head on, and then we both turned hard to the left and whirled round on opposite sides of what seemed to be an ever-decreasing circle.

The 190 bore strange markings on the side of its fuselage just below the cockpit. This painted crest looked very similar to the markings of the Italian Air Force, and I thought, This pilot is an Italian! We had not seen them since they had received some severe treatment over the Thames Estuary towards the end of the Battle of Britain. We had been looking for them ever since, for we had little regard for their fighting qualities in the air. He's mine, I thought. He's mine, and I forgot the vulnerability of a lone Spitfire and tightened my turn to get on his tail.

With wide-open throttle I held the Spitfire in the tightest of shuddering vertical turns. I was greying-out, and where was this Italian, who should, according to my reckoning, be filling my gunsight? I couldn't see him, and little wonder, for the brute was gaining on me and in another couple of turns would have me in his sights. The over-confidence of but a few seconds before had already given way to irritation at losing my opponent, and this was replaced by a sickening apprehension. I asked the Spitfire for all she'd got in the turn, but the 190 hung behind like a leech and it could only be a question of time, and not much of that!

Stick over and well forward and I plunged into a near-vertical dive – a dangerous manoeuvre, for the 190 was more stable and faster than my Spitfire in such a descent, but I had decided on a possible method of escape. At ground level I pulled into another steep turn, and as I gauged the height and watched the rooftops I caught a glimpse of the promenade, of stationary tanks, of the white casino and a deserted beach. The 190 was still behind and for a few seconds we dodged round the spires and columns of smoke. Then I made my bid to throw him off.

A short distance off-shore I could see a destroyer surrounded by a clutter of smaller ships. We had been carefully briefed not to fly below 4,000 feet over the shipping, otherwise they would open fire. I rammed the throttle into the emergency position, broke off my turn and at sea-level headed straight at the destroyer. Flak and tracer came straight at me from the destroyer, and more, slower tracer from the 190 passed over the top of the cockpit. At the last moment I pulled over the destroyer, then slammed the nose down and eased out a few feet above the sea. I broke hard to the left and searched for the 190, but he was no longer with me. Either the flak had put him off or, better still, had nailed him. I made off at high speed to West Malling.

We flew four times that day, but our subsequent fights were not as savage as the first. The Luftwaffe bested us in the air fighting and shot down more than two of our aircraft for every one lost to them, a fair indication of the all-round superiority of the Focke-Wulfs over our Spitfire 5s. They also showed that they were able to provide fighter reinforcements at short notice. Late that night my Australian wingman phoned me from Newhaven to say that he had baled out and had been picked up by a naval vessel six miles out to sea. He was unhurt, but sobered by what he had seen and heard on his journey back.

The close-support operations of Hurricanes and Typhoons were not effective because tactical aircraft can rarely participate successfully in close-locked, hand-to-hand fighting of this nature. In later years we devised tactics and communications whereby our forward ground troops were able to indicate precision targets, and in Italy, attacks were successfully carried out against enemy troops occupying houses on the other side of the street from our own soldiers. But these facilities were not available at Dieppe. When Leigh-Mallory asked for a situation report, the reply was: 'Situation too obscure to give useful report.'

Tactically, the Dieppe raid must be regarded as a complete failure, for none of its stated objectives were achieved in full measure. It is a record of poor security, of faulty intelligence, of inadequate communications between air and ground, of a confused and bloody ground situation over which central co-ordination could not be exercised. It is a story of great gallantry and heavy loss of life, and the record of the (Canadian) Essex Scottish, who brought back 52 personnel, of whom 28 were wounded, out of a force of 553, gives some indication of the desperate situation on the ground. Perhaps Chester Wilmot made the best assessment of the operation when he stated: "[the] Dieppe raid yielded bloody warning of the strength of the Atlantic wall."[1]

About this time, Cocky and his Typhoon squadron moved to Matlask, and his officers lived in a charming converted mill-house which arched over a clear chalk-stream stocked with brown trout. Our off-duty hours were spent walking up the golden stubbles after partridge, and I met a wonderful old sportsman of the Broads, Jim Vincent, who took me wild-fowling and showed me that there is far more to shooting than the mere accumulation of large bags. Cocky and I spent a delightful leave together. We chugged off to the north in my tiny Morris, staying with a number of his relations. I returned with a small black Labrador puppy, Sally, who was later to cross the Normandy beaches and make the journey in my caravan from Normandy to the Baltic.

From time to time our girlfriends came to stay in nearby pubs and hotels for a week-end or whenever we held a dance in the mess. For me these were light-hearted affairs and not taken seriously. Anything of that nature, we were firmly resolved, must wait until after the war. But one night at a party in Norwich I met the beautiful Paula Ingate, and we began to see a lot of each other. She worked in the Norwich operations room of the Auxiliary Fire Service, and after a month or so we became engaged. I did not possess sufficient spare cash to buy a decent engagement ring, so she managed without one until long after we were married.

The bombshell exploded late one evening towards the end of September. I was changing in my room before driving into Norwich to meet Paula when the squadron adjutant called up and said he had some important news which he couldn't tell me over the telephone.

"Stay where you are, Arthur," I instructed. "I'll drop in on my way to Norwich and you can tell me."

Minutes later I was with him.

"We've got our marching orders, sir," began the adjutant. "Good show," I answered. "It's about time we got back to 11 Group. Where is it? Biggin, Kenley or North Weald? We might get some

[1] *The Struggle for Europe*, p. 186.

of the new Spitfire 9s…"

The adjutant interrupted my discourse with the cold pronouncement:

"We won't get any Spit 9s where we're going, sir! This," – waving a signal form, "says we're to change places with a squadron at Castletown."

"Castletown! Where's Castletown?" I demanded, for I had never heard of the place. The adjutant had already briefed himself:

"I've found it on the map. It's the most northerly airfield in Scotland. Next to a place called Thurso. From what I can make out there are plenty of sheep up there and that's about all!"

I had promised the squadron a move south and all ranks had worked hard to produce the right results. This was a ghastly reward, and the decision would have to be challenged, if necessary at the highest level.

The next day I told my two flight commanders, Alan Laurie and Doug Collinge. Laurie had replaced Peter Pool, who was shot down over Dieppe, and the easy-going but utterly dependable Collinge had recently taken over from Crow, who had just left us to form a new Typhoon squadron. They were equally shocked by the news, but I pledged them to secrecy and flew to Coltishall to see the new group captain. He was sympathetic, but pointed out that there was little he could do to help. Squadron postings were controlled by Fighter Command, and if they had decided we should go north, there it was. I asked if I might put my case to the group commander, Air Vice-Marshal Saul, and received the necessary permission.

The group commander listened to my tale of woe. He thought it was bad luck for the squadron and had already said so to Fighter Command. It certainly looked as if we should have to go to Castletown. He looked a bit startled when I asked leave to approach the commander-in-chief, but he agreed to the request, although he was doubtful about the outcome.

A few days later we flew down to Biggin Hill to take part in the largest Fortress raid so far. We picked up well over a hundred Fortresses over the target and helped to bring them home despite some determined opposition from the Focke-Wulfs. The Biggin

Hill wing leader led my squadron and the boys flew perfectly. Our task was not easy, for the wing leader flew a faster and more powerful Spitfire 9, which was vastly superior to our 5s. But my three pilots somehow stayed with him in the leading section and provided perfect support and cross-cover when he knocked down a 190 and damaged another. The wing leader was full of praise and said he would like to see us permanently based at Biggin. Such unstinted commendation made our forthcoming journey to the north all the harder to stomach.

I phoned a staff officer at Fighter Command. Could he please arrange an interview with the commander-in-chief? He was doubtful. The commander-in-chief was not in the habit of granting interviews to disgruntled squadron commanders! I was careful to point out that I had followed the right chain of command, and both station and group commanders had given permission to seek the interview. All right, he said, be here at two o'clock tomorrow afternoon and he'd see what he could do for me.

I took Laurie with me for moral support. We put on our best uniforms and reported at Bentley Priory well before the appointed time. The staff officer was pessimistic about the whole affair. Was our visit really necessary? It was most unusual.

"It's also unusual that I should take my squadron to the north of Scotland after a year in 12 Group," I countered. "But if he's too busy to see one of his squadron commanders .

"Wait here," he interrupted. "I'll be back in a few minutes." He returned with a stooped senior officer, who regarded the two of us with a decided twinkle in his eyes.

"So you want to see the C.-in-C., Johnson? What's your case?" enquired Group Captain McEvoy.

I explained as briefly as possible.

"I'm sure the C.-in-C. will see you," said the group captain. "Wait here while I have a word with him." He was back within a few seconds. "Come in and make it snappy, he's a busy man."

The three of us filed into a pleasant, lofty room where Sholto Douglas sat behind a large desk. He was big and impassive, but courteous.

"Well, Johnson, I understand you want to see me. About this

move of yours to Castletown. Apparently you disagree with my squadron dispositions?"

I spoke my carefully rehearsed little speech. A year in 12 Group and plenty of long sea-crossings, but little of the work we liked best, air fighting. My short period of command and the promise to bring the squadron south. And now Castletown.

The C.-in-C. was silent for a few moments and then said:

"You go back to your squadron and tell them they're going to Castletown. And you can tell them you've been to see me and that I've said you'll be in 11 Group by next spring. And if you haven't heard anything by next February you can come and see me again. You will find that Castletown has its compensations. Good afternoon."

We saluted and withdrew. I had something tangible to tell the squadron, and I felt the visit had been well worth the effort. Apparently the group captain thought so too, for he was still smiling when he shook hands and wished us well.

So we left Norfolk and went to the north. We flew hard and established a local record for the amount of bullets despatched at air and ground targets. We found that Caithness contained far more than sheep, and we soon fell under the spell of its wild beauty and the warm hospitality of its inhabitants. We were too late for the salmon fishing in the Thurso, where the mess members fished through the generosity of the owner, Sir Archibald Sinclair. Although Lord Tichfield had no official connection with 610 Squadron, he wrote to say we were welcome to the hind-shooting on his nearby deer forest at Berriedale. We shot quite a few beasts, and sometimes the whole squadron – officers, N.C.O.s and airmen – dined together on venison at the Dunnet Hotel. We shot mallard and widgeon when they flighted on to Loch Heilen, and flushed the grouse from great stretches of heather-covered moorlands.

Paula and I were married during November. She was nineteen and I was twenty-five. The war years stretched ahead into infinity, and like many others we snatched some happiness together while we could. We agreed that while I remained on ops. she would continue to live at home, for I had seen too much of camp followers.

We were married in Norwich, and Cocky was our best man. Some of my pilots managed to find their way to Norwich by various means and I stayed with Cocky at the Mill-house for a day or two beforehand, where we had the usual party to mark my last days as a bachelor.

Sholto Douglas did not forget his promise. Early in January 1943 we moved back to 11 Group and were again based at Westhampnett. This time we shared the airfield with the New Zealanders of 485 Squadron, who were commanded by the tough, lion-hearted Reg Grant. The third unit of this Tangmere Wing, 165 Squadron, was led by ex-sergeant-pilot Jim Hallowes, who had won both the D.F.M. and bar on the same day during the Battle of Britain. Hardly anyone remained at Tangmere who had served there during my earlier days, but the locals still remembered, and Arthur King gave us a rousing welcome back to the 'Unicorn'.

It was almost two years since Douglas Bader had begun to lead the Tangmere Wing from this same airfield, and curiously enough another legless pilot now joined the squadron. Colin Hodgkinson lost both his legs after a crash when serving with the Fleet Air Arm, but by following Bader's example and showing the same indomitable spirit he flew operationally and soon proved to be a valuable and aggressive member of our small team. Soon after our arrival we gave a party in our quarters, Woodcote Farm, and invited perhaps sixty or seventy officers from the other squadrons and the station. After all the guests had departed, a few of us sat amongst the debris, chatting about the evening and drinking a last half pint of beer. Hodgkinson made his excuses and clumped across the stone flags of the hall and up the stairs. Suddenly there was a loud crash when the legless pilot stumbled against the banisters, and pilot and banisters fell to the flags ten feet below. We rushed into the hall to find our pilot lying on the floor. He sat up and rubbed his head. I said:

"That was a hell of a drop. Are you all right? What about your legs, Colin?"

"Oh, they're quite all right, sir," he answered.

"Are you sure? Perhaps we'd better call the doc?" I suggested.

"No, thank you, sir. You see, I fell on my head!"

We suffered our first loss of this tour when Sergeant Parker failed to get back from a *Rhubarb* operation. Other pilots were over France at the time and they heard Parker call a Mayday[1] shortly after he crossed the French coast on his return journey. The ops. room got a very accurate fix[2] from Parker's transmission. I took six Spitfires to sea to search for him. Reg Grant led a section of New Zealanders and Jim Hallowes sent off sections to escort the air-sea rescue boats. We searched until dusk and never saw a thing. Parker was the fourth pilot to be lost in three days on this type of operation.

We were badly hit by the Focke-Wulfs when, together with the other two squadrons, we flew as close escort to a dozen Venturas who were to attack a target at Caen. The bomber leader held his small force just below the cloud to keep as far above the flak as possible. This left no airspace for the Spitfires to manoeuvre above the bombers, and as they were well covered on either flank I dropped the squadron behind so that we could sweep the target after the bombing and protect the Venturas when they turned for home.

The Focke-Wulfs were ready and waiting. Their leader was very clever and did not show his hand until our cross-cover was reduced during the turn over Caen. Then he wheeled some thirty 190s down through a gap in the clouds and they were into us. When I broke round I tried to size up the situation so that I could hold the squadron together. The beehive had crossed the coast and was well on its way home, but at all costs we must hold the 190s over Caen and so prevent them getting to the bombers.

The tail of young Smith's Spitfire was shot off by a 190, but our pilot had baled out and we could see his parachute drifting down to the sea only about three miles from the French coast. One of my Polish pilots, Sergeant Lisowski, was also in trouble: I could see his Spitfire smoking badly. I called him:

"Blue three from red leader. You won't get back in that aircraft. Turn inland and bale out or crash land." This, of course, was an order, but he said:

"I'm trying to reach England."

[1] Mayday was our distress call and was derived from the French "m'aidez".
[2] Bearings taken by ground stations from our radio transmissions.

The stupid fool, I thought. He'll have to bale out in mid-Channel and in this icy water will be dead in about twenty minutes.

Then 'Pappy' Wright was hit by a cannon shell which slammed into his Spitfire, wrenched the stick from his hand and threw his aircraft upside down. He thought – I've had it, better bale out – but the Spitfire still responded to the controls and he dropped to sealevel and headed towards Tangmere

Nine Spitfires left, and the 190s still hammering away at us. The beehive was out of sight, so I called my chaps:

"Get down on the deck and fight your way out. I'm going down. Now!"

We flew only a few feet above the sullen, quietly lifting sea. It was always ready to receive a victim and I tried to turn this to our advantage. If the Focke-Wulfs wanted to fight it out, then the battle-ground would be of our choosing: when they turned with us their inboard wing-tips would be brushing the crests. They would have to pay a lot of attention to their height, and in the past the German pilots had shown a marked disinclination for this type of combat.

I counted my Spitfires. Four in my section. Alan Laurie well out on the port side with three. Seven. Where were the other two? I looked across the grey sea on the starboard side. Nothing there, and then something caught my eye well above. It was a section of two Spitfires still flying straight and level well above us. The section was led by an officer who was not a permanent member of the squadron but who was attached to us for a week or two before going to another unit. I could see a bunch of 190s behind the two Spitfires and I turned my section towards them and shouted a warning over the radio.

We were too late, for, when we straightened out of the turn, the Focke-Wulfs were breaking away from their attacks and our two Spitfires were going down. The leading Spitfire was badly hit. First of all it poured black smoke. Then it began to burn.

From our cockpits we watched the burning Spitfire. We could do nothing except wait for the parachute to flare out and then pass an accurate fix to Tangmere for the rescue operation. But instead of using these few precious seconds to bale out the man inside suddenly panicked and screamed over the radio. We had never heard this sort of thing before, and for a few shocked moments we listened to his dreadful mouthings. We were a lot of dirty bastards! It was our fault he was on fire! He was going to die! Alone. We would leave him. And not return. We...

I came out of my stupor and flicked on my transmitter switch to jam this creature's accusations. Mercifully the radio was silent and we watched the Spitfire smack into the cold sea at a shallow angle. I passed a fix to Tangmere and flew low over the sea. The heaving waters had already closed in and there was no sign of wreckage or dinghy. The seven of us flew back to Tangmere together, and did not speak again until we were on the ground.

Wright had managed to stagger back to Westhampnett, and Lisowski had, quite surprisingly, also got home. But a few days later we lost another Polish pilot, Skibinski, when we tangled with fifty or sixty 190s just inside the French coast. In this fight Reg Grant lost three of his New Zealand pilots, one of whom was his younger brother.

The squadron had now lost five pilots in almost as many days, and we could not continue operations for much longer at such a high casualty rate. Our wing leader left us, and pending the appointment of his successor I sometimes led the Tangmere Wing, for Reg Grant had been taken off ops. and I was the senior squadron commander. Our penetrations into France were considerably less than those of two years ago, and when the controller called up and told me of enemy gaggles, five and ten miles away, my reaction was to avoid combat unless sun and height would give us the perfect bounce. Such was the superiority of the Focke-Wulf over our Spitfires in the spring of 1943.

One day I was called to the telephone and found it was a staff officer from 11 Group headquarters on the other end:

"Morning, Johnson. Could I please have your total operational hours and when you last had a rest?"

"I'll have to get my log books for the hours," I answered cautiously. "What's the form?"

"Oh, just the usual routine stuff," he explained, but he was a shade too nonchalant for my liking. "Anyway, never mind about hours. When did you last have a rest from ops.?"

"Just had one," I lied. "We've just come down here from the north of Scotland. Wonderful shooting up there. Good salmon too. Just the sort of rest you want."

"I see," he replied, and I wondered whether he did.

A few hours later I answered the telephone again, and I had to wait until the line was transferred to the group commander, Air Vice-Marshal Saunders:

"Hello, Johnnie. What's all this I hear about a rest at Castletown with your squadron?"

"Well, it was far better than the usual rest, sir," I countered defensively.

"I hope it was," he answered quietly, "because I'm giving you a wing of your own. The Canadian wing at Kenley. They've got the new Spitfire 9s. Put your stripe up and get there tomorrow. And let me know if I can help in any way."

"Thank you, sir. There is one thing. I would like to recommend Laurie for the squadron. I know its unusual, but we're having a hard time with the 190s and he knows the form."

"All right," said the group commander. "I'll look into it. Good luck with the Canadians."

Alan Laurie got the squadron, and Hvinden, the Norwegian, became flight commander of B Flight. Arthur King laid on a farewell party at the 'Unicorn', and we celebrated the various promotions. I had arranged for Paula to spend the week-end there and now it would have to be put off. I telephoned her centre in Norwich and a sleepy Paula eventually came to the phone. Security regulations prevented me from telling her, over an open line, where I was going:

"I'm leaving here, darling," I explained. "But I'm not going far and not crossing the water."

"When are you leaving?" she asked.

"Tomorrow. I'm just saying good-bye to the boys. Don't you hear the noise?"

"Yes, they're singing that dreadful song again! What about our weekend?" asked the sleepy voice from Norwich.

"We'll have to scrub it, I'm afraid. You see, darling, they're promoting me to wing commander and I have to be at the new place tomorrow."

Suddenly she was no longer sleepy, but all woman and incomprehensible:

"Why can't they promote you next week?"

Chapter Ten

CANADIAN WING

I had plenty to think about as I drove to Kenley with Sally the Labrador curled up beside me. A few Canadian pilots had served in 610, but somehow in a fighter squadron of half a dozen different nationalities it had seemed comparatively easy to mould the mixture to a common purpose. It was generally agreed between squadron commanders and wing leaders that a mixed unit was happier and more efficient than one comprised of pilots of a single nationality. The Canadian fighter pilots had a reputation for toughness and they required a firm hand on the reins. I thought of Bader and how he had often sworn by the Canadians; and who could have flown better or shown greater loyalty than Stan Turner?

I wondered how the Spitfire 9 would match up against the Focke-Wulf 190. The engine of the 9 was bigger and more powerful than that of the 5, but it was mounted in the same airframe and its great tactical advantage was that, apart from its longer nose and more numerous exhaust stacks, it looked exactly like the inferior 5. From the usual combat range it was impossible for the Luftwaffe pilots to distinguish between the two types, and this suited me, for I had a score or two to settle. My personal victories only amounted to a modest eight.

I thought of my own duties as wing leader. Such an appointment to one of the crack 11 Group wings was the ambition of every fighter pilot worth his salt. I have said in an earlier chapter that fighter leadership consists not in scoring personal victories but in the achievement of success with the whole wing. My job would be to lead and to fight. To bring the greatest number of guns to bear against the enemy in the shortest possible time. To cut down losses to a minimum and to avoid the bad bounce. To control the progress of the engagement and to keep the wing together as a fighting force and not get split up into isolated, ineffective packets – by far the most difficult task. These goals could only be achieved through a high standard of flying, perfect discipline and strict radio drill.

I drove to the mess and parked the small Morris outside, much to the amusement of a party of husky Canadian pilots who were obviously comparing its size to the glittering monsters they used at home. A smart, broad-shouldered squadron leader walked out of the mess and gave me a snappy salute.

"Wing Commander Johnson?"

"That's right," I replied.

"I'm Bud Malloy. Wing Commander Hodson, whose job you are taking, is off for the day and so is the group captain. Shall we have a can of beer, then some food, and I'll take you round and introduce you to your wild Canadians."

After lunch I inspected my room. The mess seemed to be hermetically sealed and the central heating was going full blast. This, I was to learn, was a feature of the North American way of life, but I had been brought up the hard way and soon changed to a room in one of the wings which did not have the benefit of steam heat.

It was a day of low cloud and drizzle, so Malloy and I made a leisurely tour of the airfield and met the two squadron commanders and upwards of seventy pilots. The lean, slightly balding Syd Ford of 403 Squadron came from Nova Scotia, already held the D.F.C. and bar, and had established his reputation as a sound leader and an aggressive pilot. Foss Bolton of 416 Squadron hailed from Alberta and was an open-faced, friendly character who was a relative newcomer to the game, having spent the greater part of his flying career in Canada.

I was surprised to learn that they still flew in the old-fashioned line-astern formation. We had a long talk about this. I pointed out the benefits of the abreast, finger-four style. A more aggressive, offensive formation and so on. Syd Ford, who had flown the Spitfire 9 quite a lot, favoured the line astern despite my arguments. Bolton seemed to waver between the two types and perhaps could not assess a new wing leader who wanted to change things within a few minutes of arriving. I felt it was time for a decision:

"For the first few wing shows, I'll lead Foss' squadron and we'll fly in finger-fours. You, Syd, will hold your position down-sun, 3,000 feet higher, and you can fly in what formation you like providing you do your job. We'll see how it goes for the first few times and then decide one way or the other for the whole wing."

I met the tall, good-looking Keith Hodson, himself a Canadian, on the following day and he gave me a sketch of the wing's recent activities. The two squadrons had received their Spitfire 9s some months previously and during January they had lost a wing leader over France and Keith was promoted into the vacancy.

"This weather of yours has been against us. We've not had a real chance to get together. But it should improve any time now, and a good thing – the boys are getting a bit restless. They've got a fine aeroplane and I think they fly well. What they want is a few good scraps with the 190s. If you can pull that off during your first few shows they'll be right with you."

"What you mean is that I'm on approval at present?" I suggested.

"I guess that's about the size of it," grinned Keith.

The senior intelligence officer introduced himself and told me I would have to select a radio call sign. He handed me a long list of approved names and I ran my eye down it and saw 'Greycap'.

"That's it," I said. "Greycap. Sounds good and will be clear over the radio. I like it. Will you let everyone know?"

"Yes, sir," answered the 'Spy'. "But you have to change it every few months. Otherwise the Huns soon fit a call sign to a particular wing leader and they know who you are. Bad security."

I've used it ever since!

A new Spitfire had arrived a day or two previously and she was undergoing her acceptance checks in the workshops. I found the engineer officer and together we had a look at her, gleaming and bright in a new spring coat of camouflage paint. Later I took her up for a few aerobatics to get the feel of her, for this was the first time I had flown a 9. She seemed very fast, the engine was sweet and she responded to the controls as only a thoroughbred can. I decided that she should be mine, and I never had occasion to regret the choice.

Instead of the usual large squadron identification letters painted on the side of the fuselage, wing leaders were allowed to put their own initials on their aircraft. This was a jealously guarded privilege and I told my rigger where to paint J. E. J. and the blue-and-red pennant of a wing commander. The Spy overheard the conversation and took a gloomy view of the proceedings.

"I think it's a mistake to paint your initials on that Spitfire. The intelligence people say that the Huns always go after the leader's aircraft, and with J. E. J. on there you'll be very conspicuous. Why not paint the ordinary squadron letters on before it's too late?"

I laughed at him and replied:

"Look here, Spy, I've worked three years for this day, and I'm not going to be put off by you! Don't forget I've got twenty-three other Spits stacked round me, and if the Huns want a fight – that's why we're there."

During the next few days the weather continued very poor and it was quite impossible to operate the wing. But we could fly individually during some temporary breaks in the weather and I flew several times to test the two cannons and four machine guns. It was standard procedure for our guns and cannon to be harmonised to give a fairly large 'shotgun' pattern at the best firing range. The theory behind this was that, since the average pilot was not a good shot, the open pattern would give him the best chance of hitting the Huns. But a far more lethal method of obtaining a kill, provided the pilot could aim and shoot, was to harmonise the guns to give a 'spot' concentration of fire. Ford's guns were set on the spot principle, and since his combat films were some of the best ever taken, I followed his example.

Some three weeks passed and we had only flown together on two or three occasions. Once, well inside France, we saw a large gaggle of Focke-Wulfs in the far distance, but our petrol was running low and we had to return without firing a shot. My Canadians flew extremely well and their air discipline was excellent, better I thought than the average mixed squadron. But we wanted a full-blooded scrap with the Abbeville boys to weld the wing together. Our opportunity arrived on a Saturday afternoon in early April.

We were having lunch when the Tannoy announced that the wing would come to readiness in one hour's time. I walked over to the ops. block to study the details so that I could brief the wing. It was only a small show, but far better than idling away the afternoon on the ground. Crow was to lead his squadron of Typhoons across the Channel at low level, dive-bomb the Abbeville airfield and then withdraw at a high rate of knots. Our job was to climb over France as the Typhoons came out and knock down any Messerschmitts or Focke-Wulfs flushed by the bombing.

It was a simple little operation, just Crow's squadron and my wing. What really appealed to me was that we were operating in a free-lance rôle and were not confined to any particular area. The weather was perfect and we were to operate under the control of a new radar station in Kent which was rapidly acquiring a reputation for excellent long-distance controlling. It was a week-end, and there always seemed to be a stronger enemy reaction on Saturdays and Sundays than any other day.

I telephoned Squadron Leader Hunter, the senior controller of the new radar station, outlined my tactics and agreed that he would not break radio silence unless he had an enemy plot on his scopes.

Crossing the French coast just south of Le Touquet, I caught a glimpse of Crow's Typhoons well below and heading back towards England. Our superchargers cut in at 19,000 feet with an unpleasant thump and the engines surged and we eased back our throttles. At 24,000 feet I levelled out and Bolton's squadron drew abreast of me in the finger-four formation. Ford's squadron were just beginning to make condensation trails and these could be seen from a great distance and would betray our position. But before I could call him he dropped his squadron a few hundred feet and the twelve conspicuous thin white banners ceased.

Hunter broke the silence:

"Greycap from Grass-seed.[1] Twenty plus bandits climbing up inland. Steer 140."

"O.K., Grass-seed," I acknowledged. "Any height on the bandits?"

"Well below you, Greycap. They are approaching the coast and I'll try and bring you out of the sun. Continue on 140."

This was perfect teamwork between controller and wing leader. It was the first time we had worked with Hunter: he seemed to have

[1] Code name of the radar station.

Air Vice-Marshal 'Johnnie' Johnson
CB, CBE, DSO & two bars, DFC & bar

Tiger Moth

Avro Anson

Miles Master

No. 5 Flight Training School, Sealand 1940

Ju 88 shot down by Tom Pike in Arundel, April 1941

The first Me 109F to be shot down in England, May 1941

616 Squadron, Kirton Lindsey, December 1941,
left to right: LAC Arthur Radcliffe (rigger), the author and
LAC Fred Burton (fitter)

616 Squadron, Kingscliffe

Kirton Lindsey, December 1941: armourers busy on 'U'

616 Squadron, Kingscliffe, 'The Pusher'

616 Squadron, Kingscliffe, January 1942

616 Squadron, Kingscliffe, January 1942: the author (third left)
with pilots of 'B' Flight

616 Squadron, Kingscliffe, May 1942

Royal visit to 485 (New Zealand) Squadron, Kenley 1942

Ludham, 610 Squadron, September 1942; back row: Flg. Off. Brown, Flt Lt Hvinden, Flt Lt Pabiat, Plt Off. Watson, Plt Off. Malton, Plt Off. Jones, Plt Off. Pearson, Plt Off. Musgrove; front row: Flg. Off. Race, Plt Off. Sanderson, Flg. Off. Cameron, Sqn Ldr Poggs, Sqn Ldr Johnson (the author), Flg. Off. Collinge, Plt Off. Smith, Flg Lt Watson and Plt Off. Wright

Kenley Wing, late 1942: Sqn Ldr Reg Grant, Gp Capt. Dick Atcherley and
Wg Ldr (later Wg Cdr.) 'Hawk-Eye' Wells

Kenley, Canadian Wing, July 1943, left to right: Dean MacDonald, 'Trapper'
Bowen, Wg Cdr. Hugh Godefroy, Sqn Ldr Walter ('Wally') Conrad, the author

The author with Field Marshal Montgomery at Copenhagen, 1945

Marshal of the RAF, Lord Trenchard, visits Copenhagen

Administration at Kastrup, Spring 1945

Fassberg 1946

Spitfires

something of Woodhall's ability to put his information across in a quiet, reassuring manner. The whole intricate mechanics of long-range radar interception seemed to be working perfectly. Suddenly I was brimming with confidence, for I knew that Hunter and I would pull this one off.

"Greycap. Bandits have crossed below you at 15,000 feet. Port on to 310. Buster."

"O.K., Grass-seed. Port on to 310," I replied.

"Greycap. Bandits now seven miles ahead. 5000 feet below. Gate."[1]

I put the Spitfires into a shallow dive and scanned the area ahead. The sky seemed empty.

"Greycap. Another strong formation of bandits behind you. About five to eight miles. Exercise caution."

Here were the makings of a perfect shambles! We were almost on top of the first enemy formation with another gaggle not far behind. How far? Hunter had said between five and eight miles, but the radar was scanning at its maximum range and five miles could be one mile – or ten. Should I call the whole thing off and set course for Dungeness now? The decision was mine. For a moment it seemed as if we were suspended and motionless in the high sky, with the Canadians clustered around me waiting for an order.

Then I saw our quarry. One bunch of twelve 190s just below us and a mile ahead, and a further ten 190s well out on the starboard side. It was too golden an opportunity to miss. Height, sun and surprise in our favour and I had to take a chance on how far behind the other enemy formation was.

"Greycap to wing. Twenty-plus Huns below from twelve to three o'clock. Syd, I'm taking the left-hand bunch. Come down and take the right-hand gaggle. Get in!"

I turned slightly to get directly behind the 190s and remembered to make the turn slow and easy so that our wingmen could keep well up. I put the nose down and had to fight back an instinct to slam the throttle wide open. We had to hit these brutes together.

My own 190 was flying on the extreme port side of the enemy

[1] Maximum speed.

formation. We came down on their tails in a long, slanting dive. Before I opened fire, I looked to the starboard, saw Bolton's boys fanning out alongside and Ford's arrowhead of Spitfires falling down on their prey about three miles away. The attack was co-ordinated, and my task of leading the wing was temporarily suspended. Now it was up to the individual pilots to select their opponents and smack them down.

I missed the 190 with my first short burst and steadied the gun platform with coarse stick and rudder. I fired again and hit him on the wing root and just behind the cockpit. The spot harmonisation paid off and the cannon shells thudded into him in a deadly concentration of winking explosions. He started to burn, but before he fell on to his back I gave him another long burst. Then I broke away in a steep climbing turn and searched the sky behind. Still nothing there. Below me another 190 was falling in flames, and on the starboard a parachute had opened into full bloom. Hunter was still concerned for our safety:

"Greycap. Withdraw. Strong force of bandits approaching. Almost on top of you.

I spoke to the wing:

"All Greycap aircraft. Get out now! We won't reform. And keep a sharp look-out behind!"

The pilots didn't need telling twice: we poured across the Channel at high speed in pairs and fours. My section was the first to land and when I climbed out of the cockpit I was met by a small posse of officers, for the good word that we had bounced the 190s soon spread. I lit a cigarette and counted the Spits as they joined the circuit over Kenley. Sixteen down, four on the circuit – twenty. A singleton twenty-one. A long pause and a pair – twenty-three. One to come. It seemed very important that he should swing in over Caterham and land. But we had waited too long: he was either missing or at some other airfield.

The pilots walked into the briefing room still excited and full of the fight. We totted up the score with the Spies listening silently and ever ready to reduce a claim from a destroyed to a damaged or, if they had the chance, to nothing at all! The total came to six 109s destroyed for the loss of one of our pilots, who, we could only surmise, must have been clobbered by a 190 after our first attack.

I was delighted with our effort. The controlling had been superb and the Canadians had flown really well. I made out my report, called the radar station and thanked Hunter, and checked with our operations room for any news of our missing pilot. They had no information.

The next morning Syd Ford walked into my office. He laid a pair of blue Canada shoulder-flashes on my desk and said:

"The boys would like you to wear these. After all, we're a Canadian wing and we've got to convert you. Better start this way."

"Thanks Syd," I replied. "I'll get them sewn on today."

A simple gesture, but for me it had a deep significance. The flashes were sewn on and two years were to elapse before it was time to take them down.

Ford did well that afternoon when we flew to Paris to escort four boxes of Fortresses, each of eighteen bombers, from the target area. We saw the glinting bombers from a great distance, for the bright sun reflected from a hundred places on each silver aircraft. They made a most impressive sight when they pounded their stately way through the skies in battle array. Flak and fighters could not stop them. Here and there a bomber fell burning to the ground below, but the rest pressed on, determined, irresistible, blazing a new daylight trail over Europe and somehow symbolic of the country whose star they bore.

Ford's squadron guarded the last box of bombers and I led Bolton's squadron to the third box. I heard Ford say:

"190s attacking the Forts. Let's go!"

There was little point in joining him, as he was ten miles away and the fight would be over when we arrived on the scene. The squadron leader himself sent down a 190 in flames after its wheels had dropped. Magwood, one of his flight commanders, accounted for a brace of 190s and saw a sergeant-pilot shoot down a fourth, but the sergeant was bounced himself by a couple of enemy fighters before Magwood could warn him. A fifth 190 was shot down, but in addition to the sergeant the American, Ed Gimbel, who served in the R.C.A.F., was missing from the fight.

This fight brought our week-end score to eleven Focke-Wulfs

destroyed for the loss of three of our pilots. It was a good start to my tour with the Canadians.

We were released from operations for the rest of the day, but as there were still a few hours of daylight left I flew to Tangmere to see how it went with 610. Laurie met me and told me about a recent black day when they were bounced by a strong, mixed bunch of Messerschmitts and Focke-Wulfs. Four pilots were lost and the likeable Doug Collinge was missing from a subsequent operation. The pilots were a bit down in the mouth and I felt sorry for them, because we at Kenley were turning the tables on the 190s. We had a beer together in the farmhouse and I tried to cheer them up. They looked at my gleaming, rakish Spitfire with envious eyes and said how they would like a chance to fly it against the 190s.

I flew back to Kenley as the shadows lengthened across the Downs. We were detailed for an early-morning show. After a light snack and a word with the two squadron commanders I went to bed and slept like a child.

Next day we had a long penetration across Holland to escort the Fortresses attacking a target near Antwerp. It was a grey, overcast day with a fine drizzling rain, but the weather man told us that we should find clear skies at 8,000 feet. We flew to Manston, where we refuelled and lounged about waiting for our appointed take-off time. The Biggin Hill Wing, led by the indomitable Al Deere, was taking part in the same show, and we chatted together for a few minutes.

"What's all this we read in the papers about Biggin's thousandth Hun, Al?" I chaffed him, for Biggin Hill always received its fair share of publicity.

"Well, we're getting on that way, you know, Johnnie," replied Al. "Any moment now. And the Sailor[1] says that when we get it we'll have the biggest thrash ever. At Grosvenor House. We've started to make the arrangements."

"Don't forget Kenley when you send out the invitations," I rejoined. "I've got some very thirsty Canadians! See you over Antwerp."

[1] Group Captain Malan, at this time the top-scoring pilot with thirty-two victories, commanded Biggin Hill.

Manston was a large grass airfield and it was possible to take-off twelve Spitfires in line-abreast. Al's wing went off before me and I watched them disappear into the low overcast. I gave my pilots time to settle down after the take-off, and then we slid into the cloud at intervals of a few seconds to reduce the risk of collisions. Mist seethed across our wind-screens; the choppy, grey waters of the Channel were soon blotted out. It was dark inside the cloud, and when I occasionally glanced up from my instruments I could only just see the Spitfires on either side. Ten, fourteen, eighteen thousand feet and we were still in the cloud. I wished I had the weather man right here with me – no cloud above 8,000 feet indeed! Soon it became lighter and we broke out on top into a clean, blue sky. I carried out a slow orbit, watching the other five sections pop out of the cloud.

We joined together and flew above the white, fleecy blanket towards our rendezvous point with the Forts. As usual, they were dead on time: they flew on a converging course with ours, and I thought how beautiful and stately they looked when they winged their way through the high sky in a good, balanced formation. Again I split the wing, for it was too cumbersome to manoeuvre round the slower bombers. I covered the leading box whilst Ford dropped back to guard the next box. We were flying well beyond our radar cover and any Huns brought to battle would be the result of our own efforts. Bolton called up: "Greycap from red three. Twenty-plus at nine o'clock high. Look like 190s."

I looked to the right, and couldn't see the Focke-Wulfs. This was not surprising, for nine o'clock on our clock code meant directly to the left and I thought confusedly – nine o'clock, three o'clock, left or right, which is it? I had to dart a quick look at the small clock on the dashboard to make quite sure.

The 190s turned into a position about two miles immediately ahead of the leading box of Forts. This meant that they would carry out the dangerous but effective head-on attacks against the bombers. They would level out of their dive, close to point-blank range, and make their getaway by easing their sticks back slightly and passing flat over the oncoming Fortresses by a margin of a few feet. Or they might half-roll ahead of the bombers, continue to fire in an inverted position and escape in a vertical dive by simply pulling their sticks back into the pits of their stomachs. The flat, level attack called for fine judgement and high courage. I thought that most of the enemy pilots would half-roll and dive away.

We drew ahead of the leading Fortresses, but the 190s had already begun their dive and were coming down in a ragged line-astern. They were on our port side, so I began to turn to try to get a bead on their leader. I was too late, and already the second 190 was within range. I gave him a short burst, then he was gone and I completed my turn into the stream of enemy fighters behind number three. I gave him a long burst of cannon fire and could see puffs of bluish smoke whipping back from his gun ports when he fired at a bomber. Behind me were more 190s, and I hoped that the Canadians had each selected an opponent and were alive to the dangers of our position when our mixed bunch of friends and foes hurtled towards the oncoming bombers.

My 190 half-rolled, but I could see that he was still firing. I followed every twist of the enemy fighter, as if I was following him in an aerobatic display, so that I was upside down and still sending short bursts after him. I daren't think of the shambles that was going on behind me. The Yanks were firing at one and all! A great amount of lead was being sprayed about this particular bit of sky.

The enemy pilot went into his vertical dive and I had no hope of holding him, so I half-rolled back to a normal position, took a deep breath and weighed up the situation. Our Spitfires were passing through successive boxes of Fortresses at a high rate of knots. I waggled my wings violently to show the American gunners the unmistakable, curving silhouette of the Spitfire. This act of friendship was received with several well directed bursts of machine-gun fire, and I lost no time in ordering our withdrawal to a safe position.

Leaving the Fortresses, we made our way back across the Channel. There were large breaks in the cloud and great patches of moving, dark shadows on the grey sea. We slid through a large gap, picked up the white cliffs at Broadstairs and soon swept into the circuit at Kenley.

It had been quite a trip. In retrospect it was amusing and we had a good laugh about the whole confused skirmish. But on the next trip it might prove to be more serious, so I phoned 11 Group and received permission to visit some of the American bases to try and formulate some common doctrine on escort tactics. For it was quite obvious that the Americans did not want us to provide the close escort we gave our own bombers.

I flew to some of the American bases and spent the night at one of them. It was as we suspected. They didn't want a close escort where Spitfires mingled with Fortresses. They simply wanted a fighter screen thrown well ahead and to the flanks of their boxes and well out of range of their own guns. Any aircraft which penetrated the fighter screen and approached the bombers would be assumed to be hostile and would be afforded suitable treatment. This was sound logic and suited us: we should have more freedom for offensive search and action. I was able to report these details to 11 Group, and the welcome news was soon passed to the wing leaders. We gave the Fortress gunners a wide berth, for, like many others, they shot first and identified afterwards.

I spent a very lively evening with the Americans and towards midnight a tremendous game of crap dice developed on the floor of the ante-room in the officers' mess. Our own gambling activities were strictly restricted to a discreet game of bridge, when the stakes were in the region of twopence per hundred points and the few shillings won or lost were carefully adjusted on our monthly mess bills. The Canadians, I had soon discovered, were no strangers to the dice and were inordinately fond of a game of poker. But this frenzied gathering of exuberant officers who shouted, pleaded and swore at the bones was new to me and I watched the scene, completely fascinated, as hundreds of pounds changed hands on a roll of the two dice. I learnt that the Americans usually beguiled away the long evenings with this form of amusement, and on this particular occasion it seemed as if the junior officers were winning large sums from the seniors. This state of affairs, I reflected, was probably most conducive to the maintenance of good order and discipline!

A major who had already lost his wad of bank-notes strolled up and began to talk:

"You fly one of these Spitfires?"

I admitted that I did.

"Great plane that Spit. How does it stack up against the Messerschmitt?"

"It's better than the Messerschmitt or the Focke-Wulf," I replied.

"That god-damned Focke-Wulf," he exclaimed. "Why, some of those babies carry four cannons. That Messerschmitt comes in a-firing. But that Focke-Wulf comes in blazing like a neon sign!"

From this brief encounter with the Americans it was apparent that their leaders were determined to establish their theories about daylight bombing. In general, British opinion, both public and military, was that long-range, large-scale bombing operations by daylight were not feasible, and that the Americans would be better advised to turn their attention to the problem of night bombing.

In order to understand this viewpoint it should be remembered that our own Air Staff had once subscribed to the belief that our bombers, flying in tight formations, could penetrate the enemy defences by daylight and for defence would rely solely upon their own concentration of fire. At the beginning of the war Bomber Command possessed a few squadrons whose primary rôle was night bombing, but it was intended that the majority of our squadrons would operate by daylight without fighter escort.

The first few daylight bomber missions after the outbreak of war were disastrous. Even so, after one daylight raid, when exactly half the force of Wellingtons was shot down, it was implied that the operation failed because the bombers did not hold a sufficiently tight formation. On the other hand, the Luftwaffe recorded the opinion that it was 'criminal folly' to despatch such unescorted Wellington formations in a cloudless sky. But our losses continued so heavy that, after the first December of the war, Wellingtons, Hampdens and Whitleys were restricted to night bombing where there was little fighter opposition, and only the lighter bombers, Battles and Blenheims, carried out their tactical tasks by daylight. In this manner, rather by force of circumstances than deliberate intention, did Bomber Command concentrate its resources on perfecting the difficult techniques of night bombing.

Now, three years later, when the Americans set out to prove their doctrine that strong formations of escorted bombers could fight their way by day through the German defences and attack distant targets, their views were received with polite scepticism.

We had seen the very first effort of the Eighth Air Force when during the previous August a dozen Fortresses had bombed Rouen. In this spring of 1943 we often escorted large numbers of the four-engined Fortresses and Liberators to various targets in north-west Europe whose selection was restricted by the Spitfire's radius of action of less than 200 miles rather than by any other considerations. We liked to fly with the Americans, for the Germans could see the writing on the wall and reacted with great determination.

During one hot fight over the target area Foss Bolton was wounded and shot down. His place at the head of 416 Squadron was taken by the burly, assertive 'Buck' McNair, who had already been through the thick of the air fighting over Malta and was credited with ten victories.

The claims of the Fortress gunners were out of all proportion to the numbers of enemy aircraft shot down: had they been correct, the Luftwaffe would simply have ceased to exist. On one raid over Lille, for example, the Americans claimed 102 enemy fighters destroyed or damaged, whereas the German records list one fighter destroyed and none damaged. For our part we were highly amused by these fantastic scores, and thought that a goodly proportion of the claims might well be explained by the promise to the American gunners of a medal for their first kill. The claims were far less important than the fact that the bombers were getting through to their targets and often hitting them with great accuracy. No longer were the Fortress raids looked upon as a daylight bait to draw up the enemy fighters: the bombing was now regarded as the main objective.

The Americans were developing their own force of long-range fighters, and soon the twin-engined Lightnings and sturdy Thunderbolts escorted their bombers far beyond the radius of action of our Spitfires. Sometimes the Fortresses and Liberators made long penetrations beyond the range of their own fighter escort: it was on some of these operations that the Luftwaffe reacted with uncanny skill, and in one black week almost 150 bombers were lost together with their crews. Despite these setbacks, the Americans never lost sight of their goal and eventually attained it through their characteristic energy and perseverance. The bomber formations grew in size and strength, and some of the Fortresses were modified to carry more guns; but this experiment was unsuccessful. Their fighters were then fitted with special long-range tanks and the Thunderbolt was given a radius of action of almost 400 miles, while that of the Lightnings was increased to nearly 600 miles. Eventually the single-engined Mustang made its appearance over Germany: this beautiful little fighter could fly as far as the bombers.

The greatest daylight air battles of late 1943 and early 1944 were fought out over Germany between the fighter arm of the Luftwaffe and the bombers and fighters of the Eighth Air Force. Towards the end of the year the Americans could put more than 600 four-engined bombers into the air, and soon these were escorted by a great ranging pack of American fighters who perfected the fighter tactics of deep penetration. The Luftwaffe replied with 'Storm-fighter' squadrons of Focke-Wulfs who were equipped with heavy-calibre cannons. Individual, finger-four and concentrated attacks in wing strength were pressed home against the Americans with a variety of weapons, including cannons, rockets and even parachute bombs. The numbers of aircraft involved in this Battle of Germany exceeded those used in the Battle of Britain three years previously, and the fighting was of greater intensity. But the Spitfire, which had achieved immortality in the earlier battle, played no part in this great conflict now being waged over Germany. How we longed for a wing of Spitfires which would fly to Berlin and back, for fighter pilots of every nationality were agreed that the Spitfire 9 was the best close in fighter of them all. But our radius of action remained the same as before, and we had to confine our activities to short-range operations while the Americans fought this daylight battle single-handed.

In the spring of 1943 Billy Burton came home on a short leave from the Desert Air Force in North Africa, and since his wife, Jean, lived near Kenley, we were able to have them both to a lively luncheon party in the mess. Like airmen the world over, we talked of our old battles and escapades; of Cocky in North Africa and of Nip, who had been creased in a delicate portion of his anatomy by a stray bullet from an enemy fighter over Malta. Billy told me that he was returning in a few days' time and expected to be promoted to group captain and given the command of his own fighter wing. But the Hudson bomber in which he flew back as a passenger was presumed shot down over the Bay of Biscay by a prowling night fighter, and we never saw him again.

Al Deere and I were awarded the D.S.O. on the same day, and I telephoned him at Biggin and suggested that we rendezvous at the Kimmul Club in Burleigh Street for a small celebration. This convenient and hospitable little place was owned and run by an ex-captain of the Royal Flying Corps, Bobbie Page, who was, and still is, a staunch friend. During the war years it was the popular meeting-place of air-crew of all nationalities, and Bobbie's spare bedrooms were usually full. He kept a great pile of blankets in his linen-cupboard at the top of the stairs, and if you were lucky, you could grab one and bed down for a couple of hours on a settee or the floor.

Later that evening a fair number of the Biggin and Kenley pilots were packed together in the crowded bar. A smiling, handsome young officer stood alone in a corner. He wore a mackintosh so that it was impossible to determine his rank or whether he was a pilot. He eyed the various activities of the fighter pilots with some amusement and eventually spoke to me:

"What are you glamour boys celebrating?"

"Well, as a matter of fact the two wings have collected a gong or two," I explained.

"And I suppose you got that D.S.O.?" he enquired, looking at the gleaming new ribbon.

"That's right," I agreed.

"Well, you'd better have a drink with me," said this enigmatic young officer.

"Thanks," I replied. "A bitter."

I moved back to the Canadians and thought nothing more of the encounter. Later on I caught a glimpse of the stranger, who was surrounded by a animated company of bomber crews. The room was so stuffy that he had discarded his mackintosh and I could see he wore the three stripes of a wing commander. I caught a glimpse of the ribbons of the D.S.O. and D.F.C., with a silver rosette to each, and some dull-coloured ribbon before the D.S.O. Curious, I eased my way through the press and had a closer look. My suspicions were correct: the ribbon was that of the Victoria Cross. I shouldered the remaining few feet to the bar, grabbed him by the arm and said:

"And now you'll have a pint with me, Guy Gibson."

Chapter Eleven

TACTICAL WING

Although the deep thrusts of the Eighth Air Force tied down the bulk of the Luftwaffe's day fighter squadrons, there still remained plenty of Focke-Wulfs and Messerschmitts to oppose our short-range penetrations over Holland, Belgium and northern France. J.G. 26, the Abbeville boys, still operated from their bases in the Pas de Calais and were generally recognised to be the élite of the German fighter pilots. Some idea of the calibre of these men can be gauged from the fate of eleven Ventura bombers who, with their Spitfire escort, crossed the North Sea at low level to bomb an Amsterdam power station. Unfortunately, one of the Spitfire supporting wings went astray, got twenty minutes ahead of its time schedule, failed to remain at sea-level and alerted the opposing fighters before it could be recalled. A great mixed pack of Focke-Wulfs and Messerschmitts were waiting for the bombers, their Spitfire escort was soon fully engaged, and the Venturas were all shot down. The bomber leader, Squadron Leader Trent, who alone attacked the target, was subsequently awarded the Victoria Cross for his part in this tragic operation.

Sometimes the radar controllers directed my wing on to large mixed gaggles of enemy fighters, and we often saw formations of upwards of fifty Huns. In these engagements our twenty-four Spitfires fought at a serious tactical disadvantage and I went therefore to see Air Vice-Marshal Saunders at 11 Group and recommended that we build up our fighter formations to about the same number, so that we could meet the Germans on equal terms. The group commander readily agreed to my proposal, and he decided that the Hornchurch Wing should fly with us.

I flew to Hornchurch to work out the tactical details of rendezvous and types of formation with the wing leader, the dark and dashing Bill Compton. In New Zealand before the war, Bill had become a member of the crew of an auxiliary-engined ketch and planned to sail round the world to England and join the R.A.F. Near New Guinea his cruise ended when the ketch struck a reef; but after a lot of adventures Bill landed in England shortly after the war began and was an aircraftman, second class, the same day.

But our large Balbos were not successful. When the controller told me to make fairly large changes of direction to intercept the enemy formations, the two wings, totalling sixty Spitfires, were difficult to hold together as a balanced, striking force. Such a mass of fighters could be seen from a great distance and the enemy leaders simply half-rolled and dived away when they wanted to avoid the issue.

Sometimes we succeeded in bouncing the Focke-Wulfs, but I found it very difficult to control and re-form the Balbo. It was no use taking part in one brief skirmish over France and returning after a few minutes as a disorganised rabble. The Balbo must be kept together as a fighting unit, which seemed impossible to achieve in our fast-moving combats. Both Bill Compton and Al Deere led these huge formations, but we were soon agreed that the Balbos were far too cumbersome for this type of fighting. We gave up the attempt and left it to the planners at 11 Group to see that we achieved a suitable concentration of fighters in any particular area.

The group captain commanding at Kenley had served in the Desert, where he had been greatly impressed by two inseparable young Canadian pilots, Walter Conrad and George Keefer. They had fought together in the Desert Air Force for a long time, had shared the same tent and been awarded the D.F.C. at the same time. Now one of them wrote to the group captain, said they were on their way to England and could they be found a job with the Kenley Wing?

On arrival at Kenley they marched into my office to report their arrival. I was immediately impressed by these two outstanding young Canadians; the blond Conrad and the dark, curly haired Keefer, both lean and sunburned after their experiences in the Desert.

We flew hard during those summer months of 1943 and scored some decisive successes against the Luftwaffe. Our Spitfire 9s were superior to both the Focke-Wulf 190 and the latest Messerschmitt product, the 109G, and Hunter continued to supply us with excellent information whenever we flew within range of his radars. Late one summer evening on a sweep over Rouen we bounced a small mixed gaggle of enemy fighters and in the ensuing confusion saw a Focke-Wulf blast a Messerschmitt out of the sky. It was comforting to know that the Luftwaffe had their recognition troubles too.

Jamie, the New Zealander, had recently concluded a long tour of operations and now headed a small cell of planners at 11 Group headquarters at Uxbridge. From the varied intelligence information available he studied the dispositions of the Luftwaffe squadrons, and when they reinforced a particular area he countered with moves of the 11 Group wings. Jamie switched us to Coltishall in Norfolk, to Bradwell Bay in Suffolk, to Manston in Kent, to Tangmere in Sussex, to Middle Wallop in Wiltshire, or to Portreath in Cornwall, where we refuelled and then took off to search the skies of occupied Europe for enemy aircraft. The wing score mounted to a pleasing total, and suitably inscribed silver tankards were presented to our pilots who shot down the ninety-eighth, ninety-ninth and hundredth Huns since the formation of the Canadian wing. I shot down our ninety-ninth enemy aircraft, and that brought my personal score, apart from probables and damaged aircraft, up to twenty. So I found myself climbing up Fighter Command's score-sheet, which for a long time had been headed by the Sailor with his thirty-two victories.

Soon afterwards George Keefer had to bale out five miles off the French coast, and Conrad was like a man demented until every available Spitfire was over the Channel searching for his friend. George was eventually found and picked up by an air-sea rescue Walrus amphibious aircraft and was back on the job within a few hours.

The following day it was the tough Buck McNair who had to be rescued from the drink.

The Fortresses had bombed a target in the Ruhr and we flew to Manston so that we would have sufficient fuel to rendezvous with the four-engined bombers over Rotterdam. We saw them as they flew over Arnhem on their return journey: they crossed the Dutch coast without incident. They were accompanied by a strong force of fighters, and I felt that there was little point in accompanying the bombers across the North Sea. So we broke away and set course to come home via Flushing, Ostend and Calais.

We hadn't gone very far when Buck's engine began to run very roughly and he called up to say he was heading straight for Manston and taking his wingman, Tommy Parks, with him. This was standard procedure, for we never flew over the sea alone in our single-engined Spitfires if we could avoid it. They had only left us a short time when Parks called out:

"Greycap. Red leader's Spit has caught fire. He's baled out. Over."

"Can you see him, red two?" I asked.

"Yes, sir. He's in the sea, but not in his dinghy. About ten miles from the French coast. What shall I do?"

I tried to work out our best tactics before I answered the lone Spitfire pilot circling over his squadron commander. Buck was only a few miles off-shore and the strong wind would drift him nearer the enemy coast. The sea was choppy with lots of white crests, and the statement that our pilot wasn't in his dinghy sounded ominous. Parks would have a difficult task to keep sight of his leader's bobbing head in such a sea. It would be a tricky rescue.

I thought of some of the bitter fights which often took place over pilots 'in the drink'. These usually began when a small section of circling fighters were attacked by an enemy patrol, and in this respect we were as guilty as the Luftwaffe. For if you came across half a dozen Messerschmitts flying above the sea, how were you to know they were orbiting a dinghy or escorting one of their rescue launches? You looked for Huns in the sky, and when you saw them you cleared your tail, scanned into the sun and went in. Both sides would then reinforce the area with fighters, and what had originated as a small rescue operation would often develop into a hotly contested air battle. Rescue floatplanes from both sides had been shot down, launches attacked and pilots lost. Today this must be avoided at all costs.

"Red two from Greycap. Stay over him as low as you can. Low

revs and just enough power to stay in the air. Transmit for Mayday on C for Charlie and we'll get back as soon as we can. O.K.?"

"O.K., Greycap," acknowledged Parks.

We put our noses down and slanted for Manston in a long, fast dive. I called the controller at Kenley, who would have overheard our radio chatter.

"Greycap to Wytex.[1] Red leader is in the drink. I've left red two over him. What's the form?"

"Wytex to Greycap. Group has pushed out a section of Spits to relieve red two. We've got an excellent fix and the Walrus is about to take off from Hawkinge."

For the present it seemed as if the rescue machinery was working perfectly, but the whole thing depended on the relieving section of Spitfires finding Parks over a large expanse of sea. If Parks had to leave Buck alone, the chances were that he wouldn't be found again.

We landed at Manston and I was soon in the air again with a small section of Spitfires after a very snappy bit of refuelling. The remainder of the wing went back to Kenley, for we didn't want to stir up the Luftwaffe with the spectacle of a large bunch of Spitfires milling about a few miles off the coast. I called ops. again.

"Wytex – Greycap again. What's the form now?"

"Red two has been relieved. One section of Spits is over red leader. The Walrus will be there in about forty minutes."

"Thank you," I replied. "I've got three Spits with me and we'll just keep an eye on things. Any Huns about?"

"Greycap from Wytex. All quiet and nothing plotted. Keep your fingers crossed!"

We found the two circling Spitfires and I flew very low to have a close look at Buck. The mae-west was holding him upright in the water and he had drifted nearer the French coast. The sand dunes looked very close. Once again I zoomed over him, but there was no gesture from the Canadian.

After half an hour or so we saw the Walrus and we fretted for another ten minutes until it joined us. I called the pilot on a

___

[1] Code name for Kenley.

common radio frequency and recognised the voice of Squadron Leader Grace, the determined and brave C.O. of the Hawkinge rescue flight. Grace and his crews had carried out many brilliant pick-ups from under the very noses of the Germans, and he knew the business. He had a difficult landing on a rough sea, to say nothing of a dozen Messerschmitts who might suddenly streak over the sand dunes and wade into us. He carried out a wide, slow circuit to study Buck's position and then he glided down, and I thought, he's landing now, but the pilot dropped a smoke marker and the Walrus turned for another circuit. I couldn't watch this lengthy, delicate business any longer and pulled my section away so that we patrolled between the Walrus and the shore.

At long last the amphibious aircraft landed safely and taxied up to our pilot. Buck was hauled on board and the Walrus swung into the eye of the wind for its take-off run. It gathered speed and then bounced from crest to crest with the sea cascading from the hull. It reminded me of an old swan beating its wings along a stretch of river to get up the right speed for take-off. Once the Walrus was in the air, I called Grace:

"Greycap to Walrus. How's our pilot?"

"Not too bad," answered Grace. "He's burnt a bit and swearing a lot!"

We flew with the Walrus all the way back to Hawkinge, and I was alongside the amphibious aircraft when Buck was transferred to a waiting ambulance. His face looked pretty grim, but he was cheerful and recognised me:

"Don't let me lose the squadron, chief," he said. "This is nothing. I'll be back in a day or two. Promise I won't lose the squadron!"

"All right, Buck," I assured him. "Don't worry about that. We'll keep the job open for you.

I flew back to Kenley, highly pleased with the team work which had resulted in Buck's rescue from the sea. It was, of course, largely due to young Parks, who had kept his head, stayed with his squadron commander for an hour and a half until he was relieved and then had barely enough petrol to get back to Manston. And

Grace had done his stuff splendidly, like all the rescue crews we knew. I made a mental note to write and ask the officers of the rescue flight to our next party.

Buck returned to his squadron within a few days and was soon flying again. But unknown to the doctors who treated him, the searing flames had damaged one of his eyes when he fought to get out of his blazing Spitfire. Buck didn't tell us, but fought on at the head of his squadron.

It was now high summer and the headquarters of the Second Tactical Air Force had been formed for some time: its subordinate groups and wings would support 21st Army Group when the long awaited invasion of Europe took place. 83 Group, one of the tactical groups of second T.A.F., began to absorb some of the 11 Group wings, and in early August the Kenley Wing was transferred to 83 Group and renamed 127 Wing.[1]

We left Fighter Command and Kenley and established ourselves at Lashenden, a recently constructed landing-strip in Kent, although our operations were still planned and controlled from Uxbridge. 421 Squadron, another Canadian unit, had replaced 416 Squadron in the wing, and my two squadron commanders were now Buck McNair and the youthful Hugh Godefroy, who was an engineering student at Toronto University when war broke out. Only a few miles away was another Canadian Spitfire unit, 126 Wing, and both wings were commanded by 'Iron Bill' MacBrien, or to give him his full title, Group Captain MacBrien, a regular officer in the R.C.A.F. and son of a one-time commissioner of the Royal Canadian Mounted Police.

At Lashenden we lived under canvas. Our food was prepared in field kitchens and all our workshops and equipment were housed in specially built trucks so that we could break camp at short notice and move to another airfield.

One day in August we flew to Bradwell Bay and took off to escort a large force of Fortresses who were going to attack the

[1] The Kenley Wing was originally renamed 127 Airfield, but this inapt name was subsequently altered to 127 Wing. For the sake of continuity I have used the word 'wing' instead of 'airfield'.

Messerschmitt factory complex at Regensburg and the important ball-bearing industry at Schweinfurt. The Regensburg force would land at bases in North Africa, but the Schweinfurt force would return to their airfields in England. It was planned that the two raids should be separated by only a small time-interval, but bad weather over some of the Fortress airfields increased the stagger to more than three hours. Eighteen squadrons of Thunderbolts, not all equipped with long-range tanks, and sixteen squadrons of Spitfires were detailed to provide fighter cover on part of the penetration and withdrawal. Meanwhile, light bombers and fighter-bombers would try and pin down enemy fighters in the Low Countries by diversionary attacks and sweeps.

We left the Regensburg force a few miles east of Antwerp, since this was the limit of our radius of action: when we turned back we had not seen an enemy aircraft. We flew across Holland and the North Sea, refuelled at Bradwell Bay, and took to the air again to rendezvous with the returning raiders from Schweinfurt.

This was the most disastrous operation of the Fortresses up to that date. They were subjected to continuous attacks by squadron after squadron of Focke-Wulfs, and by both Messerschmitt 109s and the twin-engined 110s. The Luftwaffe pilots fought well and tried every trick in the book. Sixty Fortresses, or almost one-fifth of the total attacking force, were shot down. When we swung out to meet them we saw gaping holes in their formations and a few stragglers, lagging well behind the main formation, struggling to get home on three engines.

Individual enemy fighters were still attacking the battered Fortresses, and since they sprawled and trailed over a great area of sky I split the wing into small sections of four Spitfires so that we could each look after the stragglers. Below us a Messerschmitt 110 fired rockets into the belly of a badly shot-up bomber. I half-rolled my little section of Spitfires, aileron-turned on to the tail of the 110 and missed him because my Spitfire was bucking in the fast dive. But the three Canadians with me made sure of the 110 and we saw him crash on the ground.

The Fortresses crossed the Dutch coast and were met by more of our fighters. The combats had ceased, but I had noticed one or two damaged Fortresses break away from the main stream and fly parallel to the enemy coast. In this way their crews would not be faced with the long sea crossing for they would slip across the narrow neck of the Channel between Calais and Dover. But they would be sitting ducks for any prowling Focke-Wulfs, so the best thing we could do was to fly a dog-leg route home, sweeping down the coast to Calais before turning starboard for Lashenden.

I called the section leaders:

"All Greycap aircraft re-form. Over Ostend at angels 24." They came swinging in from all directions, six sections each of four Spitfires, who jockeyed into their wing formation in well under five minutes. It always pleased me to see the pilots form up again in such a workmanlike manner: it was the hallmark of teamwork and good flying discipline. We set course for Calais, and after a few minutes Walter Conrad called up:

"Greycap, there's one lone aircraft behind. Six o'clock. About the same height and two miles away. Looks like he's trailing us."

"All right, Walter," I replied. "Ease out a bit and keep an eye on him."

I could hardly believe that this unknown aircraft would turn out to be a Hun. It was a brave Hun who would have the nerve to stalk a wing of Spitfires in a clear, blue sky.

Wally called again:

"Greycap, he's gaining on us. He's not much more than 1,000 yards now. It's a 190!"

"Take your number two and break into him when you're ready," I ordered. "But don't wait too long!"

A few seconds elapsed, during which we all continued to fly straight and level to draw on the unsuspecting Hun. Then Walter sang out:

"Blue two, break right, now!" And I turned the rest of the Canadians to watch the unequal fight between our two Spitfires and the bold pilot of the 190.

But the enemy pilot had seen the two Spitfires break away from our main formation and he half-rolled and dived down towards

Dunkirk with Wally and his wingman, Flight Sergeant Shouldice, streaking after him. We watched the three fighters until they became mere specks and were swallowed up by the early evening haze. Someone called up and said:

"Greycap, two explosions on the ground."

I called up Conrad:

"You alright, Walter?"

An answer came back over the radio. It was from Shouldice, and he spoke very quietly:

"Greycap from blue two. I've collided with blue leader. I think he's gone in!"

"How's your Spit, Shouldice?" I asked.

"My right aileron has gone and some of the wing-tip. She's very hard to control. Over."

I had to give him some advice at once. Either to climb up and bale out over France or to try and get back to England. If he baled out over France he would probably be taken prisoner in this strongly held coastal belt. But this did not matter: the main thing was to save the pilot. The Spitfire was badly damaged and it was unlikely that it could be flown back to England for a safe landing. I called Shouldice and tried to sound reassuring and cheerful:

"You'd better head into France. Climb to 10,000 feet and bale out. We'll cover you. Over."

"I can't bale out, sir. The hood seems jammed and I can't get it open!"

"All right then Shouldice. Steer three, zero, zero for Dover. Climb as high as you can. What's your height now?"

"8,000 feet, sir."

I left the others at our original height, and taking my wingman, went in search of the crippled Spitfire. On the way down I called the controller at Kenley and asked him to alert a Walrus and the launches.

We soon found Shouldice, just off the French coast and heading for Dover. I drew alongside and could see that most of the right aileron and wing-tip had gone. It was a miracle that the aeroplane was still flying. The right wing was well down and the Spitfire was trying to swing to the right and back into France. The pilot was fighting this and was having a hard struggle; I could see he had both hands on the stick. I spoke to him again:

"We're half-way across now. Only ten miles to Dover."

This time there was no reply from him and perhaps the stick forces were so heavy that he could not move a hand to the transmitter switch. Then the right wing dropped lower and I turned steeply inside him when his Spitfire yawed dangerously to the right with the wings vertical: I saw his hands reach to the rubber ball at the top of the hood which controlled the emergency release system. Then the Spitfire fell into an uncontrollable vertical dive.

It only took a second or two to reach the sea. We watched the Spitfire knife cleanly, nose first into the water. Watched the cascading ring of spray fall back and saw the surging waters close in over the Spitfire and its pilot. I called the controller and gave a fix, but I knew the rescue boys would never find a thing.

Back at Lashenden I sat down in my caravan to write letters to the next of kin of the two pilots. Before I began to write I glanced through the 'in' tray and saw that two of my recent recommendations had been approved. Flight Sergeant Shouldice had been appointed to a commission and the promotion of Flight Lieutenant Conrad to squadron leader was notified.

One day Bill MacBrien climbed the few steps into my caravan and said:

"Got some news for you, Johnnie. How would you like Screwball Beurling in your outfit?"

"I shall have to think about that one, sir," I replied. "He's a great fighter pilot, but I hear he's very much of a lone wolf."

We all knew Beurling's history. He had joined the R.A.F. after being turned down by the R.C.A.F. and was eventually posted to our own 403 Squadron. Even in those days he was a remote, brooding lad who showed great individual promise, but whose temperament was not suited to our style of team fighting. So he was sent to Malta and there found fulfilment in his solitary yet brilliant exploits against the Luftwaffe and the Italian Air Force. In the dangerous sky over the Mediterranean island he brought his score to twenty-nine victories, and on his return to Canada he was greeted as a national hero.

I discussed the problem of Beurling with our two squadron commanders. For my own part I felt that we could not condemn this extraordinary pilot, because he had fought so well over Malta. We must give him the chance to prove his worth in the wing. I told the group captain we'd have Beurling and recommended that he go to 403 Squadron, where he had served two years previously as a sergeant-pilot.

I made it a point to meet Beurling within a few minutes of his arrival and took him along to the caravan for a quiet chat. We talked about his Malta exploits and I tried to explain how the style of our fighting differed here.

"I'm going to make you gunnery officer of the wing, George," I told him. "Try and teach the rest of the chaps how you do it. If you can settle down here you'll be a squadron commander in a few months. And with your record you could easily have a wing of your own within twelve months. What do you think?"

"I guess you fly a lot of sweeps without seeing any Huns?" he enquired.

"I should think we engage about once out of every three or four sweeps," I told him.

"They must be there then," he said more to himself than me. "Wouldn't you do better to split up into twelve pairs and fly on the deck to look for them. You'd cover a wide area that way."

"No," I answered firmly. "In the first place we must stick together because the Huns operate in packs of up to fifty. Secondly, the flak is so hot over here that if we flew on the deck we'd lose half of the boys in a week."

"You know anything about this Mustang, Wingco?"

"Not much," I said. "I hear one of the 83 Group wings is going to get them and they have a tremendous radius of action. I hear they can easily fly to Berlin and back."

"Can they now?" exclaimed the Canadian. I could read his thoughts. Give him a long-range Mustang, fill it up with petrol each day and he'd either get himself killed or would finish up with more Huns than the rest of us put together!

He changed the subject.

"Hear you've got a scatter gun, Wingco?"

"That's right," I admitted. "There it is, a B.S.A. twelve bore."

"And a bird dog?"

I thought that my well-bred Labrador would not take kindly to being called a 'bird dog,' but I only said:

"Her name's Sally."

"Guess I'll borrow them some fine day," announced Beurling. "I must get some hunting."

"Help yourself, George," I invited. "She'll follow you anywhere when she sees the gun."

A day or two later I walked across the airfield after waiting for a shot at the mallard at a little pond. It was a dark, moon-less night, but the stars were very bright. Suddenly Sally growled at a dark shape sitting on a fallen log.

"Hello, George," I said. "Bit cool out here, isn't it?"

"It's O.K.," he replied.

"Walk back with me and we'll have a beer," I suggested. "No thanks, Wingco. Guess I'll stay out here. I'm figuring out some of the angles between the stars."

Beurling and I only flew once or twice together, for soon after his arrival I left the Canadians.

September came, and this meant that it was more than three years since I had joined 616 Squadron at Coltishall as a pilot officer. All this time, except for a few weeks in hospital, had been spent with the fighter squadrons, and during the last six months I had led the wing on 120 operations. Now, after a sweep, I felt washed out and got into the habit of making straight for the caravan, pulling Sally off the bed and falling into a fitful, restless sleep.

I found the heavy flak more frightening than ever before. We always had a very healthy respect for this accurate, deadly stuff, but until now I had found time, like Stan Turner, to make some cryptic comment about it. There was never any warning of the flak.

One moment you were in a serene sky and the next the flak was alongside, reaching for and bracketing your Spitfire, and sometimes so close that you could hear the crump of the explosion above the steady drone of your engine. When you heard the flak like this it was too near, and the evil, black smoke swirled over your aircraft. Then it was time to watch the gauges and feel the tension of the controls for any sudden slackening...

I found that I was reacting differently to the presence of the Messerschmitts and the Focke-Wulfs. When we saw large gaggles, it was my job to manoeuvre the wing into the best tactical position and take the Canadians into the fight. When we saw small enemy formations I had previously detached a pair of Spitfires or a finger-four to bounce the Huns while we watched the fight and guarded our own pilots. But during this last month I had got into the habit of handing the wing over to a squadron commander and taking my own section down to fight. It was as if the Huns roused a deep personal antagonism in me and a 'probable' or a 'damaged' did not seem enough. For some reason the enemy aircraft had each to be destroyed, and more than once I found myself at ground-level in single-handed combat with no quarter asked or given. The long tour was beginning to cloud my better judgment. My score stood at twenty-four.

I hadn't developed a 'twitch' like some pilots did when they were very tired. Then the carefully controlled nervous tension expressed itself by various tell-tale signs, such as the continued flicking of an eyelid or the shake of a head. "Old So-and-So's got the twitch," we used to say. "He's had it! He'll be taken off any time now."

We all knew the meaning of fear, and felt it according to our temperaments and training. I never knew a pilot who fell outside this category: our simple duty was to control this fear and prevent its natural transition to panic. We knew fear and lived and fought with it. Once you let it give way to panic, you were finished.

Others in authority had noticed the signs. One day, when I had led the Canadians on four missions, I was lying down before the evening meal. Bill MacBrien entered the caravan. He came straight to the point: "Well, that's it, Johnnie. Your tour's over.

Godefroy takes over the wing tomorrow, so you'd better get off on some leave."

The Canadians laid on a tremendous guest night in our mess tent to bid me farewell. Air Vice-Marshal Dickson, our group commander, was present and at a late hour decided that the wing should be stood down on the following day. The usual speeches were made and it was strongly hinted that the Canadians would offer me the leadership of another wing after a rest. I was presented with a beautiful gold watch and felt like an old man retiring after a lifetime with the firm.

Chapter Twelve

GROUNDED

Paula and I spent two weeks together before I took over new appointment on the planning staff of 11 Group headquarters. In Norfolk we walked the root fields together after a few partridges. Sally worked well, and although we got a few birds I suspected that my young wife was not much interested in the sport. She regarded the despatch of wounded birds with some horror, and my dream of happy days together with Paula shouldering a light sporting gun began to evaporate. Sally limped towards me with a thorn in her foot, so I handed my twelve bore to Paula and knelt down to remove the thorn. Suddenly there was a loud bang and the Labrador and I were peppered with earth and bits of sugar beet. It was my closest shave of the war and marked my wife's last appearance in the shooting-field!

A fortnight later I reported to Uxbridge, where I became a staff officer and once again worked for Pat Jameson. Together with a squadron leader we formed a small team whose job was to plan and co-ordinate the day-to-day activities of the 11 Group and 83 Group wings, for this latter group would not assume these responsibilities until it was established in France after the invasion.

It was a most interesting job and one in which our recent experiences as wing leaders were invaluable. Our main task was to provide escort and support wings for the various bomber forces which were assigned to four different organisations. These were the Lancasters of Bomber Command; Fortresses and Liberators of the Eighth Air Force; Marauders and Havocs of the United States Ninth Air Force; and Bostons, Mitchells and Mosquitoes of our own 2 Group.

We had little liaison with Bomber Command, since their daylight operations were few and far between, although we were to support the Lancasters later on when they added their strength to the tactical bombing after the invasion. We provided what support we could to the deep penetrations of the Eighth Air Force, but their radius of action was so great and ours so small that our efforts were very restricted. We felt there was a great need for a first-class, long-range fighter like the American Mustang so that we of the R.A.F. could play our part in this new style of long-range daylight fighting. Our Spitfires had the performance but not the range to carry the daylight offensive to Germany, and, unfortunately, our Typhoons had the range but not the ability to live in the air against the Messerschmitts and Focke-Wulfs.

Our biggest customer was the Ninth Air Force, and on most suitable days we provided escort and supporting fighters to these tactical bombers when they attacked a variety of targets in Occupied Europe. Whenever possible these missions were timed to coincide with the strategic attacks of the Eighth Air Force, so that the Luftwaffe squadrons were all fully occupied at the same time. The twin-engined Marauders and Havocs met with little opposition and we found one squadron of Spitfires sufficient to escort a box of thirty-six bombers. Two years before we had found it necessary to stack twelve fighter squadrons round a handful of bombers.

At this time, the activities of the 2 Group bombers were largely directed against the hundred or so 'ski sites' which were being constructed inside the French coast to launch flying bombs against London. These were called 'Crossbow' targets and, although enemy fighters rarely opposed these short-range missions, both the light and heavy flak had to be reckoned with. Sometimes the low-level bombers of this famous group ranged to other targets and we provided the fighter escort when nineteen Mosquitoes breached the prison wall at Amiens to release many political prisoners. Unfortunately, the leading Mosquito, flown by Group Captain Pickard, was shot down by two 190s and both this great pilot and his navigator were killed.

The 'duty planner' tried to submit an outline plan of the following day's operations at the group commander's evening conference. Very often we were hard at it until the small hours, for there were many last-minute alterations owing to varying weather reports. The Americans had a very healthy respect for our weather. "When you're lost over Europe," they would say, "all you've got to do is look for the biggest, dirtiest cloud. Fly to it and make your let-down. You'll find that god-damned island below!"

The Luftwaffe were always up to some dodge or other. When the Thunderbolts escorted their Fortresses on the long daylight penetrations, the Focke-Wulfs climbed up over Holland and only attacked the American fighters. To defend themselves, the Thunderbolt pilots had to jettison their heavy, long-range tanks long before they were empty. This meant that the American fighters had to turn back before their appointed time and the Fortresses were left without fighter escort and took some bad knocks.

This move on the part of the Luftwaffe was fairly easy to counter. We studied their squadron dispositions and saw that they were concentrated at Schipol, Deelen, Eindhoven and Volkel. On the next Fortress penetration over the Holland route we pushed out three Spitfire wings from Norfolk, kept them twenty minutes ahead of the bombers and at sea-level until the Dutch coast was in sight. Then they climbed steeply and surprised the enemy fighters just taking off and assembling over their airfields.

When the weather was too bad for large-scale bombing operations, there were our own Spitfire and Typhoon wings to keep busy. Inevitably, as the weather worsened with the approach of winter, there was more talk, some of it ill-advised, of *Rhubarbs*: I felt one of the first and most important things I had to do was to change our policy concerning these costly operations. In 1941, when we had begun *Rhubarb* operations, we had flown in small numbers, usually a pair, and tried to take full advantage of cloud cover. I have related how the Germans set up decoys and how, in my opinion, our losses made this type of work, in single-engined Spitfires, prohibitively expensive.

I knew that the present set of wing leaders shared my strong views, for we had often discussed the futility of these operations. The wing leaders were the most senior officers who, in the fighter and tactical worlds, flew consistently against the enemy. There were a few notable exceptions to this rule, namely Basil Embry, who, as an air vice-marshal, flew often and saw to it that his officers did likewise. But in general the wing leaders were the men who were best qualified to discuss the tactics and hazards of their work. I checked with them once more, not as one of them but in my capacity as a member of the air staff, and the unanimous opinion was that our present policy should be radically altered.

I put forward these views to our understanding 11 Group commander, Air Vice-Marshal Saunders, at the first opportunity. Jamie supported me with the reservation that *Rhubarbs* might be worth continuing on a small scale over Holland, where the flak was less dangerous than over France, and I was ready to yield on this point. I stressed the difficulties of target identification and the numerous occasions when innocent French civilians must have been shot-up, of the vulnerability of our Spitfires to light flak and machine-gun fire, of our appalling losses and the cost of expensive aircraft and highly trained pilots. The group commander listened attentively, then decided that, as far as his wings were concerned, *Rhubarbs* over France would be a thing of the past, except for special operations.

What constituted a special operation? The answer was, when the target was of sufficient importance to merit the risks involved. Shortly afterwards I planned a special *Rhubarb*, and its origin, preparation and the pilots' reaction to it is worth setting down.

We learnt from a secret and reliable source that the German commander-in-chief, von Rundstedt, was to make a long train journey from the south of France to Paris. The train would consist of sleepers, restaurant car and flak waggon, and would be preceded by a pilot train. We were provided with a detailed time-table by our informant, and to Jamie and me it seemed that the opportunity was too good to miss. Our group commander was of the same opinion, so we got on with the planning.

It must be a small force of fast fighters, which would remain on the deck, hope not to alert the enemy defences, and would take full advantage of any low cloud cover. The train must be attacked on a long, level stretch of railway well to the south of Paris and this ruled out the Spitfires because of range considerations. The task had to be carried out by the Typhoons, and it would be on a voluntary basis. I was the duty planner, but I consulted with Jamie:

"Which Typhoon squadron shall I offer this von Rundstedt job to, Jamie?"

His answer was quick and decisive.

"609 at Lympne. They've done a few long-range jobs lately and are pretty hot at it. Pat Thornton-Brown is their C.O. I should have a word with him and see what he thinks."

I got Thornton-Brown on the scrambler telephone, and without mentioning the date or the place asked him how he would like to take part in a long-range, train-busting mission. We couldn't choose the day and time of attack because it was a special train and would only run on one specific day. He would have to fly through a heavily defended fighter belt and a lot of flak. We could hope for cloud cover, but it was October, and we could not be certain of it. The leader of the Typhoons would have to decide whether the mission was 'on' shortly before take-off, when he had the latest weather forecast and any actual weather information we could provide from previous flights on the same day.

The squadron commander accepted the task immediately and we passed full details of the train, its time-table and route and the name of its distinguished occupant over our teleprinter system. We left details of the time and type of attack to the squadron pilots, for they were the best judges of such things. The train was scheduled to enter Paris at one minute to six on a Saturday afternoon, and if all went well it would never get there.

The weather was favourable to the enterprise, with a great deal of cloud cover. Six Typhoons, led by Thornton-Brown, took-off just before tea-time, and from now on the fate of von Rundstedt was in the hands of the half-dozen young pilots.

I left our planning office and walked the few yards to the spacious, underground operations block which, with its elaborate communications system, was the nerve centre of the whole of 11 Group. I made my way to the controller's dais and paused to look at the framed stub of Winston Churchill's cigar which was a souvenir of the epic day in September 1940 when he had visited this very room and watched the progress of one of the great air battles.

I sat next to the duty controller in a comfortable seat reserved for the duty planner and watched the Waafs plotting the movements of aircraft on the large table below the dais. The majority were blondes, and some were quite beautiful. It couldn't be just coincidence, I reflected, that all the most glamorous Waaf plotters seemed to find their way to the operations rooms at Fighter Command and the groups. We never saw such a beauty chorus in the station operations rooms, and to me it was obvious that their selection called for a high degree of administrative staff work on someone's part. I remarked on this fact to the controller.

"Yes," he agreed, "a pretty face here and there makes life a lot easier." He reached for his cup of tea, sipped it and continued, "The brunette watch comes on duty a bit later!"

The afternoon slipped by and I looked at my watch. The attack should be over by this time and the boys on their way home. I estimated that they would be thundering over the outskirts of Paris. A coloured counter was placed on the plotting-table near the mouth of the Seine. The controller nodded towards the table and said:

"That's 609 crossing out."

"Can't be," I answered. "They're not due out for another ten or fifteen minutes."

"We'll soon make certain," said the controller. "We'll call them. They must be climbing up now."

It was 609 Squadron, and I phoned their intelligence officer when they taxied in at Lympne. He was excited and said that he could see all six pilots had fired their cannons. I told him to get his squadron commander to the phone since we were all anxious to know what had happened. Eventually I heard his voice at the other end of the line.

"How did it go, Pat," I asked.

"Absolutely first class, sir. We had a great afternoon. I think we got two Junkers 88s destroyed, one twin-engined Messerschmitt in flames, two 109s on the Seine, a crane damaged and a gasometer sprayed. We ran into the Huns over Bretigny, near the airfield, you know, and …"

"That's fine," I interrupted gently. "But what about old von R.?"

"Oh, yes," he answered. "I'd almost forgotten about him. We used up a lot of ammo against the Huns and the weather was lifting – blue sky south of Paris. So I called the show off and we came home, with one or two squirts at shipping on the Seine."

"Well done, Pat," I said. "We'll get von R. some other time."

It was during November that the telephone rang and Bobbie Page spoke to me from the Kimmul Club. There was a noisy party in progress, for I could hear the usual background clamour over the line. We exchanged the usual pleasantries, when Bobbie said quite casually:

"Here's a friend of yours who wants a word or two with you."

I waited a second or two, and then a Canadian voice said:

"Is that you, Wingco? You old bastard! Guess who this is?"

I replied, "I think it's Walter Conrad. But that's impossible ..."

"You bet it's Walter! Right here in the jolly old Kimmul Club. Knocking back a pint of this stuff you call beer. The Spanish vino was better!"

"Let's have the story then, Walter," I demanded. "Now. I can't wait till I see you."

"Well, you saw Shouldice and me go down after that 190 last August," began Walter.

"Go on," I said.

"We were both firing at the Hun and Shouldice couldn't have been watching me. The Hun went in and then Shouldice hit me behind the cockpit with his right wing. My Spit was sliced in two! I don't remember how I got out, but my parachute only just opened when I fell on a haystack just inside Dunkirk."

"What happened then, Walter?" I asked.

"I was pretty bruised and I had lost my shoes when I baled out. I hid in an old machine-gun trench for four days and got to feel pretty miserable."

"How did you get out of France?" I asked.

"I got in touch with a farmer, who gave me a pair of size twelve British Army boots he'd found on the beach at Dunkirk. But he wouldn't help me any more. So I told him that if I was caught by the Huns, I'd tell them who gave me the boots!"

"Yes," I prompted.

"It worked like a charm. I soon met the right people and spent the usual six weeks in one of Spain's lousy prisons. But here I am! Cheers!" And he took a long pull at his beer.

So Walter commanded his squadron after all: I was to see a lot more of both him and his friend, George Keefer.

After only a few weeks on the staff I began to feel that my own combat experience was getting out of date. The introduction of a new aeroplane or a more powerful version of an existing type, the provision of long-range tanks, the appointment of a new wing leader together with the ever-changing reactions of the Luftwaffe served to keep our own tactics very flexible. Both Jamie and I felt that we could not deal on equal terms with the wing leaders unless we kept ourselves up to date, and it was obviously our duty to be fully conversant with every aspect of fighter work. I remembered the shining example of Victor Beamish and how he had both planned and flown on the earlier sweeps.

As a typical example of how soon we could get outmoded, let me relate a story about the Tangmere Wing and how their tactics changed once they received the new Spitfire 12s.

The Luftwaffe had modified some of their Focke-Wulf 190s so that they had a very good performance at low-level. Anyone who lived on the south coast during this time will remember their sharp fighter-bomber raids on our coastal towns, when the 190s came over at sea-level and achieved both surprise and success.

Our answer to this threat was the Griffon-engined Spitfire 12, which Rolls Royce and Vickers quickly produced. At low and medium altitudes the Spitfire 12 was faster than its contemporary, the 9, and could cope with the low-flying 190s. Naturally we used the Tangmere Wing on the greatest possible number of offensive operations, and on this occasion I watched Jamie when he drafted an operation order for the wing to sweep the Rouen area at 12,000 feet.

"12,000 feet seems a bit low, Jamie," I commented. "The boys are certain to get bounced at that height."

"That's right," briefly answered the New Zealander.

"Then why don't you put them higher?" I suggested.

"Because, dear boy, Ray Harries prefers to fly below the Huns. In fact, his tactics depend on the Huns starting the attack."

I expressed profound disbelief, for I had always been a firm believer in the old axiom that the leader who has the height advantage controls the battle. The following day found me in the Tangmere briefing room listening to their small but brilliant leader. We were to sweep the Rouen-Beauvais area under radar control and I would fly wingman to Ray: in other words, I was a pilot officer again for the duration of this mission. The wing leader concluded his briefing:

"We'll fly between ten and twelve thousand feet as usual. The 190s will be above us. So just report them quietly to me. We'll pretend we haven't seen them and when they're just out of range we'll break into them."

Ray and I walked to our Spitfires. Before we climbed into our cockpits, I said:

"I always thought the chap with the height held all the cards, Ray."

"Yes, he does," replied the wing leader. "But 12,000 feet is our best fighting height. Somehow we've got to pull down the Hun to our level. Once he's down, our Spits are so much better that we can break into him, out-turn him and soon get on top of him. One day we saw twenty-five or thirty Huns above us. We drew them down, broke into them and clobbered nine. I hope you'll see how it's done today."

I could think of no suitable comment.

The controller gave us various courses to steer and eventually we were flying immediately below a gaggle of 190s. The pilots reported them quietly enough, and for a few minutes we flew some 5,000 feet below the enemy aircraft. Ray followed every move of the German leader and held us below the Huns, and I sweated it out and felt like a juicy worm being dangled before the sharp teeth of a very hungry pike. But soon the 190s made off and Ray didn't have the opportunity to demonstrate his tactics to me.

Once, I flew again with my old Kenley Wing. This was a mistake, for I flew in a subordinate position in the very outfit I had trained and led throughout the previous summer. I didn't go back again.

Most of the R.A.F. personalities I have mentioned in this narrative were known personally to me, and we served together somewhere or other during the war years. But now I am going to tell the story of a squadron commander and a young Australian pilot, neither of whom I ever met. The incident took place in the west of England, outside our own area, and we at Uxbridge had no part in the planning or conduct of the operation. I heard of the affair almost casually, as one does during a war. It is a story of great bravery and deliberate cold-blooded sacrifice. It so impressed me at the time that I jotted down the bare facts in my diary. Recently I have checked them from the few available records and the people who still remember.

Geoff Warnes joined 263 Squadron as a pilot officer in 1941. Just over a year later he became the squadron commander and won both the D.S.O. and the D.F.C. After a rest at 10 Group headquarters he returned to the squadron and supervised its re-equipment with Typhoons.

Warnes had poor eyesight, but the doctors had fixed him up with contact lenses, and one of his party pieces was to loosen these lenses and let them drop into a pint tankard of beer at his favourite pub. The locals knew the trick, but it astonished the casual visitor. Legend has it that he took a glass of stout with his early morning bath and smoked a cigar immediately afterwards. He was a gay, cheerful character. He was also a leader of men.

It was one of those dreary February days of the late winter. There was no blue sky, and no high cumulus clouds drifted across wide horizons. It was the sort of day pilots hate, when cloud and sea merge into a grey, yielding blanket and a flight over the sea meant a lot of instrument work for the leader. It was bitterly cold; below the clouds the sea looked bleak and choppy – so cold that a pilot would be dead in less than an hour unless he was rescued. So choppy that the little dinghy fighter pilots carried would soon be awash.

Warnes led nine Typhoons to Harrowbeer at first light. From Harrowbeer they took off for a fighter sweep over France, but low snow-clouds over the enemy coast made Warnes abandon the planned operation. Sooner than return empty handed they would keep low and have a look for enemy shipping to the west of the Channel Islands.

Disaster overtook the nine Typhoons when they were some ten miles west of Guernsey. They were still flying only a few feet above the sea in their wide, search formation, when the engine of the leading Typhoon cut and Warnes said:

"I'm going to ditch."

The eight pilots circled over their leader. One pilot climbed up a few hundred feet and gave a long Mayday transmission. Good fixes were obtained from the wireless receiving stations at Middle Wallop and Exeter.

A young Australian pilot, Flying Officer Tuft, who had been a member of the squadron for eight months, flew low over the ditched Typhoon and saw his squadron commander swimming towards what looked like a half-submerged dinghy. There was no flak. No enemy fighters. No sudden decision in the heat of battle. There was only the struggling man, who wore contact lenses, in the cold sea, the eight circling Typhoons, and Harrowbeer ninety miles away.

Tuff switched on his radio and said:

"I think the C.O.'s hurt and can't get to his dinghy. I'm going to bale out and help him!"

Someone said: "Don't be a bloody fool." Back in the ops. room the controller overheard some of the pilots' conversations and alerted the rescue organisation.

Tuff baled out. The visibility suddenly worsened, and although the Typhoons circled for another thirty minutes, neither pilot was ever seen again.

Early in the new year a well-known Canadian wing commander came to see me. This was Paul Davoud, who had a brilliant reputation as a clever tactician and a splendid night fighter pilot. Before the war he had been a bush pilot in Canada and he possessed a great fund of amusing stories about his flying experiences in the north-west territories.

Paul told me that the R.C.A.F. was about to send a further six fighter squadrons to England. They would be formed into two wings, one of Spitfires and one of Typhoons, and would be in 83 Group. Apart from the squadron commanders and flight commanders, the eighty or so Spitfire pilots would be raw and inexperienced, but Bill MacBrien might be persuaded to supply a few section leaders from my old 127 Wing. The squadrons would arrive from Canada during February and would get their Spitfire 9s soon afterwards.

Paul had been selected to command the new unit. He was looking for a wing leader for the Spitfire squadrons and already had suggested to the Canadian authorities in Lincoln's Inn Fields that I should be offered the appointment. The Canadians were agreeable, and the decision lay with me. If I accepted, we would see Air Vice-Marshal Saunders and arrange a date for me to leave 11 Group headquarters.

We were both interviewed by the group commander, and Paul put the case to him. The wise, kindly senior officer listened and said:

"When were you taken off ops., Johnnie?"

"Early last September, sir," I replied.

"Well, you can leave in early March after your six months' stint here. Your guess about the invasion date is as good as mine, but I should say you'll have enough time to lick the Canadians into shape."

So it was arranged that I should return to the comradeship and the carefree life of the fighter squadrons. Once more to take my place at the spearhead of a wing and know the thrills of leadership. I had enjoyed my previous six months with the Canadians and looked forward to flying with them again. During the previous years we had fought from static bases in England, but once 83 Group was established in France we should be constantly on the move across Europe. The coming tour should be exciting and full of incident.

I had sold the little Morris and bought a splendid Lagonda sports car from Ken Holden. During the winter months it had been thoroughly overhauled by the makers and was in perfect condition. I began to pack my belongings for the trip to Digby, where the new 144 Wing was forming. There was one man I wanted with me for the forthcoming trek across Europe, and I phoned the C.O. of 616 Squadron. I came straight to the point:

"Is Fred Varley still with the squadron, old boy?"

"Yes sir, he is," replied the squadron commander. "He often talks about the old days when he looked after you and Wing Commander Dundas, and wonders who cleans up the mess in your rooms these days!"

"I'm leaving here and taking another Canadian wing next week," I explained. "We shall be crossing the drink sometime, and I could use Varley again. Could you let me have him?"

"I'll call him to the phone," replied the squadron commander, "and you can have him if he wants to come."

Varley joined me at Uxbridge within a few days, and soon afterwards I said my good-byes to the group commander and staff officers. The three of us – Varley, the Labrador and I – wedged ourselves into the front seat of the Lagonda and set out for Digby and the Canadians.

Chapter Thirteen

BEFORE THE BIG SHOW

We spent the week-end with our families before driving to
Digby; Varley at Nottingham, where he lived, and I at Melton
Mowbray. Paula joined us from Norwich: during our few hours
together I told her that I had left the security of a staff appointment
and was about to begin another tour of ops. She had married a
fighter pilot and had always taken it for granted that I would want
to see the thing through. My father, who at the age of sixty paced
the streets of Melton Mowbray as a War Reserve police officer, was
quietly proud that I was returning to the fray.

On the following Monday we drove the few miles to Digby in
Lincolnshire, and leaving Varley to get on with the unpacking, I
went in search of Paul Davoud. I soon found him and we waited
together in his office until the three squadron commanders could be
found. I had not previously met any of these officers.

George Hill, a wiry, tousle-headed veteran of twenty-six, from
Pictou in Nova Scotia, commanded 441 Squadron. He was one of
the few recipients of the D.F.C. and two bars and he had shot down
his first Hun during the Dieppe raid. Later, in North Africa, George
led the famous 'treble one' (111) Squadron and piled up a score of
fourteen victories. He was a man of strong character who knew his
own mind and stated his opinions with forthright candour. He
would be a good man in a tight spot, and I couldn't have a better or
more experienced squadron commander.

The quiet, well-built 'Brad' Walker commanded 442 Squadron,
and also held the D.F.C. He had already completed one tour of
fighter operations from England and had led his squadron when it
was based in the Aleutians before coming to Digby.

The third squadron commander, Wally McLeod, was a tall, alert,
cool-eyed man of almost thirty from Regina in Saskatchewan. He
was credited with thirteen victories, most of which he scored over
Malta, where he was a contemporary of Buck McNair and

Screwball Beurling. He moved about the room with a restlessness which I came to know well during the following months. Wally had the reputation of being a deadly shot and very fast on the draw.

"A killer, if ever there was one," I thought. "I'm pleased he's with me and not on the other side. He might be inclined to stick his neck out too far, so I'll watch him."

We drove to the three squadron dispersals which lay about the perimeter of the airfield and I had the first opportunity of meeting the pilots who were to fly with me during the coming months. They had read and heard of the fighter exploits of their fellow-Canadians, and I was bombarded with questions:

"How long will it be before we are operational, sir?"

"Shall we move to Tangmere or somewhere down south before the invasion?"

"What's it really like in a dog-fight?"

This last question struck a chord in my memory, and I recalled my own desperate search for advice and encouragement when I first flew the Spitfire so many years ago. The young, eager Canadians clustered about me, anxious to know something of what lay ahead, and I took a long breath and plunged into a history of our tactics since we first took the offensive at the beginning of 1941.

The ever-increasing speeds of fighters and the coming introduction of faster, jet aircraft made it quite obvious that our large, unwieldy wing formations of up to thirty-six Spitfires would soon be a thing of the past, except for offensive operations which were planned well ahead. While we continued to operate from England, we would usually fly in wing strength, but these formations were getting more and more difficult to hold together in the air.

Once based in France, our mobile radar system would not give us a lot of warning of the approach of enemy formations: if the Luftwaffe kept at low-level, there would be no warning. Certainly, once on the Continent, the vital time factor would not permit the lengthy take-off and assembly procedures which we used today. When our ground troops found themselves in a tight spot they would want our support in the shortest possible time, and a flight, or at the most a squadron, would be our usual fighting strength. No doubt there would be occasional wing shows, but the experiences of the Desert Air Force clearly indicated that small, manoeuvrable formations would be the order of the day. The reign of the wing leader, which had lasted since early 1941, was drawing to a close and squadron and flight commanders were emerging as the key figures in our changing pattern of fighting. From now it would largely be a squadron commanders' war. This trend of smaller fighting units was to continue, and later in Korea, when Sabre-jet met Mig 15, it became a flight commanders' war.

Apart from the squadron and flight commanders, we were desperately short of experienced leaders. Our achievements in the air would be matched against those of the other Canadian wings who had flown together for a long time. We should undoubtedly suffer some casualties in our first few operations, and if we lost a section leader, there were no reserves in the wing. We made out a strong case for half a dozen experienced leaders from the other Canadian units, and these officers soon arrived. Amongst them was the young, smiling Flying Officer McLachlan, who was so small that we called him 'The Wee Mac'.

The Wee Mac had flown with me from Kenley, and I knew him as a good pilot and a steady, experienced leader. He loved aeroplanes and flying as other men love women. If someone wanted a parcel collected from the north of Scotland, or if there were mess bills to be paid on the other side of the country, it was The Wee Mac who climbed into his Spitfire to do these odd jobs. At Digby he often came into my office to ask if there were any flying jobs for him. It did not matter where he had to go, when he would return, or what type of aeroplane he had to fly. He simply wanted to get into the air.

Our ground equipment was brought to Digby by road convoys and our brand-new Spitfire 9s were flown in from the maintenance units. I flew six or seven from the grass airfield, and selected one which I thought handled well and had a sweet-sounding engine. Once again my initials and wing commander's pennant were painted on the engine cowling, and, as with her predecessor of a year ago, I never had occasion to regret the choice.

I had to remember that, apart from our air fighting rôle, we were now classified as a fighter-bomber wing: when the time came we would be required to strafe enemy troops and vehicles and carry out dive-bombing operations. In France our first and most important task would be to clear the skies of enemy aircraft and so let our ground forces get on with their job without being harassed by the Luftwaffe. Once air superiority was established, we should have to get on with the more mundane tasks of a fighter-bomber unit.

To assist us in our ground-strafing activities a system of 'contact cars' had been devised. These cars advanced with our own troops and reported the positions of any serious enemy opposition, such as tanks, armoured vehicles and heavy artillery. In a fluid situation they were also of the greatest value in keeping the various headquarters informed of the exact positions of our spearheads. The R.A.F. member of the contact car was usually a very experienced squadron leader, on a well-earned 'rest' from flying duties, who had a radio and told us, in pilot's language, of the position, type and size of enemy targets. These contact cars simplified our identification problems, especially as our ground troops would often mark an enemy target with coloured smoke.

Our dive-bombing missions would be to assist our bombers in their efforts to isolate the battle area. Operations carried out in support of a carefully planned isolation campaign would aim at the destruction of essential road and rail bridges, viaducts and centres of communication on the perimeter of the battle area so that the Germans could not easily move their ground forces and armour into any particular sector. Dive-bombing was an important part of our training, especially as the 'boffins' had recently discovered that fighter-bombers could knock out a bridge with far less weight of high explosive than the light or medium bombers.

For this dive-bombing our Spitfires were fitted with racks under each wing and the aeroplane was stressed to carry two 500-pound bombs. The theory of dive-bombing was to put your aeroplane into a steep dive, aim it at the target and release your bombs about the same time as you pulled out of the dive. Unfortunately, the bombs did not possess the same line of flight as our Spitfires and if you aimed directly at the target, then the bombs fell short. You also had to make the necessary allowance for the prevailing wind on any particular day. Our latest gyroscopic gunsights automatically computed the amount of deflection you should allow when attacking an enemy aircraft, but we had no such assistance to determine the distance or time you should allow before releasing your bombs. Some leaders counted 'one, two, three', and then released their bombs. Others counted to 'four', and some devised a system whereby the bombs were released when the target passed through a certain portion of the gunsight.

The first time I saw my lean Spitfire with two bombs hanging on its slender wings, I decided that I was never going to be crazy about this phase of our work. The Spitfire seemed to be intolerably burdened with her load, and the ugly, blunt bombs were a basic contradiction of all the beauty and symmetry of the aeroplane. Perhaps I was unduly sensitive after flying Spitfires for a long time. It was one thing to dive-bomb with a heavier type of fighter-bomber strapped to your back, which weighed almost seven tons and literally descended like a bomb, but it was quite another matter to force this relatively light, sensitive aircraft into a screaming dive against a ground target

"What do you think of it, Wally?" I said to McLeod as we stood together inspecting a bombed-up Spitfire.

"Not much, sir," replied the veteran from Malta. "If we'd got two decent long-range tanks to hang under the wings, instead of those things – pointing to the bombs – "we could go to Berlin with the Yanks and get stuck into some real fighting."

We made it our business to find out what the chances were of improving the radius of action of our Spitfires. Normally we carried a small jettisonable 'slipper' tank under the bellies of our aircraft; but we heard recently that the Americans had fitted two Spitfire 9s with under-wing tanks and had flown them across the Atlantic. We found out, from Vickers, that apart from the external tanks the Americans had fitted further internal tanks in the wings and, unfortunately, this modification reduced the strength of the wing below that necessary for combat purposes.

The days passed quickly at Digby, and I made every effort to get acquainted with the eighty Canadian pilots in the three squadrons. On some evenings when the work was over, we filled the Lagonda with Canadians, dined in some pleasant country inn and talked nothing but 'shop' as we sipped our pints of ale. These trips were invaluable, as the formalities of our daily round could easily and sensibly be put aside and we could get to know each other in a suitable atmosphere. At closing time we made our way back to the mess for a final drink in the bar before turning in. Sometimes the piano was man-handled into the bar and the singing was led by a young flying officer, Johnnie Marriott, who possessed an inexhaustible stock of British and Canadian songs, and also a fine voice in which to render them.

After two weeks of hard training at Digby we moved south to an airfield near Bournemouth, and took the opportunity to rehearse the operational procedure for the move of a tactical wing. First of all the advance party, which consisted of about half our ground crews and vehicles, left Digby and drove in small, well-camouflaged convoys to the new base. Immediately they arrived they set up a skeleton wing head-quarters, including flying control, and prepared to receive the Spitfires. Meanwhile we continued to fly from Digby and carried on with our training. Immediately we received word that the advance party was ready to operate the squadron, we flew to our new airfield and within a few minutes of landing were refuelled and ready for the air again. The rear party, back at Digby, rounded up all our equipment, loaded their three-tonners, set course for the south and within two days had joined up with their comrades of the advance party.

Soon we carried out our first operation together. We found a dozen enemy aeroplanes on an airfield near Paris and left at least half of them blazing wrecks. Within three weeks of receiving their Spitfires, the newcomers from Canada had flown like veterans and kept level heads under fire. The wing moved to Tangmere and we took our place in the daily air onslaught against Germany and Occupied Europe.

After a few trips it was apparent that the enemy fighters were more difficult to flush than ever.

Although we were an 83 Group wing, our operations were largely planned and controlled by 11 Group. This arrangement was to continue until 83 Group had established its radar and control organisation in France. So I made a special visit to the 11 Group headquarters, at Uxbridge, and had a close look at the estimated Luftwaffe dispositions within our own radius of action. A considerable number of Luftwaffe fighter squadrons were shown as still operating from various airfields, and our intelligence people were certain their estimates were accurate. Then I went to Jamie:

"We don't see much of the Huns these days, Jamie," I complained. "Yet the Spies swear that they still operate from France. Are we missing them because we fly too high?"

"Perhaps you're right," answered Jamie. "The Typhoon pilots, who operate lower than you, often get stuck in. But I think the real trouble is that the Hun is concentrating against the Forts and ignoring our short-range stuff."

"Let's try some low-level tactics, Jamie," I proposed.

"Yes, it might work," said the New Zealander. "We think that when we put the tactical bombers on the Hun airfields he tries to get all his aeroplanes off before the bombing starts. Perhaps they stay on the deck and make for Germany."

"The next time we escort the Marauders, I'll take a section down on the deck well ahead of the bombers. We'll sweep the Hun airfields at tree-top height and find out where the brutes get to. Will you fix it up on the next operation order?"

"All right," agreed Jamie. "I reckon you want to be about twenty minutes ahead of the bombers. You should just about catch them taking off. Watch the flak!"

Except for an occasional low-level exit from France, we had never operated on the deck in clear weather. The route must be carefully planned so that we avoided known concentrations of flak and the large, industrial towns. It would be too hazardous to fly directly over the enemy airfields, and I would have to try and position our Spitfires well to one side so that we could spot any aircraft taking off. I should be almost fully occupied with hugging the contours of the countryside and map reading. The remainder of the section would keep a good cross-cover and would search the sky for enemy aircraft.

This type of low-level operation was very different from the wretched *Rhubarbs* of previous years. We flew in good weather and we crossed the heavily defended coastal belt at a safe height. When we made our let-down from a clear sky we knew our exact position and which areas to avoid. We found that the further inland we penetrated the lighter became the flak, always provided we avoided towns and airfields. The increased radius of our Spitfires meant that we could get as far as the Rhine on this type of flight. We called them Ranger operations.

On our first Ranger I positioned my section of Spitfires well inland when the Marauders crossed the coast at Ostend. We went down to tree-top height in a fast dive and I found it a pleasant and thrilling experience to fly low over the neat pastures and villages of Belgium. Sometimes, peasants working on the land would look up at the sound of our engines and wave frantically when they saw our R.A.F. roundels or recognised the silhouettes of our Spitfires. To them, perhaps, our flight represented a sign of their long-awaited liberation.

We streaked over the peaceful countryside. Almost brushing the tops of the trees. Easing the stick forward to thunder down into the valleys. Climbing parallel to the slopes of the rising ground and swerving gently to avoid church steeples and high chimneys. Here and there we saw the stippled brown-and-green camouflage of Wehrmacht vehicles and staff cars as they were driven along the cobbled roads. We gave them no heed, for we were after bigger game and their turn would come later.

We approached a thickly populated area with Brussels on our right flank and the old university town of Louvain to our left. We could run into trouble here, for the two airfields near Brussels were well defended. We eased towards Louvain.

"Greycap from red two. One twin-engined aircraft at twelve o'clock. Same level."

The Dornier 217 was quite alone and our Spitfires were rapidly overhauling it. It was a piece of cake! McLeod drew level with my Spitfire, and I had a nasty suspicion that he was going to draw ahead and commit an unforgivable breach of flying discipline. But he remained alongside, and so I said:

"It's yours Wally. Let's see how you do it."

He closed for the kill while the rest of us hung back to watch the dual. It was all over in a flash. There was no tearing pursuit. No twisting and weaving as the bomber tried to escape. It was a classic example of fine shooting with a master of the craft in the Spitfire. Wally nailed his victim with the first burst, and the Dornier pulled up steeply so that we saw it in plan view, hung for a moment in the air, and then fell on its side and crashed with a sheet of flame near the back gardens of a row of cottages. We swept on our way, over the burning wreckage of the Dornier.

"Well done, Wally," I said. "Re-form. There may be more about."

We continued our search over Belgium and Holland. But we saw no more enemy aircraft on this day, so before we climbed back into the vault of the sky we loosed off a few rounds at several German staff cars and transports. It was good strafing practice and we left six or seven vehicles smouldering beside the roads.

Two days later we tried the same tactics and almost came to grief. The tactical bombers were operating in the Paris area and I led a section of Spitfires down to the deck to sweep the numerous airfields scattered round the circumference of the French capital. After twenty minutes at low level I was lost, although I knew we were a few miles south of Paris. I put away the map and concentrated on flying the various courses I had worked out before leaving base. About another five minutes on this leg and then a turn to the west to avoid getting too close to Paris. Our horizon was limited to about three miles over level country but was considerably reduced when we dipped into a valley.

We crossed a complicated mass of railway lines which indicated that we were close to Paris. We sped across a wide river and ahead of us was a heavily wooded slope, perhaps rising 200 feet from the river. We raced up this slope, only a few feet above the topmost branches, and found ourselves looking straight across a large grass airfield with several large hangars on the far side.

The gunners were ready and waiting. The shot and shell came from all angles, for some of the gun positions were on the hangar roofs and they fired down at us. I had never seen the like of this barrage. It would have been folly to turn back and make for the shelter of the wooded slope, for the turn would have exposed the vulnerable bellies of our Spitfires. Enemy aircraft were parked here and there, but our only thought was to get clear of this inferno. There was no time for radio orders. It was every man for himself, and each pilot knew that he would only get clear by staying at the very lowest height.

It seemed that our exits were sealed with a concentrated criss-cross pattern of fire from a hundred guns. My only hope of a getaway lay in a small gap between two hangars. I pointed the Spitfire at this gap, hurtled through it and caught a glimpse of the multiple barrels of a light flak gun swinging on to me from one of the parapets. Beyond lay a long, straight road with tall poplars on either side, and I belted the Spitfire down the road with the trees forming some sort of screen. Tracer was still bursting over the cockpit, but with luck I should soon be out of range and I held down the Spitfire so that she was only a few feet above the cobbled roadway. Half a dozen cyclists were making their way up the road towards the airfield. They flung themselves from their bicycles in all directions. If you're Frenchmen, I thought, I'm sorry, but I've had a bigger fright than you.

I pulled up above the light flak and called the other pilots. Miraculously, they had all come through the barrage, and when the last one answered I pulled the Spitfire into a climbing roll with the sheer joy of being alive.

We landed at Tangmere, and never has a cigarette tasted so delicious. Even the usual lukewarm, dark brown Naafi tea was welcome on this occasion. As we stood in front of our Spitfires, talking about our various experiences of but half an hour ago, a few staff cars, full of V.I.P.s, swung along the perimeter track and stopped alongside us. Eisenhower got out of the first car, followed by Leigh-Mallory, now chief of the recently formed Allied Expeditionary Air Force. They were accompanied by our new group commander, Harry Broadhurst, who had gained great distinction as a fighter pilot during the early years of the war. 83 Group was not his first big command, for he had recently led the highly successful Desert Air Force. Broadhurst saw from our dress that we had just returned from a show. He said to the general:

"Come and talk to these chaps, sir, they've just landed."

Eisenhower was immediately interested and said to me:

"Did you have any luck over there?"

I thought quickly, for we had not fired a shot, and what words could describe our desperate encounter with the flak?

"No, sir," I answered. "Our trip was uneventful."

About a month before the invasion I had a strange experience. We had bounced a small gaggle of Focke-Wulfs. I tried to follow their leader when he half-rolled, but I lost him in a vertical dive. I pulled out at ground-level and for a few seconds turned steeply to make sure there was no Hun on my tail. Then I straightened out of the turn and began to build up speed before climbing to re-form the Canadians. Suddenly my eyes were attracted by a dark shadow which tore across the sunlit fields at high speed. As it sped over walls, roads and small copses it lost its shape momentarily, only to regain it over the flat fields. It took perhaps two seconds to realise that it was the shadow of another aircraft flying on a parallel course. Somewhere up-sun was the substance of the shadow. I wrenched my Spitfire into a near-vertical climb and then swung into the low, early-morning sun. Below me was a Focke-Wulf with its tell-tale shadow some four hundred yards away.

I eased below the 190. Every few seconds the enemy pilot weaved slightly to cover his blind spot. I hung behind, taking full advantage of the contours of the gently rolling country below. I would wait until he relaxed. Then I would clobber him. Gradually his weaving motions became fewer and he flew very low up the wide valley of a river. I had to fly slightly higher than the 190 because there was no room below him. I narrowed the gap between us. Some instinct made me focus my eyes ahead of the Focke-Wulf. Two hundred yards ahead some high-tension cables stretched across the valley. At our present heights the Hun would slip under the cables and I would hit them. I brought the Spitfire down until I was only a few feet above the river. The slipstream from the Focke-Wulf hit me squarely and I fought hard for control – sandwiched between the surface of the water and the sagging cables. Once on the other side the cunning German pilot pulled his 190 into an easy climbing turn so that he could watch the fun. This manoeuvre cost him dear, for I cut across the wide arc of his turn and hammered cannon shells into his engine and cockpit. Large pieces flew off the doomed aeroplane. The pilot jettisoned his cockpit canopy, but I hit him again and again. The 190 struck the ground wing first. Then it cartwheeled several times before coming to rest in a blazing wreck.

Unfortunately, we lost George Hill during this fight. He shared in the destruction of a Focke-Wulf and then crash-landed when his engine cut. George was seen to climb out of his Spitfire and run for cover. I did not see him again until long after the war, when we met in Canada. He avoided capture for a month, but then he was picked up by the Germans. Because they thought he might know something of our invasion plans, George was subjected to some very brutal treatment by the Gestapo.

We decided that the right man to replace George Hill was an American named Danny Browne. During the previous year he had often flown as my wingman and he soon became a resolute section leader. Dark and good looking, he was a splendid companion and proved himself to be an outstanding squadron commander. He was fond of discoursing about the value of the Yankee dollar, but when the opportunity arose to transfer to the U.S. Army Air Force, at a substantial increase in pay, he elected to remain with us.

We had another vacancy for a squadron commander since Walker's tour was over and he was returning to Canada. I was searching for a suitable replacement when Wing Commander Dal Russel, from Montreal, came to see me. Dal had come to England in the early days of the fighting and as a mere boy had won his first D.F.C. in the Battle of Britain. During the summer of 1943 he had led a Spitfire wing and we had often flown together. I held him in the greatest respect. Blond, handsome and always debonair, he had all the attributes of the popular conception of a fighter pilot and was a great favourite with the ladies. For the past few months he had been a staff officer at 83 Group headquarters. Now he came straight to the point:

"I hear there's a squadron going, Johnnie. What about it?"

"But, Dal, you're a wing commander," I replied. "You've led your own wing. Wait a bit longer and you'll get another. Why drop rank now?"

"I don't mind that," he answered. "All the wing leaders' jobs are filled and I'd like to fly with you. I want to get on ops. before the big show. It can't be far away."

"What does Harry Broadhurst say?" I asked.

"I've tackled him and he's quite agreeable," replied Dal.

"All right, Dal. When can you start?"

"I'll collect my gear from group and take over the squadron tomorrow."

So Dal Russel joined our company. I was very pleased, and not a little flattered, at this development. He was a very popular man with the Canadians and a good leader, and would be invaluable during our coming march across Europe. I knew that I was lucky to have three squadron commanders of the calibre of Russel, Browne and McLeod.

Some few days later I took two squadrons, McLeod's and Browne's, to sweep the Lille area before an attack by Marauder bombers. After we had patrolled the target area for some minutes I spotted a solitary 190 some several thousand feet below my formation and flying on the same course as ourselves. It was an ideal target for one of my inexperienced boys and I decided that the first pilot to report it would have the pleasure of shooting it down. We flew steadily on for at least a minute and I began to get a little irritated at this lamentable lack of watch-keeping by twenty-three pairs of eyes. There was always the risk, too, that the enemy pilot would spot our formation, half-roll and be lost to us. I decided to give the chaps another thirty seconds in which to spot the Hun. Still there was no report from the twenty-three keen pilots. I lost height gently until I was only just above the enemy aircraft and considered that I was fully justified in having a crack at it myself.

"Greycap wing. For the past two minutes there's been a solitary 190 below us. I am going down for a squirt with my section. The rest of you stay up here."

This instruction was received, as I expected, in a stony silence.

As I closed to firing range the enemy pilot must have seen one of us, for he immediately jettisoned his canopy and began to climb over the side of his aircraft. When I opened fire, he dropped away and pulled the rip-cord of his parachute. The 190 plunged into a ploughed field. Flying low overhead, I saw the enemy pilot release his parachute and stagger to his feet, apparently none the worse for his abrupt descent.

I climbed back to height, the wing dropped into their appointed positions and without any chatter we pressed on. I could only hope that the eternal lesson of the necessity for keeping a sharp look-out had been driven home.

Between Mons and Douai I spotted two sections of five or six Focke-Wulfs flying very low, but they soon disappeared into the ground haze of this May morning. I sent down two sections of four Spitfires, one led by Wally McLeod and the other by The Wee Mac, to try and find the 190s. Soon afterwards we heard The Wee Mac's section chattering amongst themselves as they carried out a head-on attack on six 190s, but there was no word from McLeod.

We had been airborne for a long time, and after a few more minutes I gave the recall order. I instructed the Spitfires to withdraw immediately, as we had a long flight back to base and also had to contend with a stiff headwind. Some twelve or fifteen minutes later I was crossing the French coast when I heard quite distinctly, but very faintly, over the radio:

"Take that, you bastard!"

Although the voice was faint, the intonation was quite definitely Canadian, and I was quite sure that it was Wally's voice. I called him on the radio, but there was no response, and eventually after a flight of well over two hours I landed sixteen aircraft at Tangmere. We were followed by three aircraft of The Wee Mac's section and three aircraft of McLeod's section.

First of all I concentrated on the three pilots of The Wee Mac's section, since he had not returned. He had led the four Spitfires down into the haze and after some searching at low level they had seen dimly, at a range of about one mile, six 190s. The little flying officer had stalked the six enemy aircraft, but their cross-cover was excellent. They suddenly broke round into the Spitfires and carried out a head-on attack. The Spitfires held their course and the two formations closed very rapidly. After the first attack a general free for all dog-fight ensued in which two 190s were shot down, but The Wee Mac could not participate in this as his Spitfire had been seen by his comrades to go down in flames after the head-on attack. So died a very courageous little officer.[1]

Saddened by this news, I then listened to an account of the exploit of the three members of McLeod's section. They, too had intercepted a small formation of 190s, but the enemy aircraft had escaped into the murk after they had seen the Spitfires jockeying for a favourable position. The three aircraft had then re-formed, but were unable to locate their leader, so when they heard my recall instructions, they set course for Tangmere. Yes, they had also heard the muttered oath over the radio and they were sure that it was the voice of their squadron commander.

I was certain that McLeod had singled out an opponent and chased him towards the frontiers of Germany itself. By this time I knew sufficient of the character of the man to know that, once he had his teeth into a Hun, he would never let go until one or the other had been vanquished. Many a good fighter pilot had been lost under similar circumstances, and I was most anxious not to lose an experienced squadron commander on the very eve of the invasion. I walked into the dispersal hut and called the controller. Had they any news of the whereabouts of Squadron Leader McLeod? Yes, indeed they had! He had just landed at an airfield in the south-east of England and had shot down a 190. Blast the 190, I thought, he'll have plenty of those to shoot at before very long. I asked for the exact time of McLeod's landing, and when I received this information I calculated that he had been airborne for almost three hours, and this was stretching a Spitfire 9s endurance to a very fine point.

He grinned sheepishly as he clambered out of his cockpit at Tangmere. I got it off my chest as soon as possible, and later that day I had all the wing pilots in the briefing room and discoursed on the importance of cross-cover and a good look-out at all times, on the necessity of keeping together and the strict requirement for

[1] The Wee Mac has no known grave, but his death is commemorated on the R.A.F. Memorial at Runnymede.

obeying instructions. I said that the days of the lone wolf went out with the First World War, and, as far as I was concerned, they had never formed any part of our doctrine in this war over Britain and Occupied Europe. Screwball Beurling had demonstrated over Malta that an aggressive, single-handed fighter pilot could knock down a reasonable bag of enemy aircraft, given the opportunities and a fair share of luck. No pilot, though, however skilful, could consistently shoot down aircraft and guard his own tail at the same time. I went to some lengths to emphasise that I was not decrying Beurling's exploits but simply stating that I could not countenance single-handed exploits in my own outfit. We fought as a team, and if the circumstances broke up the team and its members found themselves alone, then, to use a descriptive Canadian phrase, "we got the hell out of it".

During these few weeks before the invasion we flew hard on a wide variety of operations. We hung bombs on our Spitfires and began a typical day's work with dive-bombing attacks against bridges and viaducts. After lunch we slung long-range tanks under the bellies of our fighters and roamed across France hunting for trains, transports and armoured vehicles. Perhaps our daily effort would end with dive-bombing or strafing attacks against radar stations on the enemy coast. For every operation we carried out in Normandy, we struck at least twice in other areas so as not to give the game away. At the time all these tasks seemed unrelated, but they were part of a well-conceived master plan which aimed at denying transport and radar facilities to the Germans. Sometimes we were switched from these pre-invasion tasks to dive-bombing attacks against V1 launching-sites in the Pas de Calais. These were difficult targets to hit, because they were well camouflaged and heavily defended by flak. My Canadians came through all these operations without loss, but on one occasion we had to pull songster Johnnie Marriott out of the drink.

When we made our run-up to the launching-site we were bracketed by many bursts of heavy flak. On a fighter sweep I would have climbed the squadron a few thousand feet, changed direction once or twice and so confused the enemy predictors on the ground below. But this time I had to make a steady approach to the target at a constant height, wait until the launching-site appeared under my port wing, then half-roll, ease out into a steep dive and release our bombs from about 4,000 feet when we pulled out of the dive.

Near the target the flak increased, and so did my respect for the bomber boys who had to put up with this sort of thing on all their missions. At last the target passed under the wing of my Spitfire. When it appeared again I half-rolled. We plunged down and the light flak came into its own. I released the bombs, braced myself to take the 'g' and zoomed up. The flak followed suit. I was not surprised when Marriott piped up:

"Greycap from red two. I've been hit! Temperature's going up."

We were almost over the French coast. Marriott had little chance of escaping if he baled out over this thickly defended area. I decided to get him as far across the Channel as possible.

"O.K., Johnnie," I replied. "Stay with her as long as you can. I'll get the Walrus to meet us. Red three, transmit for Mayday."

I circled round Marriott's Spitfire as it gradually lost height. He was flying very slowly with low revolutions to keep down the critical oil and coolant temperatures. Every few seconds a puff of white smoke belched from his exhaust stacks.

"How's it going, Johnnie?" I asked him.

"O.K., sir. Temperature's off the gauges. But she's still ticking over."

The Spitfire was down to about 2,000 feet. Marriott would want this height to bale out and there was always the danger that the aeroplane would start to burn.

"Step out, Johnnie," I ordered. "We'll pick you up in no time.

"O.K., sir," he cheerfully replied.

We saw his parachute spill out. Then he clambered into his dinghy and waved when I passed a few feet above him. I left a section of Spitfires to circle his dinghy, but these were soon relieved. After landing, the controller told me that Marriott was already in the Walrus and heading for a coastal airfield. It was a perfect rescue operation.

Later that day, Johnnie Marriott returned, none the worse for his ducking. He was a likeable lad, and, as I have already said,

217

possessed a good voice. We celebrated his return with a party, and he burst into song after his first pint. He was still singing when the party broke up, and was attempting another ditty when he was not ungently eased into bed.

Towards the end of May we moved again, and this time we found ourselves at Ford on the Sussex coast. Paul Davoud's command, which consisted of a Spitfire wing and a Typhoon wing, was altered so that he would not control two wings with different aircraft and varying tasks. So we left Paul, and Bill MacBrien once again became our group captain.

Recently vast convoys of trucks, armoured vehicles and tanks had poured into the Portsmouth and Southampton areas and now overflowed into the surrounding countryside. Our piece of Sussex became an armed camp and the Ford airfield held three wings of Spitfires and some night fighter squadrons. Beer was very scarce, since most members of this great enterprise seemed partial to a few pints. The pubs closed early, but landlord Arthur King always found something for our thirsts.

We airmen were possessed of a great confidence which seemed to increase with the approach of D-Day. One memorable evening the senior officers of the Second Tactical Air Force dined by candlelight in the Tangmere mess. General Eisenhower was the guest of honour and the portraits of an earlier generation of fighter pilots smiled down upon our company. I thought of the long road we had journeyed since my first days in this very mess with the South Yorkshire Squadron. I thought of Douglas Bader, long since a prisoner of war but whose shining example was always before us.

Early one morning Fred Varley, Sally the Labrador, the twelve bore, the wild-fowling piece and my caravan left and were swallowed up in the assembly area. Left to fend for myself, I desperately missed Varley's cheerful personality and his frequent brews of strong tea.

On 5th June the group captains and wing leaders were briefed by Harry Broadhurst on the next day's invasion. He spoke of our many tasks in great detail, and made no bones of what he expected from us. It was late evening when I drove back to Ford, where the

Canadians were waiting to hear from me. Our particular task was simple, to protect the eastern flank of the assault from enemy air attack.

When I walked back to my quarters, my own personal reaction was one of some relief. We should soon be based in France and not faced with the two-way Channel crossing we had made day after day during the previous three years. We had lost a great number of pilots in the drink. A great armada of heavy aeroplanes roared over head. Sometimes, through breaks in the low cloud, I saw the Lancasters pounding their way through the night to herald the invasion of France.

Chapter Fourteen

NORMANDY

We were called well before dawn, and, driving across the darkened airfield to the Ford mess for an early breakfast, we heard the roar of powerful engines as the first formations of day fighters made their way to Normandy to relieve the night patrols. After a hurried meal we strapped ourselves into the cockpits of our Spitfires. I took the three squadrons across the Channel, over a choppy grey sea, to patrol the line of beaches being assaulted by British and Canadian troops. Throughout the previous night Lancasters of Bomber Command, followed by American heavies, had dropped vast quantities of high-explosive on the enemy's coastal defences. Airborne troops had parachuted into the area to prepare landing-zones for glider reinforcements and to secure the flanks of the bridgehead by assaulting enemy strongpoints from the rear. Already the Normandy coast-line from the Orne river to Carantan at the base of the Cherbourg peninsula was ablaze as the spearheads of our invading forces fought to secure a foothold. I thought of these things as we sped across the Channel. Surely, by this time, the German High Command would have diagnosed the Allied intention to invade Normandy. Even at this moment, fighter squadrons of the Luftwaffe might be in the air on the flight from Germany to reinforce their depleted forces in France. The Luftwaffe possessed plenty of airfields within striking distance of the assault area. They had always been a flexible organisation and capable of rapid reinforcement. Perhaps the scale of fighting would be similar to the stirring air battles fought over Dieppe. Tense and eager in our cockpits, anticipating bitter opposition, we made an accurate landfall on the Normandy coast.

From the pilot's viewpoint, flying conditions were quite reasonable – better than we expected after the gloomy forecasts of the previous two or three days. The cloud base was at about 2,000 feet and the visibility between five and six miles. Calling the wing leader of the formation we were about to relieve, I told him that we were already on our appointed patrol line. Had he seen anything of enemy fighters? "Not a bloody thing," he replied, "although the flak is pretty hot if you fly a few hundred yards inland."

Amongst the mass of shipping below us was a fighter direction ship. I called the R.A.F. controller on my radio and asked if he had any plots of enemy formations on his table. The controller came back with the guarded reply that, for the moment, he had no positive information for me.

We swept parallel to the coast beneath a leaden grey sky, and I positioned the wing two or three hundred yards offshore so that we should not present easy targets to the enemy gunners. Our patrol line ended over the fishing village of Port-en-Bessin, while farther to the west, beyond our area of responsibility, lay the two American assault beaches *Omaha* and *Utah*. When we carried out a wide, easy turn to retrace our flight path, a wing of American Thunderbolts harried our progress and for a few uneasy moments we circled warily round each other. Formations of different types of Allied aircraft had attacked each other during the preceding months, but in this instance recognition was soon effected and we continued our flight to the south of the Orne. For the present there was little doubt that we were the undisputed masters of this little portion of the Normandy sky, so for the first time that morning I was able to turn some of my attention to the scene below.

Off-shore, the sea was littered with ships of all sizes and descriptions, and small landing-craft ploughed their way through the breakers to discharge their contents at the water's edge. We could see a fair number of capsized vessels, and afterwards learnt that the various obstacles erected by the Germans below the high-water mark were considerably more formidable than had been expected. Not content with the erection of these steel obstacles, the Germans had attached underwater mines to them and so added to the hazards of our landing-craft. Further out in the bay, cruisers and destroyers manoeuvred to lie broadside on to the assault beaches: we could see the flashes from their guns as they engaged the enemy defences well inland. As I watched the naval bombardment I realised that we flew constantly in an air space between the naval gunners and their targets. No doubt the shells were well above our height of 2,000 feet, but I made quite certain that we did not exceed this altitude.

Swimming tanks, a recent innovation, were launched from their parent ships well out to sea. From the air, it seemed as if these amphibious tanks had a fairly long and rough sea journey before they reached the beaches. During the last lap of their journey the tanks opened fire against adjacent enemy positions, and this must have come as a considerable surprise to the defenders. Here and there the enemy appeared to be putting up a stiff resistance: we saw frequent bursts of mortar and machine-gun fire directed against our troops and equipment on the beaches. Small parties of men could be seen making their way to the beach huts and houses on the sea front, many of which were on fire. But the greatest danger to us pilots lay in the mass of Allied aircraft which roamed restlessly to and fro over the assault areas. Medium bombers, light bombers, fighter-bombers, fighters, reconnaissance, artillery and naval aircraft swamped the limited air space below the cloud, and on two occasions we had to swerve violently to avoid head-on collisions. Towards the end of our allotted patrol the controller asked me to investigate bogey aircraft flying down the Orne from Caen, but these turned out to be a formation of Typhoons, so we resumed our cruise above the beaches.

Four times that day we made our way across the Channel, and never a sign of the Luftwaffe! We arrived back at Ford from our last patrol as dusk was falling and had to wait for a few minutes for the night fighters to take off and maintain the vigil over the beach-head. Tired and drained, I drove to the mess for the evening meal. All my pilots were there. All had flown on this day and some had participated in all the missions. They were very quiet: it was apparent that they were bitterly disappointed with the Luftwaffe's failure to put in an appearance on this day, which was one of the most momentous in our long history of war. We had geared ourselves for a day of intense air fighting, and the actual result had been something of an anti-climax. I could not let them go to bed in this mood of apathy and frustration, and I gathered them together for a short 'pep' talk. Although we had not succeeded in bringing the enemy to combat, I said, it was still a brilliant triumph for the Allied Air Forces as it marked our complete dominance over the Luftwaffe – an ideal we had striven to attain for more than three years. I glanced at my audience. Lounging in chairs, propped up against the walls, rather dirty and many of them unshaven, they received this somewhat pompous statement with the cool indifference it merited. I tried another approach.

"We know that the Luftwaffe squadrons in this area are not very strong. In fact, the latest order of battle estimates that they have only about 200 fighters and less than 100 fighter-bombers. But they still possess many crack squadrons of fighters based in Germany. You can bet your last dollar that some of these outfits will move into Normandy immediately, if they haven't already done so. You'll have all the fighting you want within the next few weeks, and perhaps more! Don't forget that we shall soon have our own airfield in Normandy and then we shall really get at them. And now we'll force a beer down before we turn in."

We repaired to the bar, where we partook of no more nor less than one pint each, and on this note called it a day.

The Luftwaffe staged a few isolated appearances on the following day, but we were completely out of luck. We flew to a very rigid, pre-planned time-table, and the pilots who knocked down the enemy aircraft merely happened to be in position when the enemy launched his attacks. On a normal free-lance fighter sweep, I could use my own judgment to route our flight where we should be most likely to intercept enemy formations. But on our beach-head flights we had very strict instructions not to leave the patrol area, since a feint attack by the Luftwaffe might otherwise draw off the Spitfire wings, leaving the mass of shipping relatively unprotected.

Our first patrol was quite uneventful, and after some forty minutes of stooging up and down we were relieved by George Keefer's wing. George called me in his usual brisk, business-like manner to say that his boys were in position, and as we withdrew across the Channel we left our radios on the same frequency so that we could listen to their chatter. We had barely turned towards Sussex when we heard George giving orders for his pilots to attack a dozen juicy Junkers 88s which had popped up out of the clouds and were heading towards the shipping. We had to endure their jubilant cries as the blazing bombers fell to the sea below. It was the same sad story on our afternoon patrol. Once more George had assumed responsibility for the protection of this part of the Normandy coast, and again we had only just left the area when he hurtled his Spitfires into a formation of Focke-Wulf fighter-bombers. All this was very distressing and we felt that we were not having our fair share of the pickings. But there was nothing I could do to improve our chances.

On the last flight of this day, the controller asked me to send a section of Spitfires a few miles inland to ascertain whether or not the enemy was bringing up substantial ground reinforcements. Leaving Wally MacLeod to lead the remainder of the wing, I took four Spitfires on the reconnaissance mission. Low cloud, which here and there rolled down almost to the tree-tops, prevented accurate observation, and after a few minutes I decided to rejoin the wing. We were only a mile or two from the coast when I saw some activity in a cornfield below. Six or eight British tanks were manoeuvring for an attack against a similar number of Tiger tanks which crouched, squat and sinister on the edge of a small orchard. The British were moving quite slowly: from the air, it seemed as if they halted to fire and then pressed on against the enemy positions. The Germans, on the other hand, fired rapidly from their static positions and their superior 88-mm. guns scored some hits on the British armour. One of our tanks was already ablaze. Fascinated, we watched the drama below, and I was immediately struck by the great contrast between the speed and pattern of our intricate air battles and this cumbersome, unwieldy but equally deadly affair on the ground. The British continued to receive the worst of the exchange, and although our cannons would have little effect against the tough armour of the Tigers, I manoeuvred my formation for a flank attack against the enemy targets. Our support was unnecessary, however, since four Typhoons appeared on the scene and without further ado proceeded to launch a rocket attack against the Tigers. The enemy tanks were soon hidden from our view by the debris thrown into the air from the impact of the rockets.

During the early morning of 8th June, before we had begun the day's work, I was called to the telephone and heard the familiar voice of the commander of 11 Group. He had just received word that the first airfield in Normandy was completed – would I send over a couple of good pilots as soon as possible to see if the strip was fully operational and whether the ground crews were organised to cope with rapid refuelling and rearming? I sent Dal Russel and his wingman, who were soon back with the splendid news that all was well. I passed this information to the group commander, who then asked me to take the Canadians on a fighter sweep well to the south of the beach-head. We were to land and refuel at St Croix-sur-Mer, the new airfield, and carry out a further patrol before returning to Ford.

I was very anxious to sweep as far south as the Loire river, since we knew that the Luftwaffe possessed some airfields in this locality and I felt quite certain that they had reinforced the sector. But once more the weather was against us and low cloud prevented the execution of our planned route. When our fuel ran low we swept across St Croix at 1,000 feet to have a good look at the general layout before landing. We had to make a fairly tight circuit to avoid the barrage balloons hoisted over vulnerable concentrations on the beaches. It was a most curious sensation, preparing to land on territory from which we had been accustomed to receive all types of shot and shell during the previous four years. R.A.F. servicing commandos guided our Spitfires to their various dispersals and were busy refuelling the aircraft before we had left our cockpits. In less than twenty minutes they were ready for the air again.

Meanwhile, we gathered together and lit the inevitable cigarettes. Keith Hodson, who was in charge of the airfield, drove alongside in his jeep and advised us not to stray far from the strip.

One or two enemy snipers were still at large and they could make life unpleasant. There were several minefields scattered about the locality and a country stroll could end in disaster. Only that morning an airman had walked into an abandoned enemy strongpoint and had found some discarded German uniforms. To impress his colleagues, he donned one of these garments and shouted to them as he stepped out of the pillbox. His gestures were unfortunately misinterpreted and he was shot stone dead.

We walked into a nearby orchard, where a control organisation had already been established. Soon we were greeted by a deputation from the nearby village of St Croix. The local countryfolk had seen our Spitfires land, and since it was something of an occasion they brought with them gifts of fruit, flowers and wine. A few German dead still lay where they had fallen in this pleasant glade; their waxen faces looked strangely peaceful. Occasionally, enemy shells thumped into the adjacent fields, but the peasants paid little heed and stolidly continued to till their ground. I noticed several strong coveys of partridge scuttling about and was thankful for the foresight which had induced me to pack a twelve bore in the caravan. No doubt a few plump partridges would make a welcome change from compo rations, come September. And so the Royal Air Force came back to France for the first time since our abrupt departure in 1940, almost four years to the day.

After a leisurely snack I walked to the edge of the orchard, which was flanked by a narrow secondary road. Here a continuous nose-to-tail procession of trucks, tanks, armoured vehicles and the like made a slow progress to the front lines after disgorging from the various ships on the coast, little more than one mile from the airfield. For some time I watched this unending stream of vehicles, and the incalculable value of our complete air superiority was clearly demonstrated to me. Had a similar scene been enacted in the enemy's territory, then the column would have been gutted immediately by our fighter-bombers which ranged to and fro over Normandy seeking such a target. In fact, we could always tell which side of the lines we were on by noting the remarkable contrast in the activity and spacing of road traffic.

We took to the air again after lunch, and although our patrol was again uneventful we felt reasonably satisfied with the day's work. We had landed and refuelled in France, which made an important milestone in our progress. Even if the assault on the Normandy coast had failed to flush the Luftwaffe, perhaps the ensuing battle for France, which was yet to come, would produce some reaction.

Soon we took off from Ford for the last time. Our ground crews and equipment had arrived safely in Normandy, had established themselves at St Croix and were ready to operate the wing. We stuffed our meagre belongings, consisting of a spare shirt, a change of underclothes and shaving-tackle, into various odd corners of our Spitfires, thanked the ground crews who had serviced our Spitfires at Ford, and thirty minutes later were on the strip at St Croix. I was very pleased to join forces once more with Varley and my Labrador, Sally, who had also arrived on the scene. Varley had sited my caravan alongside the clutch of operations vehicles in the orchard, and he greeted me with a cup of his special brew of tea.

I did not fly again on this day, but spent my time on the ground checking the small group of vehicles which formed the nerve-centre of the wing. The two army liaison officers were hard at work marking up the various friendly and enemy ground positions on the large-scale maps which hung on the sides of our briefing tent. Our Spies were busy with the many reports and summaries of enemy activity, and I was delighted to hear that the expected Luftwaffe reinforcements had arrived and were now based on various airfields to the south and south-east. Intelligence estimated that more than 300 enemy fighters had been flown in to oppose us, and *Jagdkorps 2* could muster about 1,000 aircraft of all types. I gave instructions for the various Luftwaffe dispositions to be carefully plotted on an appropriate map, for we would pay them a social call at the very first opportunity. The signals personnel had established good communications with 83 Group, which would control our activities in the air. It was apparent to me that the many tactical moves we had rehearsed continually in England had paid a handsome dividend. The machinery of the control organisation was working smoothly and efficiently. We were the very first wing to be based in Normandy: as such we possessed a far greater radius of action over France than those Spitfires still operating from southern England. We should be able to strike deep into enemy territory, and if the enemy squadrons did not take to the air we should seek them out in their lairs and write them off on the ground. Highly satisfied, I jumped into my jeep to inspect the airfield. After making certain that the three squadrons were well prepared for a spell of intensive flying, I returned to my caravan, where Varley and I unpacked my personal belongings.

Varley had already spent two or three nights in Normandy and repeatedly told me that the customary evening barrage was quite unpleasant. According to him, a few enemy reconnaissance and bomber aircraft put in an appearance immediately it was dark and every gun on the beach-head opened up at the intruders. Varley suggested that perhaps the safest place for my bed would be in a narrow slit trench, but I am afraid that I paid little heed to his advice and was determined to sleep in the caravan – a decision I was to regret before many hours had elapsed.

I turned in quite early, as it had been a strenuous day and I wanted the benefit of a good sleep for the activities of the morrow. I was rudely awakened by the loud staccato chatter of a Bofors gun situated some twenty yards from my caravan. Faintly, I could hear the typical unsynchronized drone of a few enemy aircraft, and so great was the clamour of our barrage that sleep was quite impossible. I might as well get dressed and see what it was all about. To the south-east the sky was bright from some large fires, but the enemy pilots were directing their attentions against the mass of shipping lying off-shore. The naval gunners opened up with everything they possessed, and orange tracer ripped across the sky in fantastic criss-cross patterns. Pieces of hot shrapnel fell upon my caravan, and the thousands of anti-aircraft guns concentrated in the relatively small area made the general din almost unbearable. Searchlights swept the sky but were hampered by the low cloud base, and occasionally the earth reverberated to the impact of bombs. Deciding that the tin roof of my caravan offered little protection against this sort of thing, I went in search of Varley, so that together we could move my bed to a more secure position; but the wise fellow had long since gone to earth, and the Labrador with him.

I dragged my sleeping-bag from the bed and struggled into it underneath the rear axle of the caravan. This would at least afford me some protection from the shrapnel. But sleep was quite out of the question, as the Luftwaffe sent over sporadic raids until the small hours and, to my regret, our gunners did not appear to suffer from any lack of ammunition! The dawn found me cold and miserable – I crept out of my damp sleeping-bag and walked across the soaking grass to the mess tent for a hot drink. I wondered how my three squadron commanders, Browne, Russel and McLeod, had fared during the firework display, and went in search of them. I had some difficulty in tracking them down, but eventually I found them, warm and snug, in a stoutly constructed underground dug-out which had been built in the orchard by the Germans. I watched them for a few seconds as they lay in a deep slumber and resolved that the coming night would find me alongside.

Twelve of us were sitting at readiness in the cockpits of our Spitfires prepared for a quick scramble. I had decided to fly with Wally McLeod's squadron and he was leading the other flight of six aircraft. Should the enemy show any activity in the air, his movements would be picked up by 83 Group's radar and plotted on the operations table at the group control centre. 'Kenway', the code name for the centre, would then telephone through to our operations caravan and order the readiness squadron into the air. The signal to take off would be a Very light fired from the operations caravan. Once we were airborne we should receive our instructions over the radio direct from Kenway. After half an hour in the cockpit, gloved and masked ready for an immediate take-off, I was rather drowsy as a result of my lack of sleep, but my cramped uncomfortable position sufficed to keep me awake. Suddenly a red Very light soared into the air from the orchard. Switches on, my fingers pressed the starting button and the Merlin roared into life. Then I was travelling down the narrow taxi-track and made the right-angled turn on to the steel-planked runway at too high a speed, for the starboard wing tilted down at a dangerous angle. A few seconds later and the twelve of us were airborne in a ragged, straggling gaggle, but the boys were already picking up their battle formation.

"Greycap to Kenway. Airborne with twelve Spits. What's the form?"

"Kenway to Greycap. Bandits active five miles south of Caen at low level. Please investigate."

"Greycap to Kenway. Roger. Any definite height on bandits?"

"Kenway to Greycap. No, but they're below 5,000 feet. Out."

There was scattered cloud between five and six thousand feet, and above, the sun blazed from a clear sky. If Kenway's information was correct, they were probably a raiding party of fighter-bombers. I eased the Spitfires through a gap and flew immediately below the cloud base.

"Stay down-sun, Wally, and keep as near to the cloud base as you can. I'll drop down a few hundred feet."

"Greycap from blue three. Bandits at nine o'clock, 2,000 feet below."

"Roger, blue three, I have them. They're heading towards us. Turning port."

The bandits were a mixed gaggle of Focke-Wulfs and Messerschmitts. About a dozen all told. Now they were immediately below me, heading towards Caen. They were not higher than 2,000 feet, and the sun was behind us. We had all the makings of a perfect bounce.

"I'm going in, Wally!" I exclaimed. "Cover my section. Take any of the bastards who climb above me."

My section was streaking down but still well out of range when the Huns saw us, probably because we were conspicuous against the background of white cumulus cloud. They broke round into our attack in an experienced manner and I realised they were led by a veteran.

"Get in, Wally. These brutes are staying to fight."

Now twenty-four fighter aircraft twisted and jockeyed for an advantageous position. My number two called up:

"Greycap! Keep turning. There's a 190 behind!"

I kept turning and saw the ugly snout of the 190 over my shoulder. But he couldn't draw a bead on me and soon he was driven off by a Spitfire. I made a mental note to buy my number two a drink back at St Croix.

The enemy leader must have given the order to withdraw, for his aircraft dived towards the ground and set course for the south. Then I spotted four 190s flying in a wide, evenly spaced finger formation, but the starboard aircraft was lagging badly and, in this position, could not be covered by his colleagues.

"Red two. Cover my tail. I'm going to have a crack at the starboard 190."

"O.K., Greycap. You're clear. Nothing behind."

Flying a few feet above the bocage country, I narrowed the gap between my Spitfire and the 190. His three comrades were still well ahead of him and he was an easy target. I slid out to one side so that I would not have a low line-astern shot and pulled slightly above him to avoid some high trees as I concentrated on firing. I hit him with the first burst on his engine cowling. More cannon shells ripped into his cockpit and the 190 plunged into the ground only a few feet below. We were over a strongly defended area, for as I pulled up into a steep climb we were engaged by a considerable amount of light flak. Gaining altitude, I spiralled my Spitfire and caught a last glimpse of the remaining three 190s. Oblivious to the fate of their comrade, they continued to streak away at low level, and after making quite certain that they were not going to return, the two of us flew back to St Croix in a wide abreast formation.

Back at our airfield I learnt that Wally had smacked down a 190 and that Don Walz had accounted for a third victim. It was a pity the Huns had seen us launch the initial attack: if we had achieved complete surprise, we could have knocked down half a dozen. Still, three victories were better than none, and the engagement marked our first success from St Croix. My own personal score now stood at twenty-eight.

Most unfortunately Walz, together with three other pilots, was shot down later that day. At the time we knew nothing of the circumstances, only the bare fact that a complete section of four aircraft had failed to return from a scramble. The four aircraft had taken off late in the evening and eventually located a force of Focke-Wulfs, which they attacked. In the fading light they were not aware that they had engaged a far superior force. The Germans, realising their advantageous position, stayed to fight, and all four Spitfires were shot down. Walz's own aircraft was hit in the engine and the petrol tanks exploded. He lost little time in baling out and landed safely in a field. After some adventures on the ground he was eventually assisted by the local peasants and returned with the tragic story. The incident was specially grievous for Dal Russel, whose young brother was one of the three pilots killed on this mission.

Once again the weather clamped down with low cloud and rain. Flying was quite out of the question, and we took the opportunity to make ourselves comfortable at St Croix. Our dug-out was warm and dry, and offered ample protection from the nightly barrage, which continued unabated in its intensity. The mayor of the local village came to see me and, with one of the French-Canadians acting as an interpreter, told me that the Germans had abandoned a number of sound cavalry horses in the locality. He had also 'collected' some saddles and bridles, and suggested that we might care to take over two or three of the steeds for our own recreation. One of my pilots, Johnny Irwin, had some knowledge of horseflesh, so together with the mayor and Varley we drove into St Croix to inspect the animals. They were not exactly the type of immaculate charger one would see at a Trooping, but from my Yeomanry days I knew something of the subject and they appeared to be sound in wind and limb. Irwin confirmed my diagnosis. He and I rode back to the airfield in some style, whilst Varley drove the jeep. With these animals we enjoyed a lot of amusement and some hard exercise. On one occasion I astonished our senior army liaison officer, who belonged to a crack cavalry regiment, when I turned up at 83 Group for a conference on my steed. Wally adopted the pastime with some zeal and rode as he flew – flat out. He soon discovered that it is far easier to stay on a horse's back at a gallop than in a canter, and proceeded across the Normandy pastures either flat out or at a sedate walk.

Our mess was located in a large tent on one side of the orchard. We lived exclusively on the tinned compo rations, and soon became bored with this monotonous but adequate diet. The Canadians deplored the absence of fresh meat, milk and fruit juices, and wanted good fresh bread instead of the hard biscuits. Each day a twin-engined Anson landed at St Croix from Tangmere carrying mail, newspapers and urgently required small spares. I sat down in my caravan to write a note to Arthur King back at the 'Unicorn' in Chichester. I told him of the dreariness of our food and asked him if he could arrange to deliver to Tangmere a supply of fresh vegetables together with bread and perhaps some meat. If he could get this stuff to Tangmere, the pilot of the Anson would do the rest and we should be very grateful.

The following day the Anson turned up with a crate of tomatoes, loaves of new bread, fresh succulent lobsters together with a reasonable supply of stout. Arthur maintained this private supply organisation until we moved out of the narrow confines of the beach-head area and we were able to purchase what we considered to be the necessities of life from local sources. One day a small party of press correspondents came to see the wing and I invited them to stay for lunch. They were somewhat reluctant to accept my offer as they had considered driving to Bayeux, where a reasonable meal could be obtained. However, they took a keen interest in the proceedings when the lobsters and local wine were set before them. Naturally, they enquired as to our arrangements for the supply of such essentials and I told them of our base organisation in Sussex which centred upon Arthur King.

Some few days later, the story was published in one of the national newspapers. It had an amusing sequel, since Arthur was visited by a representative of His Majesty's Custom and Excise, who solemnly told him that an export licence would be necessary if he persisted in this sort of thing!

Since its introduction to the Service in 1939, the versatile Spitfire had participated in many diverse rôles and had fought over a variety of battle-grounds. It had appeared as a fighter, a fighter-bomber and as a tactical reconnaissance and photographic reconnaissance aircraft. Now it fulfilled yet another rôle, perhaps not so vital as some of the tasks it had undertaken in the past, but to us of supreme importance. Back in England, some ingenious mind had modified the bomb racks slung under each wing so that a small barrel of beer could be carried instead of a 500-pound bomb. Daily, this modern version of the brewers' dray flew across the Channel and alighted at St Croix. The beer suffered no ill effects from its unorthodox journey and was more than welcome in our mess.

Now we met and fought the Luftwaffe daily over the Normandy countryside. Whenever the weather permitted, they were active over the battle area, and we ranged far to the south so as to cut them off before they could attack our ground troops. They generally operated in small formations – rarely of more than a dozen aircraft. Consequently, we resorted to sweeps and scrambles in squadron strength and the wing seldom flew as a complete formation. Thirty-six aircraft would be unwieldy and too conspicuous. I flew once or twice each day, leading the various squadrons in turn so that I did not lose my intimate association with all the pilots. The wing's total score of confirmed victories now stood at a pleasing figure and my own personal score at twenty-nine, all of which were single-engined fighters. There was widespread speculation about how long it would be before I equalled the Sailor's record of thirty-two victories, but I refused all discussion on the subject and would not countenance it in my own mind. Should we continue to be successful in our fights with the Luftwaffe, and should they still operate at the same intensity, then I should have many opportunities for combats in the immediate future. My job was to lead the pilots into combat and to make sure that our team knocked down the maximum number of enemy aircraft. My personal score and any records attached to it were quite a secondary consideration. I did not intend to take undue risks and was quite content with our present rate of progress. Nevertheless, on a sweep on 23rd June I missed a golden opportunity of adding a further scalp or two to my belt.

It was an excellent flying day and I was at the spearhead of Wally's squadron. He was leading a section of two aircraft on my starboard side. High in the heavens the sun blazed down from a blue sky, but there was a great deal of fluffy white cumulus cloud at 6,000 feet. This cloud was broken, and covered about half the countryside. Sometimes it continued unbroken for five or six miles, and then we would fly over a clear expanse where we could see the ground below. After crossing the enemy's flak belt, just south of the Caen-Bayeux road, I dropped the squadron to the base of the cloud, for I didn't want to be silhouetted from above against such a tell-tale white background.

We had just left Alençon on our port side when I saw a bunch of bandits at three o'clock. They were a formation of Focke-Wulfs and travelling in the same direction as ourselves. Like me, their leader had elected to fly just below the cloud base so that he could not be bounced from above. Under these circumstances I had only two methods of attack to choose from. I could take the squadron down to ground level and try to creep up on them from below with an attack into their vulnerable bellies, or I could climb through the cloud, fly on the same course as the enemy and strike from the sun when they appeared from the broken cloud cover. I adopted the high tactics, and with throttles wide open we climbed through the cloud and swung high into the sky. Now we were on the same course as the enemy formation and I could see that five or six miles ahead the cloud ceased in a ragged line. If my timing was right and if the Huns continued to fly a straight course, then we should reach the edge of the cloud at the same time.

Obligingly, the enemy leader held his original course, and twelve or fourteen Focke-Wulfs swept into view. Telling blue leader to attack the aircraft on the port side, I took the six Spitfires of red section down in a fast dive on the starboard Focke-Wulfs. As the range closed I glanced back over my shoulder, a thing I did automatically, to make certain no enemy aircraft were above us. The sky was empty, but as I focused my eyes back on the enemy I saw they had commenced a turn to starboard. Wally was on my starboard side some two hundred yards out and the 190s were now nearer to him than to me. He was well within range and hit a turning 190 with his very first few cannon shells. Flames leapt from the cockpit; the aircraft fell over on to its back and dived vertically into the ground. Surprise was now gone, but the Germans were confused by our sudden arrival and remained turning and twisting in the area. There was yet another 190 ahead of me. He was swinging to port, but not too steeply. An easy shot. Just a little deflection. One glance back to make sure no one was on my tail. All clear. Eyes back on the 190. Thumb on the firing button. But already cannon shells are tearing into his engine cowling and wing root. Mortally damaged, the 190 joins some of its comrades in their funeral pyres below, but I have not fired a shot! The 190 was attacked from below, and a Spitfire, the killer, zooms into the air a hundred yards ahead of me. Another search, as I had not fired my guns. But the enemy aircraft had either fled or were burning in the fields. I gave the order to re-form, and feeling more than a little frustrated, set course for St Croix. I had spotted the bandits, had brought them to account, several had been destroyed, but I, the leader, had not fired a single shot. Back at St Croix, I walked over to Wally's Spitfire. The armourers were already rearming it.

"That 190 of yours was a piece of good shooting, Wally. I suppose you clobbered the second?"

"Yes, I got a couple of them. Did you see the second one, chief?" This last with a disarming grin.

"I not only saw it, Wally, I was about to shoot the — down," I replied.

"Hard luck, sir! I saw a Spitfire behind the 190, but I thought I'd better make sure of it. Of course, I didn't know it was you!"

"Anyhow, the great thing is for someone to hack them down. I've never seen better shooting. Just how many rounds did you fire?"

"I don't know yet. Let's see what the armourers say."

We learnt that Wally had only fired thirteen rounds from each of his two cannon. Each gun carried a total of 120 rounds, so that

Wally had used only about one-tenth of his ammunition. It was a remarkable display of both flying and shooting skill and, as far as I know, the performance was never equalled.

Once more the Luftwaffe changed their tactics and we began to meet fairly large formations of enemy fighters. Sometimes they numbered as many as fifty aircraft, but their leaders could not control such unwieldy formations and we were quite content to operate in squadron strength. One of the enemy leaders was easily identified in the air as he invariably flew a long-nosed Focke-Wulf when leading his gaggle of Messerschmitts. From various pieces of information available to them, our Spies deduced that the pilot was a fairly well-known veteran known by the un-Teutonic name of Matoni. We met him in the air on several occasions, but he was an elusive sort of character, skilful, dangerous and difficult to bring to combat unless the affair was of his own choosing.

The presence of Matoni was something of a challenge, and we would have welcomed a joust with him. Once airborne, we formed the habit of calling Kenway and asking whether there was any news of Matoni today. Some of my Canadians made rude remarks over the radio in the hope that the German listening service, which doubtless monitored our radio conversations, would pass our comments to the enemy pilot. But I was never successful in having a crack at him.

The story of Matoni and our vain quest for him came to the ears of the eager-beavers of the press. They were ever alert for a personal human story of this type, and several of them came to see me. I gave them the facts as set down in this record and went to some pains to explain that the old-fashioned 'duel to the death' epics of the First World War were just not possible under the conditions imposed by our type of team fighting. Despite my explanation of the affair, the story was suitably garnished and published in the popular press. It was front-page news, and its substance was that I had challenged Matoni to a personal combat over Normandy. This breach of faith on the part of certain war correspondents meant that I was subjected to a great deal of unmerciful chaffing by my comrades. It also caused me some personal unhappiness, for Paula wrote to say she thought I was taking quite enough risks without sticking my chin out any further.

The Matoni episode had an interesting sequel. The story found its way into the German newspapers and was brought to the attention of the enemy pilot. But by this time he had been shot down, wounded and lay in hospital. I heard from him shortly after the war was over, when he wrote from an address in the Ruhr and regretted that he had been unable to accept the 'challenge'. But perhaps it was not too late for him to pay his respects? In my reply I asked him to dine with us, but he never turned up.

One of my pilots had spotted some likely looking cavalry horses from his Spitfire. He told me that they were wandering about in the grounds of a large château which we estimated to be very near to the front lines. We decided to have a close look at these animals, and if they were better than those we possessed, we would bring one back. Accordingly, one sunny afternoon I threw a saddle and bridle into the back of the jeep and with Johnny Irwin struck across country for the château. Gradually, the nose-to-tail traffic on the choked, dusty roads thinned out and after passing through four or five small villages we found ourselves the sole occupants of a long, straight, cobbled road. I stopped the jeep and we had a close look at our large-scale map. We were very near the front line, but if my map was marked correctly, then we were about one mile behind our forward troops. It was very quiet, and the distant muted chattering of gunfire merely served to accentuate the silence and loneliness of our position. We continued along the road in a state of some uneasiness. Perhaps our army liaison officer had not been too careful when he marked my map, or perhaps the enemy positions had changed in the last few hours. Once again I stopped the jeep and anxiously studied the map.

"Good afternoon. Bit out of your way, aren't you?"

I almost leapt out of the jeep at the sound of the voice. A figure in a worn battledress had appeared from the ditch by the side of the road. He proved to be a lieutenant from a Scottish infantry regiment and I introduced ourselves and explained the purpose of our visit.

"Exactly where?" I enquired, "are the most forward British positions?"

"Right here," he replied. "My chaps are providing a forward screen and there is nothing between us and the Germans. The Hun is dug in on the other side of that village."

Yes, he had seen the German cavalry horses and confirmed that they were still in the grounds of the château whose lime-washed wall we could see gleaming through a belt of trees.

"The Hun seems to think we are using that place as a forward headquarters and lobs a few mortar shells at it every hour or so. He's a very methodical chap, y'know." He looked at his watch.

"In fact, he is due to have another crack in about ten minutes. Why not have a cuppa? We're brewing up, and you can catch your horse afterwards."

I refused his offer, since, should we be lucky enough to catch a horse, Irwin would have a long hack back to St Croix. As we drove down the lane, he shouted one final piece of advice.

"Don't go into the village or you'll be shot at, and watch out for the mortars. They're bloody uncomfortable."

We drove down an unkempt drive lined with tall poplar trees and saw our quarry in a small paddock to one side of the house. I parked the jeep under the trees and with bridle and saddle we walked across a ragged lawn to the paddock. Suddenly the oppressive silence of the afternoon was broken by a high-pitched unpleasant whistling noise and the topmost branches fell to the ground as a salvo of mortars slashed their way through the trees to fall on the château perhaps one hundred yards from our position. Saddle and bridle were abandoned and we ran for the cover of the trees. A second salvo again hit the building and one or two fell short and dangerously near to where we lay face down beneath the trees. Our position, I decided, was definitely untenable. A narrow stream meandered through the grounds and a small brick bridge supported the drive. Grabbing Irwin by the arm, I pointed to the bridge and together we raced across the few yards of shrubbery and lawn. We flung ourselves face down into the stream, which was not more than a foot deep and groped for the safety of the arch. We reached the security of this position as a third salvo from these multiple-barrelled mortars tore through the branches. Suddenly the attack ceased with the same abruptness with which it had begun. Wet, dirty and very frightened, we clambered from our ignominious position and took stock of the situation.

Once more we walked to the paddock and succeeded in catching one of the nervous creatures, which was branded with the double flash of the S.S. After Irwin had started his long ride back to St Croix, I opened the gate of the paddock so that the remainder of the horses could escape into the countryside and get away from the horrors of the mortar fire. Then I started the jeep as I was not anxious to remain near the doomed château and be subjected to further treatment from the mortars. I stopped for a word with the lieutenant and told him that our mission had been successful. But he was highly amused at the sight of an exceedingly dirty and wet wing commander.

Chapter Fifteen

COMBAT

Flying with Dal Russel's outfit, we brought off a sharp encounter with a squadron of Messerschmitts. Near Argentan we spotted the 109s flying south just above the treetops. We were well astern of the enemy formation, hoping for complete surprise. I took the twelve Spitfire pilots to a height within a few feet of the ground. Slowly and cautiously we narrowed the gap. Spitfires were positioned behind individual Messerschmitts so that each of us had a definite target. If our luck held, we had a splendid chance to put down the lot. Blast! At a range of a quarter of a mile, the Luftwaffe pilots spotted our Spitfires and carried out the only possible tactical manoeuvre by breaking steeply into our attack. They climbed as they turned, and we hung on to their tails to prevent them from gaining a height advantage. The enemy leader broke up his formation into several small sections of two aircraft and the little air battle began to spill over the countryside as Messerschmitts and Spitfires jockeyed for an advantage. Although I could no longer lead a co-ordinated attack, the radio gave me a degree of control over the squadron.

"These boys are staying to fight. Get into them! Number twos, you know the form. Dal, I'm climbing up after two 109s."

"O.K., Johnnie. I'm sparring with two more down here." The two Messerschmitts were climbing up and I hung on to their tails, 300 yards behind and slightly lower so that my Spitfire would be in the leader's blind spot. I could only hope that his number two would not see me. The leader reduced the rate of his turn, but continued to climb steeply. He was taking his section into the eye of the sun, would probably stall turn and bring the two aircraft down-sun in a fast dive searching for an unwary Spitfire. I glanced at my airspeed indicator. It told me that I was climbing at less than 100 miles per hour. Already my aircraft felt slack and clumsy.

Any more of this steep climb at such a low speed and I should stall and spin. But the enemy pilot has opened fire; wisps of smoke spurt out from his cannon. Unaccountably, a solitary Spitfire is flying in front of the Messerschmitt. My own wingman, well trained and efficient, has sized up the situation and called out to me:

"Nothing behind, Greycap. You're clear."

All my concentration was now on the Messerschmitt. No time to lose. Any second the lonely Spitfire would be sent down in flames. Cannons thundered above the roar of my engine as I pressed the button. The Messerschmitt was hit immediately in the belly of the fuselage and beneath the cockpit. For an infinite fraction of time it appeared to hang in space. I was now very close and could see the cockpit. Hungry flames spurted from the engine cowling and licked at the perspex canopy. There was no sign of the enemy pilot. He was probably dead already – slumped in the bottom of his seat. Now the aircraft fell into a steep dive. As I circled to watch its fall, I felt no pang of remorse. It was merely one less to contend with in future, and to me was as impersonal as an enemy tank. Hurtling down, it narrowly missed colliding with a Spitfire, and Dal swore violently as he wrenched his aircraft into a tight turn.

"What's going on up there, Johnnie?"

"Sorry, Dal," I replied. "Greycap to red two. What happened to the other 109?"

"He half-rolled to the deck," he replied. "Shall we go after him?"

"No, let's call it a day."

Two days after this fight I knocked down a further two Messerschmitts which offered little resistance, and my personal score now stood at thirty-two victories. My opportunity to pass the Sailor's record occurred on the last day of June, when, flying with 44 Squadron, Kenway told me that a squadron of Spitfires was having a rough time with enemy aircraft some six or seven miles away. Could we lend a hand? Could we! As we sped south, we saw the dog-fight silhouetted against a background of towering white cumulus cloud. Spitfires, Messerschmitts and Focke-Wulfs climbed, turned and dived and, to me, it seemed as if the Huns had a height advantage. There were certainly more of them. Leaving six Spitfires as top cover I took the other six over the combat area. My two section leaders, red three and red five, soon picked out suitable targets, and with their wingmen to guard their tails, I sent them down to attack. My own wingman, Bill Draper, and I were left alone with the six Spitfires of blue section well above. Ahead of us was solitary Focke-Wulf and I tried my usual low astern tactics.

"Greycap from red two. Two 109s turning in behind us. They're quite a way behind."

"How far, Bill?"

"Well over a thousand yards. You have a crack. I'll tell you when to break."

I tried to concentrate on the 190 ahead, but the ugly threat of the two yellow-nosed monsters behind made this impossible. Life itself depended on Bill's ability to assess the range of the pursuing Messerschmitts. He had sounded very confident over the radio, but I almost pulled a neck muscle in the endeavour to look over my left shoulder. I abandoned all thought of the 190 ahead.

"What's the form, Bill?"

"They're gaining. Break port. Now!"

But I was well into my turn before the 'Now', and the arc of our flight meant that I could see their leader's sinister yellow nose over my shoulder. After two steep circling turns we turned the tables on the 109s and began to close in from astern. But they realised the significance of our tighter turns and evaded the issue by half-rolling and diving steeply to the deck. In such a manoeuvre they held a decided tactical advantage, since our Spitfires simply could not hold a dive at the same high angle. So we gave up the chase.

Our skirmish had drawn us away from the scene of the original mêlée and now we found ourselves over a layer of white cloud. A perfect backcloth on which to spot enemy aircraft, and I climbed our small section still higher. A 109 sprang out of the cloud, climbed and levelled out 2,000 feet below. We were ideally poised for a surprise attack, well hidden in the strong sun. Bill had not seen the 109. Nor should he, for it was his job to guard our tails, mine to search and strike.

"One 109 at ten o'clock, Bill. Going down. All clear?"

"All clear, Greycap. I'm covering you."

This was perfect teamwork. I could pay undivided attention to the Hun below and I hit his ugly yellow nose with a long, steady burst. Thick black smoke poured from the Messerschmitt, but he continued to fly and darted for the protection of the cloud. We tore after him and I reflected on the wisdom of this move. I did not know the depth of this layer of cumulus cloud and it could reach to the ground. My blind flying instruments had toppled in the dive and I was losing height very rapidly. If the cloud was very deep, then perhaps there wouldn't be sufficient height to recover when we rocketed out of its base. But I was committed to the chase and we plunged into the swirling white blanket. For a second of time, which seemed an eternity, the cloud held and imprisoned my bucking Spitfire. The glaring whiteness blinded me, but my fears were groundless, as the layer was very thin and I dropped into a safer world, bounded by wide horizons of green and gold patchwork fields. The 109, conspicuous by its trailing banner of smoke, was some 800 yards ahead and I closed in for the kill. But the Messerschmitt was out of control, and at a shallow angle struck the ground. For a moment I had thought the enemy pilot was trying to pull off a crash landing. If so he was far too fast, for the aircraft hit the ground at well over 200 miles an hour. For a short distance it careered across the uneven surface of a meadow. Then it hit a dyke, tore into a stout hedge and pitched into the air once again. The wings and tail were torn apart. The fuselage twisted as it fell to the earth, where it disintegrated into a thousand pieces.

We flew back to St Croix at low level, only varying our height when we had to climb to 6,000 feet to clear the enemy's efficient flak belt west of Caen. I felt exhausted and was anxious to get down, so that I could stretch out on my bed and relax. We had pursued the enemy and had been hunted ourselves. During the last short encounter with the Messerschmitt, all my energy and impulses had been geared high in the scale of violence; I had taken a deliberate and calculated risk when I dived through the cloud, and now the reaction set in. On the last few miles of the flight back to the airfield, with the ever vigilant Draper guarding my flank down-sun, I felt drained and fatigued. It was the first time this had occurred in the air.

Back at St Croix, there was a good deal of hand-shaking and

back-slapping, since the Messerschmitt brought my total of victories to thirty-three. The news soon spread, and within an hour a batch of Allied press and radio correspondents arrived on the scene for their stories. I tried to explain to the correspondents that it was my job to see that the Canadians brought down the maximum number of enemy aircraft. In carrying out this job I had topped Sailor Malan's score of thirty-two confirmed, but otherwise there was little similarity between our two tasks. Malan had fought with great distinction when the odds were against him. He had matched his handful of Spitfires against greatly superior numbers of Luftwaffe fighters and bombers. He had been forced to fight a defensive battle over southern England and often had to launch his attacks at a tactical disadvantage when the top-cover Messerschmitts were high in the sun. He had continued the fight until the outcome of the Battle of Britain was decided and had flown on operations well into 1941 until he was relieved for a well-earned rest. On the other hand, I explained, I had seen little or nothing of the defensive type of fighting. I had always fought on the offensive, and, after 1941, I had either a squadron, a wing or sometimes two wings behind me. I never had to contend with the large formations encountered in Sailor's heyday when he had been unable to select the best opportunity to strike. Generally, my tactics were to flush, to stalk and to kill our opponents. It was a different type of fighting, and our only disadvantage, compared to the circumstances prevailing in his time, was that we invariably operated over enemy territory when a single bullet in a vulnerable part of our Spitfires could mean, at the best, a prison camp until the end of the war.

This day also marked Danny Browne's last mission with the wing. Young and green, he had joined us at Kenley early in 1943, and in fact had first flown over France in my leading section of four Spitfires. For his excellent work over the past fifteen months he had been recommended for the D.F.C., and this award was soon to be gazetted. Now he was to return to the United States for a rest and would have the opportunity to see his folks in New Jersey. Like many other exiles, he was desperately anxious to see his homeland once more, and for the past few days had talked of little else but the size of the first steak he would devour, the heat of the New Jersey sun and the long-leggedness of the hometown girls. Once there, he would soon become sated with such an existence, and like many of his brother pilots from North America, he would not be really content until he fought with us again. I told him all this on our last evening together, but he laughingly replied that, if I ever saw him again, it would be in the United States. He was supposed to be rested for at least six months, but exactly eleven weeks later, when we were based in Holland, he reported to me for another tour of operations.

We had been in Normandy well over three weeks, but the German bastion at Caen still held firm and prevented our ground forces from breaking out into the open country south of the city. Our fighter-bombers and light bombers of the Second Tactical Air Force had attacked enemy strongpoints on the outskirts of Caen many times, but the well-disciplined, tough German troops continued to put up a most stubborn and effective resistance. Early in July it was decided, despite some stern opposition in high quarters, to reduce enemy ground opposition by saturating them with a heavy attack by Lancasters of Bomber Command.

Would the fiasco of Cassino in Italy, when the bombing attacks had created impassable obstacles to our own advance, be repeated at Caen? Was not the condemnation to death of many innocent French civilians unnecessary and a basic contradiction of the very principles we fought for? Would not the heavy bombers be more suitably employed in their strategic rôle of reducing the industrial might of Germany? Despite the various military and moral considerations, and the conflict of opinion amongst our most experienced air commanders, the decision was made to attack Caen. Late one fine July evening, as the sun dropped to the western horizon, the attack began.

Although Spitfires provided a target-cover force for the hundreds of Lancasters and Halifaxes, our presence was unnecessary, for the Luftwaffe did not react to the attack. As the bombers made their run-in from the sea, I positioned my Spitfire to the west of the town so that I could watch the progress of the attack from a down-sun position. Our own ground troops had been withdrawn to a line some distance from the target area so that they would be in little danger of bombs which fell short of the targets. We had been told that all the targets were contained in an area approximately two miles in length and just short of a mile in depth. But well before the smoke and debris from the first bombs which hung over Caen in the calm evening sky had obstructed the scene from our view, it was quite apparent that a number of bombs had fallen well outside the target area. As I watched the terrible destruction wrought on this French city I could not help but wonder whether we were using a sledge-hammer to crack a nut. We were all aware of the military necessity to break the enemy at Caen so that our ground troops could eventually deploy into open country. But we were not so sure that this object could only be achieved by the wholesale destruction of Caen and the death of a great number of its inhabitants.

Some of the bombs were fused to explode up to six hours after the attack, so that there would not be too large a time-lag before the ground forces went in early the next morning. Flying low on the fringe of the attack, I distinctly saw a German tank thrown into the air, like a child's toy, and turning over and over before it fell to the ground.

Instead of turning to the north to set course for England after dropping its load, one of the Lancasters came down in a fairly steep dive towards the strongly defended enemy-held territory south of the city. I watched this manoeuvre in some amazement as the Lancaster would soon find itself a solitary target for the German flak. Perhaps the aircraft had had its controls shot away or damaged and could only fly in this fashion. But wait, the bomber has now levelled out and is still flying due south only a few feet above the main Caen-Falaise road. Amazed, I watch its antics. What the hell is the pilot up to? I soon discover the object of the low-level flight. This road, which is one of the enemy's main supply routes, is packed here and there with stationary tanks, armoured cars and vehicles. As it sweeps down the road, both front and rear turrets of the bomber are in action and the gunners are firing long bursts into the enemy vehicles. There is a considerable amount of light flak, but the pilot obviously scorns this small stuff, since he is accustomed to a nightly barrage of heavy flak over the industrial cities of Germany. For him this affair is a bit of a lark, and like a schoolboy away from the vigilance of his prefect, he is making the most of his freedom. Now the Lancaster carries out a slow wide turn to re-trace its flight northwards to Caen. Majestically, it ploughs along over the straight road with rear and front guns blazing away. Enemy drivers and crews abandon their vehicles as the Lancaster pounds along and dive for the shelter of the hedgerows. But what is this? Another Lancaster has appeared on the scene and is carrying out similar tactics. The first Lancaster is flying north. The second is steaming south. Both are over the centre of the highway and both avoid each other with a careful little swerve. Speechless, I watch the rôle of fighter-bomber being carried out, and most effectively, by the four-engined heavies. But now it is all over. The original glamour boy has climbed away to the north for his homeward journey and the second is pulling up from his strafing run. I fly alongside the Lancaster as it settles down for the flight back to Lincolnshire and wave to the gay adventurers inside. We have seen two bomber missions this evening which will never be recorded in any official log! Long after the war I discovered that the pilot of the first bomber was an ex-bricklayer from Scotland called 'Jock' Shaw. At the time of my story he was the proud captain of his own Lancaster, and was to win the D.F.C. and bar. Later he served as my adjutant.

Two days after the bomber attack, Caen was in British hands. We decided to drive there and see the results of the bombardment at close quarters. The streets were still choked with rubble and we had the greatest difficulty in manoeuvring the versatile jeep past blocks of stone and gaping craters. We had been told that the original plan to send an armoured column through Caen on the morning following the attack had to be abandoned. We could fully understand the reason. Bulldozers struggled to clear the blocked roads, and we had to stop the jeep and continue our journey on foot. Here and there fires still raged: pathetic groups of silent French folk struggled with the debris in a forlorn attempt to find the bodies of some of their friends and relatives. A sickening stench of death pervaded, and the people to whom we spoke said that few Germans were killed as there were no enemy positions in the bombed area. We had seen the destruction wrought by the Luftwaffe on London, Sheffield, Coventry, Liverpool and Manchester; but those scenes paled when compared to the magnitude of this disaster. We thought that the French had been made to suffer without sufficient justification.

We cut short our visit, made our way back to the nearby beach, where we lay in the sunshine and swam in the stained waters in an endeavour to forget the broken bodies, the shattered homes and the brooding despair which lay heavily on Caen.

Some weeks before D-Day, the three squadron commanders of 144 Wing and I had laid a wager with our opposite numbers in 127 Wing that we would shoot down more enemy aircraft than they during the period D-Day until D plus 30. With less than twenty-four hours to go we led by the uncomfortable margin of one victory – fifty-one to fifty. Tough, stocky, aggressive Tommy Brannagan, who was born in Scotland before his family moved to Canada, had succeeded to the vacant post of squadron commander of 441 Squadron caused by the departure of Danny Browne, and I led the unit on the last day of the wager in an all-out effort to increase our slender lead. I decided to take the squadron to patrol the Alençon area, since we knew that this Normandy country town was the supply centre for Von Kluge's Seventh Army, and during the past few days the Luftwaffe had attempted to protect it from air attack. My hunch was correct, and we pulled off a pleasing bounce against a dozen Focke-Wulfs well below us. This time, the enemy pilots were taken completely by surprise: it was not till five had been shot down that the others turned to give battle. For a few seconds we sparred with the remainder until I spotted a 190 on the tail of a lonely Spitfire. My pilot had little idea of his acute danger: he was flying his Spitfire straight and level as if he had been over the prairies of Canada. As I drove my Spitfire round in a greying-out curve of pursuit, I could see wisps of smoke from the Focke-Wulf's cannons and a large chunk of aileron flew off the Spitfire. There was no time for accurate, steady ranging if I was to save my pilot, so allowing plenty of lead, I 'hosepiped' the 190 with a long continuous burst. When I saw my cannon strikes registering, I held the same deflection with coarse stick and rudder. The tactics paid off. My opponent's aircraft started to burn and its nose pitched into the air preceding the fatal stall. But I was more concerned with the pilot of the Spitfire, who, fortunate chap, continued to fly in the same haphazard manner. I pulled alongside and recognised the pilot. He was a flight lieutenant who had recently joined us. I knew him to be a good pilot, but this was not sufficient in these dangerous skies. He had served for a long time as an instructor in Canada and would have to learn to keep a better look-out if he was to stay in one piece. But, for the present, a word of encouragement was obviously needed.

"Greycap to blue four. You all right?"

"I think so, Greycap. I've lost a lot of starboard aileron and I've been hit in the wing. But she's flying quite well."

"Good show. I clobbered the chap on your tail. You can buy me a long drink when we get back."

Back at St Croix, we added up the score from this furious little encounter. We had accounted for a total of seven enemy aircraft for the loss of one of our pilots, who unfortunately collided with a Focke-Wulf. Immediately it was dark, I was on the phone to 127 Wing: they had not met with the same good fortune, so we had won our wager by a comfortable margin. I suggested that they should bring the booty, which included a case of champagne, to our mess and assist us in its disposal. The invitation was accepted with alacrity and we celebrated the event with an exceedingly good party. Unfortunately, it was completely spoilt for us by some dreadful news brought by Bill MacBrien, our group captain. The organisation whereby Bill co-ordinated the activities of the three Canadian Spitfire wings had proved too cumbersome for tactical operations in the field and was to be disbanded.

In future, a group captain would command a wing of three or four squadrons with a wing commander as leader. The new organisation would be more compact and flexible and the group captain would have a more reasonable span of control. Bill continued to explain the new organisation. As the junior Canadian

Spitfire wing, we were to be completely disbanded. 441 Squadron, led by Tommy Brannagan, was to be attached to a British wing. Dal Russel's 442 Squadron was to be transferred to 126 Wing and Dal was to be very deservedly re-promoted to wing commander. Our third unit, Wally McLeod's 443 Squadron, was to join 127 Wing and I was to go there as wing leader. We received this news in a stunned silence, for although we had not served together a very long time we had fought some exciting battles and had built up a fine esprit de corps. We had started from scratch with our first mission in late March, and had proved our ability by accounting for more enemy aircraft than the longer-established 127 Wing. But the decision, we could see, was sound and logical.

It fell to the lot of Tommy Brannagan and his boys to mark our last day together with a resounding and spectacular victory. Leading his squadron into an equal number of Focke-Wulfs, Tommy's tactics were so successful that only two of the enemy managed to get away. Ten 190s was a record to be proud of; especially as our only casualty was an enemy cannon shell in the wing of a Spitfire. Shortly after this outstanding fight, Brannagan was awarded the D.F.C. Unfortunately, he was hit by flak soon afterwards, broke his arm when he crash landed behind the enemy lines and was subsequently taken prisoner.

I drove slowly round the airfield, stopping at dispersals, the repair and maintenance sites, the armament depot, the cookhouses, the operations vehicles and the many small but essential sections which, when blended together, put the Spitfires into the air. Apart from the squadrons and myself, the remainder of the wing personnel were being shipped back to England, and after the excitement of our Normandy days they did not relish this prospect. They were keen to remain with the Second Tactical Air Force and take part in the adventurous trek across North-West Europe, through France, Belgium, Holland and into Germany itself. Officers and airmen were all downcast, and stood about the airfield in forlorn groups waiting for our Spitfires to take off from St Croix for the last time.

But we all had something to remember. During our short span of active operations we had taken part in a great enterprise. We had shot down seventy-four aircraft and either probably destroyed or damaged many more. On the debit side, we had lost fourteen pilots, two of whom we knew were safe. I was taking my own Spitfire to 127 Wing, and when I climbed into the cockpit a crowd gathered round me to wish me God-speed. I was deeply touched by this spontaneous demonstration from my Canadian friends. Slowly, I taxied on to the runway, opened the throttle and climbed above the haze into the clear sky. For once, I was alone. After a slow turn I put the Spitfire into an easy dive across the airfield and could see the white blur of their faces when I passed a few feet above their heads. Happy, aggressive Canadian wing! I saluted you with an upward roll.

Chapter Sixteen

FIGHT FOR FRANCE

127 Wing, which, as the Kenley Wing, I had led during the previous year, now consisted of four Canadian Spitfire squadrons, and some of the pilots who had flown with me still remained, including Walter Conrad, whose miraculous escape over Dunkirk has already been described.

I did not fly on this first day, for I was busily occupied in settling down and getting to know the pilots and key personnel. I had a long session with Bill MacBrien and learnt that a recent spate of flying accidents was causing him some concern. A few days before there had been a most unfortunate mid-air collision when the wing leader, Lloyd Chadburn, had lost his life. In addition, two pilots had been killed when they scrambled from either end of the single runway and met head-on half-way along its length. We could not afford to lose valuable, experienced pilots in this manner, so Bill asked me to pay particular attention to flying discipline and accident prevention.

It was a grey, dreary sort of a day with leaden skies and limited visibility. Sometimes we heard the angry chatter of our anti-aircraft guns as they fired against enemy fighters. The Luftwaffe was taking advantage of the weather conditions and attempted to press home isolated raids against opportunity targets in the crowded beach-head. 416 Squadron provided the readiness sections which were scrambled to deal with this unorthodox behaviour of the enemy, and succeeded in shooting down seven aircraft. One of these combats took place directly over our airfield, providing a tremendous tonic for our hard-working ground crews, who seldom saw the more spectacular results of their labours. This 190 crashed just short of the runway, but the enemy pilot baled out successfully: as he drifted down, I raced the jeep across the open ground so that I was alongside him when he hit the deck. He turned out to be a small, weedy looking character, and his recent experiences had not improved his general demeanour. Our army liaison officer, a husky Canadian infantry captain complete with webbing and revolver, took charge of the proceedings and the wretched pilot probably thought that his last moment had arrived. Just as we were about to move off with our captive, a posse of British Army personnel arrived on the scene. Their leader announced that since the Army was responsible for the safe custody of all prisoners of war he intended to relieve us of our prize. I pointed to a brace of Spitfires which, with wheels and flaps down, were making their final approach to land.

"The pilot leading those two Spitfires shot down this chap a few minutes ago. My pilot would like to meet him, and I insist on taking him along if only for a few minutes."

The Army objected and quoted various rules and regulations. Fortunately, I was the senior officer present and Forbes-Roberts, our victorious pilot, had the pleasure of meeting his victim, an opportunity which seldom occurred. The enemy pilot wore a new type of mae-west which would be of little use to him in the prisoner of war stockade: he was persuaded, without undue difficulty, to hand it over to Forbes-Roberts. This garment, suitably autographed by everyone present, provided a fitting souvenir of an unusual incident.

Before he left the Desert Air Force, Air Vice-Marshal Broadhurst had acquired a captured Fieseler Storch. This aircraft accompanied him to England and now was often seen over the beach-head. In addition to the pilot, the Storch carried one passenger: at this time it was perhaps the most versatile little aircraft in the world. It could land or take off in a much shorter distance than any contemporary British or American aircraft, and was ideally suited for hedge hopping between the many airfields, radar sites and headquarters. The Storch was always to be seen with a V.I.P. passenger in the back seat on the fringe of the big bombing attacks. Its versatility can be judged from the manner in which the pilot landed the aircraft on his frequent visits to Crepon. If the wind was blowing across the strip, then the Storch would land in this direction rather than along the length of the runway and sometimes the pilot would put it down alongside our dispersal. Naturally there was always the danger that it might be mistaken for an enemy-piloted Storch, but this contingency had been provided for by painting the aircraft a bright yellow colour with prominent R.A.F. roundels. As a further precaution all gunner formations had been warned of the daily activities of the little aircraft.

One day we were told to put a strong patrol of Spitfires over the airfield, since the Storch would shortly arrive with a V.I.P. in the back seat. Soon it came into view flying only a few feet above the hedges. As it came to a halt, we were delighted to see the Prime Minister, complete with cigar, in the back seat. We had the rare privilege of meeting Mr Churchill and listening to an impromptu speech in which he told us of the progress of the war.

On another Storch flight, General Dempsey, commander of the Second British Army, was the passenger. He had asked our group commander to show him one of the big bomber attacks on Caen from the air, and, together, general and air vice-marshal flew above our lines. At a height of only two or three hundred feet the Storch ambled along at a modest sixty miles an hour. Suddenly the frail little aircraft was struck several times by shells from our own light flak. Later it was discovered that it had been hit in eleven places; but for the moment the pilot's chief concern was to get his aircraft down in one piece before it was shot out of the sky. The crime had taken place over a field of corn; Broadhurst carried out one of his more rapid descents, and at a slow speed brought the damaged aircraft over the boundary hedge. It was now apparent to both pilot and passenger that they were landing in the very centre of the gun sites and that the gunners, determined not to be robbed of their prey, were continuing to fire their weapons from near horizontal positions. Indeed, there was some danger that they might eliminate each other! The Storch came to a grinding standstill in the cornfields. Broadhurst and Dempsey jumped out of the aeroplane. Then they saw a large Canadian lieutenant, complete with Sten gun, racing towards them with a set, determined expression on his face. The air vice-marshal turned to the general and shouted: "Wave your red cap and show the brute we're friendly."

We were delighted to learn that our ground forces were about to make a determined attempt to break out from the confines of the beach-head and advance to the south and south-east. For more than two months we had been restricted to a small, congested, dusty area and we were ready for a change of scenery. We should be required to take part in a phase of very active operations, and we were to make sure that pilots and Spitfires were on the top line.

The Allied ground forces were now poised for their assault and once more the strategic bombers laid heavy carpets of bombs to reduce enemy resistance. American heavy bombers killed, stunned and demoralised the Wehrmacht to such an extent that the defences between St Lô and Coutances were prostrated. Pressing south towards the Loire river, the Americans then turned towards the Seine, thus outflanking von Kluge's Seventh Army. There was still time for von Kluge to withdraw his divisions across the Seine, but he had received direct orders from Hitler himself not only to stand and fight but to counter-attack. Meanwhile, the British and Canadian armies drove to the south from Caen and in mid-August the town of Falaise was captured. With the exception of a small gap between Falaise and Argentan, the Allied forces held a perimeter of steel round the Germans. Von Kluge's counter-attack had failed, and through this narrow gap he must withdraw his divisions or suffer annihilation from the air.

The gap of the Falaise pocket was some twenty-five miles across. The stage was set for the Second Tactical Air Force, with our own 83 Group well in the van, to crack down with all its might. Harry Broadhurst was undoubtedly the R.A.F.'s most able and experienced officer in the planning and conduct of air-ground operations, and he had already made careful plans to deal with such a situation.

Tactical reconnaissance pilots began to report the first enemy movements which were to lead to the destruction of the German Seventh Army. These pilots brought back vital information about certain roads which were packed with enemy vehicles attempting to reach the comparative safety of the far bank of the Seine. This meant that we were approaching the very climax of our air-ground operations in Normandy, the aim of which was to destroy the German forces where they stood and not chase them half across Europe. The failure of the British ground forces to break out at Caen before this had been the subject of some severe criticism and had created some unfortunate disunity between British and American commanders. But some of us had been privileged to hear Montgomery's oft-repeated battle plan to destroy the German forces in Normandy. The two months of build-up, of reconnaissance and probing, of attack and counter-attack, were over. The day was at hand to silence the critics.

Broadhurst's twenty-two squadrons of Spitfires and Typhoons, armed-up with bombs and rockets, were at readiness on their airfields. The pilots were anxious to be let off the leash. Every second that elapsed before we struck meant that more of the enemy would get across the Seine. But a confused ground situation held us back.

Elements of the Polish Armoured Division, which formed part of the Second Canadian Corps, reported their position at Chambois when they were, in fact, some distance away at a place with a very similar name. The identity of the east-bound columns at Chambois had to be established beyond all doubt. Our group commander gave this vital task to his most able and experienced ground-attack leader, and Charles Green roared off in his Typhoon and flew low over the suspect transports. Soon afterwards he was talking to his group commander.

"What are they, Charles?" said Harry Broadhurst.

"Huns, sir," replied the wing commander.

"How low were you?" said the air vice-marshal.

"Fifty feet, sir," answered Green.

"Are you absolutely sure they're Germans?" persisted the senior officer.

"I saw their black crosses – and the square heads of the drivers!" was the classic reply.

When the Spitfires arrived over the small triangle of Normandy, bounded by Falaise, Trun and Chambois, the Typhoons were already hard at work. One of their favourite tactics against long streams of enemy vehicles was to seal off the front and rear of the column by accurately dropping a few bombs. This technique imprisoned the desperate enemy on a narrow stretch of dusty lane, and since the transports were sometimes jammed together four abreast, it made the subsequent rocket and cannon attacks a comparatively easy business against the stationary targets. Some of the armoured cars and tanks attempted to escape their fate by making detours across the fields and wooded country, but these were soon spotted by the Typhoon pilots and were accorded the same treatment as their comrades on the highways and lanes.

Immediately the Typhoons withdrew from the killing-ground, the Spitfires raced into the attack. The tactics of the day were low-level strafing attacks with cannon shells and machine guns against soft-skinned transports, including all types of trucks, staff cars and lightly armoured vehicles. Here and there amongst the shambles on the ground were a few of the deadly Tiger tanks, and although the cannon shells would have little effect against their tough armour plate, a few rounds were blasted against them for good measure. As soon as the Spitfires had fired all their ammunition, they flew back at high speed to their airfields, where the ground crews worked flat out in the hot sunshine to rearm and refuel the aircraft in the shortest possible time.

Throughout this day, and on all subsequent operations in the Falaise gap, the Luftwaffe failed to provide any degree of assistance to their sorely pressed ground forces. Faced with the threat of losing their forward airfields to our advance, they were busily occupied in withdrawing to suitable bases in the Paris area, so our fighter-bombers enjoyed complete air supremacy over the battle area. Quick to exploit such a great tactical advantage, Broadhurst issued instructions that until such time as the Luftwaffe reappeared to contest our domination of the Normandy sky all his aircraft would operate in pairs. This was a wise decision, for it meant that pairs of Spitfires and Typhoons could return to the fray immediately they were turned round on the ground. Detailed briefings were unnecessary since all pilots knew the area and the position of our own ground troops. Valuable time was saved and it was possible to put the maximum number of missions into the air. Before Falaise, an individual fighter pilot had rarely flown on more than three or four missions on any one day, but now it was not uncommon for a pilot to fly six times between dawn and dusk.

The trees and tall hedgerows, in full foliage, afforded some cover to the Germans, who tied large green branches and shrubs on to their trucks in an effort to conceal them from the eyes of our pilots. A gleam of reflected sunshine on metal here, a swirl or eddy of dust there, or fresh tracks leading across the fields were sufficient evidence to bring down the fighter-bombers with their assorted armoury of weapons. When darkness fell and brought some relief to the battered Germans there was time to take stock of the situation and to add up the score. My own pilots had amassed a total of slightly more than 200 destroyed or damaged vehicles, plus a few tanks attacked with doubtful results. For once, the weather was in our favour, and the forecast for the morrow was fine and sunny. The pilots turned in immediately after dinner, for they would require all their energy for the new day. As they settled down to sleep, they heard the continuous drone of our light bombers making their flight across the beach-head to harry the enemy columns throughout the short night.

The Canadians were up well before the dawn, and the first pair of Spitfires retracted their wheels as the first hint of a lighter sky flushed the eastern horizon. The Germans were making strenuous efforts to salvage what equipment they could from the debacle and get it across the Seine. Such enemy action had been anticipated: some of the Typhoon effort was diverted to attacking barges and small craft as they ferried to and fro across the river. Once more the Spitfire pilots turned their attention to the killing-ground and attacked all manner of enemy transports wherever they were to be found. They were located on the highways and lanes, in the woods and copses, in small villages and hamlets, beneath the long shadows of tall hedges, in farmyards and even camouflaged with newly mown grass to resemble haystacks. During the previous night many of the enemy had decided to abandon a great proportion of their transports: they could be seen continuing the retreat on foot and in hastily commandeered farm-carts. Sometimes the despairing enemy waved white sheets at the Spitfires as they hurtled down to attack; but these signs were ignored; our own ground troops were still some distance away and there was no organisation available to round up large numbers of prisoners.

On this day, 19th August, my Canadians claimed a total of almost 500 enemy transports destroyed or damaged, of which many were left burning. Even so, this score was not outstanding, since Dal Russel's wing easily outstripped us with a score of more than 700. Afterwards, our efforts in the Falaise gap gradually petered out, for the transports and personnel of the German Seventh Army had either been eliminated or had withdrawn across the Seine. The Falaise gap ranks as one of the greatest killing-grounds of the war, and is a classic example of the devastating effects of tactical air power when applied in concentrated form against targets of this nature. During these few days, pilots of the Second Tactical Air Force flew more than 12,000 missions and practically wiped out no less than eight infantry divisions and two armoured Panzer divisions. The Second Tactical Air Force had in fact turned an enemy retreat into a complete rout.

After the fighting had ebbed away from Falaise, we decided to drive there and see the results of our attacks at first hand. We thought that we were prepared for the dreadful scenes, which Eisenhower later said could only be described by Dante.[1] On the last flights the stench from the decaying bodies below had even penetrated through the cockpit canopies of the Spitfires. Another, and perhaps the most important, object of our visit was to bring back a suitable German staff car, since it was obvious that we should soon be on the move across France, and a comfortable Mercedes would provide a welcome change from our hard-riding jeeps. After we left Falaise behind, all the roads were so choked with burnt-out German equipment that it was quite impossible to continue the journey. The bloated corpses of unfortunate domestic animals also lay in our path, so we took to the fields and tried to make some progress across country. Each spinny and copse

[1] *Crusade in Europe*, p. 306.

contained its dreadful quota of dead Germans lying beside their wrecked vehicles, and once we came across the body of what had been a beautiful woman lying sprawled across the back seat of a staff car. We found our limousines, which consisted of Renaults, Citroens, Mercedes and strangely enough a smooth Chevrolet. We had brought ropes, jacks and a few jerrycans of petrol, but it was impossible to extricate any of the cars. Soon we abandoned our search and left the fields and lanes, heavy with their rotting burden in the warm sunshine.

A few days later Kenway telephoned to say that the Luftwaffe, operating from their bases near Paris, were putting up a fighter screen over the Seine in order to protect the retreating German troops from more air attack. The controller suggested that if two squadrons patrolled well to the south of Paris and then approached the Seine from the east, we might have some luck. This was too good an opportunity to miss, for we had seen little air fighting during the past two weeks. We had not flown in wing strength for some time, and it would be a pleasant change to operate in our true rôle after the carnage of Falaise. Beating up the German Army was part of our job, but it was a poor substitute for the clean, exhilarating thrill of the dog-fight.

The pilots were soon briefed, and once more I led 443 Squadron with the Spitfires of 421 stepped up a few thousand feet down-sun. It was a fine, cloudless day: above the layer of haze, our view was unrestricted. We flew in our well-proven finger-fours, but shortly after the climb, my number two called to say that he had a rough engine and was returning to Crepon. The small, wiry French-Canadian, Larry Robillard, who led the section on my starboard side, asked if he should detach a number two from his section to fly with me. Because I did not anticipate any strenuous air combat, I declined his offer and we flew on. After the low-level attacks of the previous days and the sickening stench of death at Falaise, it felt good to be flying high through the clear sky. No longer were we restricted to a tight air space only 1,000 feet above the ground and condemned to attack cumbersome transports which crawled over the surface of the earth. Today we enjoyed the boundless horizons, and we were after big game.

We swept well to the south of Paris, then curved north to fly down-sun with the sprawling city on our port side. Should the enemy fighters make their appearance from the south, we should be in a vulnerable position, for they would have the advantage of the sun. So I warned the wing to keep a sharp look-out. We completed our northerly leg of the flight and again carried out an easy turn to port to make our run up to the Seine. We had held this course for a few seconds when I spotted a gaggle of at least sixty aircraft well ahead, the highest of which were at the same altitude as ourselves.

A distance of some five miles separated us from the other formation, and there were so many of them that I felt they must be a bunch of American fighters. Still, you could never be sure, and it was a simple matter to take out a little more insurance in the form of an extra 2,000 feet of height. The mass of aircraft milled about the sky some three miles ahead, and they were certainly not behaving like our American friends. I eased our Spitfires a few degrees to port to hide them in the sun and called the pilots:

"Greycap to wing. Sixty-plus at twelve o'clock, three miles. They may be Huns. Green leader, keep us covered."

Our quarry were very near, and their turning, wheeling manoeuvres brought their top section about 2,000 feet below. Above us the sky seemed empty. I kicked on hard top rudder and with opposite stick held the wings of my Spitfire vertical so that I could have a good look at them. Recognition came, and with it the usual shocked, heart-in-mouth feeling which was always the same – exactly the sort of sensation you get when your car slides out of control on a greasy road. Then it was gone. We were boring into them and I was talking into the microphone to bring the whole wing down in one fell swoop. As I turned and dived, I called the leader of the top-cover squadron:

"Green leader, I'm taking my section into the top bunch. There's plenty more below. Get in!"

We gained complete surprise and I lined up my sights on an unsuspecting squat 190 which carried a long-range petrol tank below the fuselage. My first burst of fire was a little too low to hit the aircraft, but the shells tore into the ancillary petrol tank, and this exploded. Burning petrol engulfed the Focke-Wulf in a blinding sheet of flame and screened it from my sight. There was little point in watching it plunge to earth, for no pilot could live in that inferno and the ciné camera would provide all the evidence I required. I spiralled the Spitfire in a tight turn, for we had lost surprise with our initial attack and now found ourselves heavily out-numbered. Our preliminary, co-ordinated attack had split up with its customary abruptness into a series of individual dog-fights, which fanned out over a wide area. I was about to rock my wings for my number two to draw up to the line-abreast position when I remembered that I was alone. Seven or eight questing Messerschmitts appeared at the same height and I decided that this was no place for a lone Spitfire. With swift movement I flicked the aircraft on to its back and pulled the stick back into the pit of my stomach. She protested in every sinew as we thundered down with the speed building up to a dangerous figure, but I held her in the dive and only eased out when we were 1,000 feet above the ground. I followed this manoeuvre with a couple of steep turns to make certain that I had not been followed and saw a solitary Focke-Wulf just below me.

I turned in behind the enemy aircraft, stalked him from his blind spot and poured a three-second burst into his thin, dark grey belly. As I climbed above him the Focke-Wulf clawed into a vertical stall, seemed to stand for a fraction of time on its tail and then fell in a slow, easy spin. The crash would attract the unwelcome attentions of his comrades, and I circled very warily at ground-level, straightening out at the completion of each turn to make a dart towards the Seine and then turning again. More Focke-Wulfs were ahead of me and a small formation of Messerschmitts was well out on my starboard flank. I put the Spitfire into a steep climb and at full throttle climbed back to 8,000 feet. Here I could see no sign either of friend or foe; but an empty sky was always a dangerous sky, and I felt that it was high time I joined forces with a few of my Canadians. I called Larry Robillard:

"Greycap to Larry. I'm at 8,000 feet just east of the Seine.

Where are you?"

"Larry to Greycap. In the same area at 15,000 feet. Shall we come down?"

"No, stay there. I'll climb up to you and rock my wings."

"O.K., Greycap," Larry acknowledged.

Cautiously, and always turning, I climbed to join Larry's section. Craning my neck, I caught a glimpse of six aircraft glinting in the sun. These must be Larry's Spitfires.

"I can see you Larry. I'm at eleven o'clock to you. Re-form."

I pulled my Spitfire well ahead of the six aircraft and learnt of my error the hard way when wicked tracer flashed over the top of my cockpit. Instinctively, I broke to port in a desperate, tight turn, and over my shoulder saw the lean nose and belching cannons of a Messerschmitt as its pilot tried to hold a bead on my turning Spitfire. My fate would be decided by the tightness of our turns and I pulled the stick back until the Spitfire shuddered with a warning of the flick-stall. I was blacking-out. I eased the turn to recover a grey and dangerous world. Keep the height at all costs. No breath to spare to call Larry. The leader of the Messerschmitts knows the form. He has placed a pair of aircraft on either side of me whilst he and his number two stick grimly to my tail. The flanking Messerschmitts whip into action with head-on attacks. But they are not good shots and the greatest danger lies from their leader. The moment I ease out of the turn he will nail me. But I cannot turn for ever, and if I am to live I must somehow climb and so get the extra power from the blower.[1] The sun is at its zenith and I wrench the Spitfire in a steep climb into its sheltering glare. The blinding light will hide me. But my Spitfire quivers as she takes a cannon shell in her starboard wing root. Another turn. Another soaring climb into the sun until with an unpleasant thump the blower cuts in. Now I have sufficient power to draw away from my pursuers, and I am able to increase the gap with another long haul into the sun. Soon I am out of range of the Messerschmitts, but they continue to climb steadily after me. Now that I have reached comparative safety, I toy with the idea of a stall turn followed by a fast dive and a head-on

[1] Supercharger.

attack against their persistent leader. But I dismiss this scheme. Fortune has already smiled upon me, and there will be another day.

I flew back to Crepon and asked the runway controller to check whether or not my landing gear was fully down, since I did not know the extent of the damage to the Spitfire. He assured me that it appeared to be serviceable, so I put the aircraft down on the strip and taxied into the dispersal. Larry was there to meet me.

"I looked all over the place for you, sir, but couldn't find you. Any trouble?"

I described the results of my error when I had mistaken Messerschmitts for Spitfires. Larry grinned and shrugged his shoulders with a Gallic gesture.

"Never mind! You're back in one piece and your two Huns bring the total to twelve. Three of our chaps are still missing."

This was the first time I had been hit by an enemy fighter. The vicious fight had shaken me, and I took to the air again as soon as possible. My own Spitfire was being patched up and I had to fly another aircraft. When we flew over a strongly held German position, those dirty soot bags of heavy flak burst around our formation and the Spitfire pitched violently when it received a chunk of shrapnel in the tail unit. She felt sluggish and heavy on the controls, so I handed over the lead and flew back to our airfield. At a low forward speed on the circuit she was decidedly uncomfortable, and I was relieved when we were safely on the ground. The damage was not extensive. A few holes in the rudder and elevators, and a control cable almost severed. The flight sergeant hovered about.

"You want to fly again, sir? I'll soon have another aircraft ready."

"No thanks, Flight," I replied. "I think I'll call it a day. What I really want is a good, long drink."

Events now moved rapidly. Two days after our fight over the Seine, Paris was liberated, and in early September the Welsh Guards were the first to receive the tremendous welcome which awaited us in Brussels. The battle for France was over.

A new airfield had been found for the wing at Illiers L'Evêque, some forty miles west of Paris. Bill and I flew up to reconnoitre it before we moved the squadrons. It was pitted with bomb craters, but some of the holes had been filled in so that a narrow runway lay across the grass surface. And so we left the beach-head which had been our home for almost three months. We carried out this move with the utmost speed, for our ground forces were advancing so rapidly that we feared we should soon be out of range of the front lines.

Chapter Seventeen

ADVANCE AND CHECK

We were able to operate from Illiers on only two days before the leading elements of the British forces were well beyond the limited range of our Spitfires. Until such time as a suitable airfield was found for us, our flying was restricted to training flights.

Our airfield lay in the midst of some good farming country. The corn had been reaped and lay about the large stubble fields in golden stooks. For a few days we enjoyed shooting of a different variety from that of Normandy. The partridge had not been shot for a long time, and the coveys were strong and plentiful. Five or six dubious twelve-bore guns were rounded up for the shooting syndicate. Cartridges were not a problem, since we had a plentiful supply for trap-shooting purposes, when pilots were taught the elementary principles of deflection shooting. Sally came into her own and retrieved many runners which otherwise would have been lost. Fred Varley and his colleagues shook their heads in dismay whenever they saw us set out on these expeditions, for they knew that they would be required to pluck and dress the game. On one occasion we came back to the mess late in the evening with more than fifty brace, and two days later all the officers dined on roast partridge assisted by liberal supplies of vintage champagne which had been presented to us by a wealthy local Frenchman. The countryside abounded with game, and the hares, partridges and pheasants which fell to our guns made a pleasant change from rations. Some of the nearby chalk streams were well stocked with grayling and brown trout. We did not possess a fly rod, but various methods were soon devised whereby these game fish were brought to the pot. We lived well at Illiers and made the very most of the golden autumn days. The dust and sweat of Normandy seemed very far away.

We remained at Illiers for more than three weeks, and already the shooting, the fishing, the trips to Paris were beginning to lose their attractions. Sometimes we heard news of the forward-based wings, which made us anxious to get on the move again and take part in the daily round. Wally McLeod was desperately keen to get into the air again and continually badgered me for news of our next move. He found it hard to relax and made no secret of the fact that he was out to increase his score of twenty-one victories. Officially, he was recognised as the top-scoring fighter pilot of the Royal Canadian Air Force. Although Screwball Beurling had destroyed a greater number of enemy aircraft, most of his victories were attained whilst he was serving in the Royal Air Force. This was a very fine point of distinction and simply meant that Wally was the top scorer of the R.C.A.F., but Beurling held the record for Canadian pilots. Wally intended to settle this untidy matter once and for all, simply by passing George's total.

Sometimes Wally would accompany us when we walked across the stubble in search of game. But several times I found him in our darkened ciné-projection caravan analysing his combat films and trying to discover whether or not he could have despatched his previous opponents with even fewer rounds of ammunition. He had the cannons of his Spitfire stripped and checked. He worked on his aircraft until it shone like a jewel in the sunlight, and his sole topic of conversation was air fighting.

The Luftwaffe were now in the process of making a most remarkable recovery after their defeat in Normandy and their hurried retreat to airfields east of the Rhine. The month of September witnessed a great effort by the German aircraft industry, and the production of single-engined fighters attained record proportions. Fighter squadrons received ample supplies of aircraft: many of the units which had been decimated in France were re-equipped and able to return to the battle. A tremendous attempt was made to increase the size and efficiency of the fighter force, even at the expense of the bomber and night fighter components. The German High Command was confident that their V weapons would be sufficient for offensive operations, and a proportion of bomber pilots were quickly converted to the fighter rôle. So the Luftwaffe was far from being a spent force: indeed, back at Illiers we heard ominous reports of the first appearances of fast, jet aircraft. Such was the state of the Luftwaffe when on 17th September more than 1,000 troop-carriers together with almost 500 gliders took part in the greatest airborne operation yet attempted. The aim of this operation was to establish a bridge-head across the Rhine by securing three important river crossings over the Maas, the Waal and the Neder Rijn. Once these crossings were secured, together with others of secondary importance, our armoured columns would be able to drive up a narrow corridor from Eindhoven to the Rhine and link up with the most northerly elements of the airborne forces. We soon learnt that the British troops of the First Airborne Division, who had been dropped almost eight miles west of their objective at Arnhem, were faring badly. There were not sufficient transport aircraft to carry the whole of the First Airborne Division on the first day, and the vital reinforcing airlift, on 18th September, was delayed by bad weather. Moreover, the German counter-attack was heavier than had been anticipated, and the division was soon badly split into three isolated pockets. Intelligence reported that the Luftwaffe had deployed squadrons of jet fighters to Holland to oppose the airborne landings, and during breaks in the weather large formations of enemy aircraft had been reported in the area. It was against this sombre background that we received orders to move to an airfield in Belgium to help deal with the rejuvenated and aggressive Luftwaffe.

Bill MacBrien immediately departed by road for our new base in Belgium, closely followed by the three-tonners of the advance party. Soon we received word that they had arrived at Le Culot, an ex-Luftwaffe airfield ten miles south of Louvain, and the squadrons flew there in separate formations. It was a parky September evening with a keen edge to the wind when we landed our Spitfires on the bomb-scarred runway. Bill drove up as we switched off our engines and suggested that we report to the briefing tent immediately. Our army liaison officer was grave when he outlined the events which had led to things going wrong at Arnhem.

Early the following morning we flew over the Arnhem area. Once again we operated in squadron formations so that we could maintain standing patrols over Arnhem throughout the daylight hours. My own Spitfire was unserviceable because of a faulty radio, so just before our take-off I hurriedly transferred to another aircraft. Unfortunately, this machine suffered from a slight glycol leak, and the minor defect meant that the oily coolant formed a thin film of viscous liquid over the windscreen. This hampered my forward vision, and, to make matters worse, the weather still continued to be most unfavourable for intensive operations. Cloud formations were stacked in unbroken layers; the usual blue vaulted dome of the sky was a grey, dark mass. I tried to fly between two layers of cloud, but often they merged together and I had continually to change both height and course to keep the twelve Spitfires together as a fighting unit. Occasionally we ran into heavy rainstorms. By this time the windscreen was completely coated with glycol and I suffered from a complete lack of forward view. I yawed the aircraft from side to side by first kicking on port and then starboard rudder, so that I had some inkling of what lay ahead, but the whole flight required a great deal of instrument work and I was unable to keep a careful look-out. It was in these circumstances, after descending through a gap in the sprawling clouds, that we ran head-on into a large formation of Messerschmitts. They, too, were completely taken by surprise, and it was not until the two formations actually met that we realised what had happened. Quickly I turned our Spitfires after them, but already they had disappeared into the cloud and we did not see them again.

The various reasons for the failure at Arnhem are well known. Some personal and official accounts of the operation have suggested that the lack of close support from the fighter-bombers of the Second Tactical Air Force was one of them. The headquarters and some airfields of our own 83 Group were located only a few miles south of Arnhem, so that a few comments on Operation *Market* as we saw it may not be out of place.

Throughout the campaign in north-east Europe, it was the job of the Spitfires to keep the sky clear of enemy aircraft whilst the Typhoons got on with their close-support operations. To drop bombs or launch rockets within a few yards of our own ground troops is not a simple matter, and the Typhoon pilots had a far more difficult and dangerous task than we Spitfire pilots, who usually cruised about the sky well above the light flak. For the provision of effective close support from fighter-bombers is not merely a matter of spraying the general area with rockets or bombs. The pilots must be provided with very detailed information about their target, including flak defences, camouflage and its exact distance and bearing from our own troops. The nearer this form of support to our own ground positions, the more accurate this information must be.

When flying on close-support missions, the pilots got their information before take-off or, if they were airborne, from our contact cars. On the ground the army liaison officers briefed us from large-scale maps, and experienced fighter-bomber leaders made it a rule to sketch their target and its surroundings from memory before take-off. The contact-car system was well suited to a fluid ground situation, for the briefing it provided was usually accurate and up to date.

'Cab ranks' of eight or more Typhoons had repeatedly demonstrated that they could take on enemy tanks, armoured cars or self-propelled guns, provided the pilots were properly briefed and the weather was suitable. The pilots realised that in such a rôle they became little more than flying artillery and they suffered heavy casualties from the flak. They knew that our troops were fighting an enemy who possessed far better and more lethal equipment, especially in the form of 88-mm. guns and Tiger tanks. It could be logically argued that our own close-support operations were far from an economic proposition when valuable aeroplanes and highly trained pilots were pitted against less-costly ground targets. However, the Typhoon pilots were not concerned with economics and pressed on with their job.

Why didn't such an efficient and well-practised system meet the requirement at Arnhem? Our nearest Typhoon wing of three squadrons was based but forty miles to the south at Eindhoven, and other wings were located near by. Between 17th and 25th September the weather, although sometimes poor, was usually suitable for the Typhoons, and the record shows that during this period they flew on every day except one. The bleak fact is that when the ground situation at Arnhem was very serious and when enemy resistance was increasing, our Typhoons from Eindhoven were operating against trains and other targets well to the south of Arnhem. How had this extraordinary situation developed?

Although our own commander-in-chief, Coningham, was usually responsible for day-to-day operations in this area, he had no control over Operation *Market*. Both planning and control were exercised from a combined headquarters in England, and little attention appears to have been given to the requirements for close support from our fighter-bombers.

During the actual drop on 17th September, and on all the seven subsequent reinforcement and re-supply operations, we of Second T.A.F. were banned from the Arnhem area because the planners feared a clash between British and American fighters, despite the fact that we had been fighting alongside each other for almost two years! Back in England, the bad weather often imposed delay and uncertainty on the timing of the transport aircraft flights, which in turn meant the cancellation of our own planned operations.

Throughout the first critical days of the battle no detailed information concerning the ground situation was available to us. This was hardly surprising, for the radio frequency allocated to the First Airborne Division clashed with that of a powerful British station, and vital messages from the paratroopers were never received.

When we heard that the plight of the First Airborne Division was desperate, the Typhoons were sent to patrol the area on free-lance missions known as armed reconnaissances. On these flights the pilots searched for and identified their targets, without other assistance; but armed reconnaissances, which had paid such handsome dividends on the cluttered roads of Falaise, were unsuited to the thick woods which surrounded Arnhem. The leaves had not fallen from the trees, which offered ideal concealment from air attack to the German tanks and guns. At Arnhem the Typhoon pilots wanted up-to-date briefings from the contact cars or from their army liaison officers more than at any other time during the campaign. They also required coloured smoke fired from our forward ground positions to mark the hidden targets. These aids were not provided: when the fighter-bombers flew over the paratroopers they only had a hazy idea of the situation below. Late one evening we heard that it had been decided to withdraw the bridge-head, and slightly more than 2,000 survivors of the 10,000 who had landed but a few days before were brought back across the Neder Rijn.

It would be quite wrong to suggest that the Typhoons could have saved the day at Arnhem, for the basic cause of failure was that the First Airborne Division was landed too far from their objective. But there can be no doubt that, had the requirement for close support been planned by experienced officers, then our own fighter-bombers could have provided far more protection to the beleaguered paratroopers. This lesson was undoubtedly learnt, since our own commander-in-chief controlled all air operations during the subsequent crossing of the Rhine. This was completely successful, and the close-support operations were models of precision and timing.

Despite the failure at Arnhem, the bridge over the Waal river at Nijmegen had been secured, and our forward troops were positioned in this area. The Luftwaffe continued to appear, sometimes in fairly large formations, and we maintained our patrols in this sector. Ironically enough, the weather had improved after the evacuation of the remnants of the First Airborne Division.

One day I was on patrol with Wally's squadron between Arnhem and Nijmegen. There was a thick, heavy cloud base at 12,000 feet, but below this height the visibility was excellent and we could see long distances over the rain-soaked flat landscapes of Holland and Germany. Suddenly I felt a tingle of excitement as Kenway broke the silence.

"Kenway to Greycap. Bandits active in the Emmerich area. They appear to be flying down the Rhine towards you. Steer 130."

"Greycap to Kenway. Roger. How many?"

"A small gaggle, Greycap. Not more than a dozen. Out."

By this time I had turned the Spitfires to the south-east and we flew over the course of the Rhine itself. We held our altitude at the very base of the cloud so that we could not be bounced from above. The Rhine was swollen by the recent heavy rains and the storm-lashed fields of Germany to the east looked dark and foreboding. It was a grey, sombre scene and its brooding quiet seemed threatening and sinister. I tried to shake off this unpleasant mood when the ever-vigilant Don Walz broke my reverie.

"Greycap from red three. Nine 109s below."

"O.K., Don. I have them. Wally, take the starboard gaggle. I'll take the — on the port."

The enemy were flying on the same course as ourselves and were in two small line-abreast sections, one of five aircraft and the other of four. We were twelve Spitfires and had all the essentials of tactical success – speed, height and surprise. We tore down into a line-astern attack, and just before we closed to firing range I saw the leader of the enemy starboard section pull his Messerschmitt into a vertical climb. I knew this manoeuvre. The enemy pilot would half-roll at the top of his loop, having gained vital altitude. He would then aileron-turn his Messerschmitt and come down in a fast dive searching for a Spitfire. My own target was very close, but before I blasted him with my cannons I found time to cry:

"Watch that brute, Wally. He knows the form!"

I hit my opponent with a good heavy burst. He started to burn immediately, but I was thinking of the danger from above. I blacked out momentarily as I pulled my Spitfire, with throttle wide open, into a vertical climb. To gain height I was carrying out a similar manoeuvre to the Messerschmitt, but as the horizon fell away and my speed dropped I realised the vulnerability of my position. It would be far better to complete the last, slow portion of the loop within the sanctuary of the cloud rather than in the sky, where I would present an easy shot to the Messerschmitt. I stretched the arc of the loop to the maximum and with a sigh of relief saw the grey vapour swirl round my Spitfire. I was upside down in the dark cloud. But this did not matter, for I only had to ease the stick forward and the Spitfire would continue its arcing flight and soon fall into the clear sky. I plunged out of the cloud in a dive with the speed building up and aileron-turned the Spitfire on to an even keel. I went into a tight circle, but there was no sign of either Spitfire or Messerschmitt, and Wally didn't answer to my repeated calls on the radio.

On the ground lay the burning wrecks of aircraft, and although I flew across these at high speed, they were so disintegrated that I could not identify them as either friend or foe. My fuel was running low, so I made my way across the Maas, over the water-logged fields, past the city of Eindhoven and over the border into Belgium. Mine was the eleventh Spitfire to land from our mission, and the other ten pilots were waiting for me. Wally was not amongst them. The pilot who had flown nearest to Wally told me that he had last seen his leader streaking after the looping Messerschmitt. The wingman had attempted to follow, but the 'g' forces had made him black out in the tight pull-out, and when he had recovered he could find neither his C.O. nor the Messerschmitt. I cross-examined all the pilots, but no one had seen Wally or his quarry after the break up of our initial attack.

"What do you think his chances are, sir?" one of the Canadians asked me. I tried to sound cheerful.

"Knowing your C.O., I feel certain that he wouldn't let go of the 109 until the issue had been decided one way or the other. There was no other aircraft in the area and they must have fought it out together, probably above the cloud. To start with, he would be at a bad disadvantage, for the 109 was already several thousand feet higher. Perhaps he was hit and has crash landed near the Rhine. You chaps get your lunch and I'll see if 83 Group have any news."

I walked to my caravan and phoned the duty controller. He was an old friend from the Kenley days and knew Wally. There was no news of our missing squadron commander, but he would check all sources of information immediately. How did the fight go? I replied that we had destroyed five of the Messerschmitts, but the price of our success might be high.

After the last patrol of the day I called the controller once more, but there was no information concerning the fate of Wally. I walked through the darkness to our mess tent. The ten pilots who had flown with me rose to their feet as I entered, and ten pairs of eyes asked the unspoken question.

"Sorry chaps, but there's no news of your C.O. We can only hope that he's a prisoner or, better still, is walking back."

They sat down with gloomy faces, and a despondent atmosphere prevailed in the tent. It was up to me to jerk them out of this.

"Don, get the C.O.'s jeep and all of you change into decent

uniforms. We'll rendezvous here in half an hour and have a meal and a drink or two in Louvain. We can pile everyone into two jeeps."

They were spruced up well within the appointed time and we drove through the black night into Louvain. It was our first excursion into this old university town, and we knew nothing of the amenities of the place. After some reconnoitring, we parked our jeeps and entered a small establishment called *Le Café des Sept Coins*. Inside it was cheerful and warm, but the animated conversation ceased at our entry. There was a complete silence as we threaded our way past the crowded tables to the bar. Our blue uniforms were strange to the local populace. But the proprietor, an affable little man by the name of Marcel, singled me out for interrogation as I ordered a round of drinks in my halting French. I explained that we were fighter pilots of both the R.A.F. and the R.C.A.F.

Marcel held up his hand for silence and announced to his customers that he was greatly honoured with a visit from the Royal Air Force. Moreover, we were Spitfire pilots and that afternoon had been in action against the hated Germans. We had achieved a great victory, and so on.

All this was rendered with splendid Gallic zest. The best in the house was at our disposal.

"What food will you have?" asked Marcel.

"Steak," replied the Canadians.

"And to follow?" enquired Marcel. "I have plenty of provisions."

"More steak!" said the Canadians. "Medium rare."

Madame and her two daughters emerged from the kitchen and the necessary introductions were made with a degree of formality. Soon tender steaks were placed before us and we fell to, since we were very hungry. Afterwards, as I sipped a liqueur and inhaled a good cigar, both provided by our generous host, I glanced round the table at my small band of Canadians, none of whom was more than twenty-two or twenty-three years of age. Their high spirits and vitality had responded to our pleasant surroundings and already they were engaged in deep conversation with the citizens of Louvain. For a few moments my own thoughts focused on the morning's fight with the 109s. I feared that Wally was dead. I drank a silent toast to his memory and the encounters with the Luftwaffe we had shared together.

As the evening wore on, the tempo increased and we were entertained by various songs from our Belgian friends. We responded with some of our more suitable ditties and towards midnight the café was heavy with smoke and warmth. Abruptly, the swing doors burst open to admit several gendarmes headed by a *sergent de ville*. Their faces were solemn. What, the sergeant demanded, was all the commotion about? He could hear the din from the other side of the city square. Marcel explained the situation and we were introduced to the officers of the law. The tall sergeant threw back his heavy cape, reached for his hip pocket and produced a large notebook. For one uneasy moment we thought the book was to be used for official purposes, but the sergeant extracted a few franc notes, ordered a round of drinks, and proposed the health of the Royal Air Force.

Eventually it was time to take our leave of this hospitable little tavern. We struggled into the two jeeps, feeling considerably lighter in heart than when we had left Le Culot a few hours previously. It was raining quite heavily as we sped through the deserted cobbled streets of Louvain. The second jeep roared past mine, swerved and heeled over at a dangerous angle as it negotiated a tricky bend in the road. Peering through the rain-lashed windscreen, I saw a body pitch out of the leading jeep directly in front of me. I swung the wheel over to the right and braked violently to avoid the unfortunate pilot in the road. My vehicle skidded out of control, struck the steep pavement at the edge of the road, pitched violently into the air and fell over on its side. Fortunately, we were all thrown clear and we hit the greasy cobbles in loose, relaxed bundles of flesh. Apart from a broken finger, a cracked head and a cut or two here and there, we were none the worse for our mishap. We heaved my jeep on to its four wheels, but before continuing our journey I issued strict convoy instructions to the other driver. We would proceed in line-astern at a steady pace of not more than thirty miles an hour, and there would be no overtaking. We arrived safely at Le Culot in the early hours of the morning, where we rousted the squadron's doctor from his warm bed to minister to our cuts and bruises. The injured were bandaged or sewn up to the accompaniment of cries of encouragement from their more fortunate comrades, but soon it was all over and I sent them packing to bed to catch a little sleep. The doc had brewed up a pot of steaming coffee and we sipped a mug together after the others had departed. He opened the conversation.

"Bad thing about the C.O. He will be hard to replace; the boys would follow him anywhere. What do you think happened?"

"Hard to say, Doc," I replied. "The sky's a big place once you're split up, but I think the Messerschmitt got him. It was always all or nothing with Wally."

"Anyhow, your party was a good thing and you certainly got it out of their systems. They'll be all right now."

"Yes. I figured that a good old-fashioned thrash was the only thing for them. Good-night, and thanks for patching up the lads."

I walked across the wet grass to my caravan, undressed, removed a pained Sally from my bed and immediately fell into a deep sleep.

After the war I learnt that Wally was found dead in the wreckage of his Spitfire, which crashed near the scene of our fight.

The airfield at Le Culot was overcrowded with many squadrons of fighters and we had to make long tortuous journeys by the taxi-tracks to reach the uneven, bomb-damaged runway. We were not sorry when Bill told us that we were to move to a less-congested airfield: he asked me to make a survey of the new base as soon as possible. Our new home was a grass meadow which was known by what we considered to be the most inappropriate name of Grave.

I was able to report to Bill that the airfield was serviceable and ready for operations, but the grass surface was soft and would probably become water-logged during the winter months. The squadrons flew in and we started to dig ourselves in for the winter. At this time Grave was the nearest airfield to the enemy lines, so we took particular care to disperse the aircraft as far from each other as possible. We were quite certain that the Luftwaffe would not fail to respond to the challenge of a well-stocked airfield under their very noses.

We had barely arrived at Grave when Harry Broadhurst phoned Bill and said that the two of us were to put on our best uniforms and report to his headquarters by six o'clock that evening. We were to meet a highly important personage. Driving along the muddy cobbled roads to Eindhoven, we speculated on who this was likely to be. Perhaps it was Eisenhower, perhaps Tedder, Monty, or some high-ranking politician. There were endless streams of vehicles proceeding in either direction, but a few miles north of Eindhoven it was apparent that something was amiss since all the transports had come to a standstill. Round the next bend we could see that several trucks had been set on fire and some had been knocked into the deep dyke which flanked the road. We knew that this road formed the axis of our narrow corridor from Eindhoven to Nijmegen and it was obvious that it was under fire from an enemy battery. I jumped out of the car and spoke to the driver of the truck immediately ahead.

"What's the form down there? Is the road under fire?"

"That's right, sir. The Jerries have got the — range nicely and are plonking their — shells in the middle of the — road."

For a few minutes we sat and watched the scene ahead. Some trucks ran the gauntlet without injury, although the road was subjected to almost continuous shelling. We made slow progress towards the head of the column until only the driver I had spoken with remained in front of us. He timed his dash to commence immediately after a salvo of shells had fallen and then let in his clutch with a grinding clash. Fascinated, we watched his progress. He negotiated a slight bend and approached the danger zone marked by a number of wrecked and burnt-out trucks. Through the leafless, evenly spaced poplar trees we could still watch his attempt; but his vehicle, travelling very fast, was hit squarely by an 88-mm. shell. It careered across the cobbles, struck a poplar tree, and pitched on its back into the dyke. By this time we were breathing fairly hard, and clenched the back of our driver's seat.

"O.K., driver," exclaimed Bill. "We'll have a crack at it. Press on!"

We slid down the road.

"Faster!" cried Bill.

"Much faster!" I supported.

We hung on to the driving seat as the car swayed and skidded over the greasy road. What a bloody way to be clobbered in the fifth year of the war! But we were lucky, and as we roared through the death trap we caught a glimpse of brave stretcher-bearers working desperately in the doubtful shelter of the dyke. In silence we drove on to Eindhoven. The dangers of day-to-day front-line warfare, of which we saw practically nothing, had been well demonstrated to us.

Harry Broadhurst and his key staff officers lived comfortably together in a delightful country house which belonged to a member of the Phillips family. Here we found that the guest of honour was none other than the King, and we had the rare opportunity of meeting him in a most friendly and intimate atmosphere. The King was keenly interested in the conduct of the campaign, and, as an airman himself, he asked many searching questions about the German jets which had recently made such a dramatic appearance over the battlefields of north-west Europe.

Soon after this, Bill flew to England for a few days' leave and I was left in charge of the wing. I thought it would be a good thing to have a look at the airmen's lines, and set out on a tour of inspection. The troops had adapted themselves to their bleak surroundings with customary initiative, and most of their tents contained far more comforts than were decreed by the official scale of equipment. Many of them had devised and built ingenious cooking-stoves, which the Canadians used to supplement their British rations. Five years of war had not acclimatised their North American palates to our starchy, bulky food: Bill had made several strong representations to have his airmen supplied with the lighter, more balanced United States rations. The complicated supply organisations of the British and United States Forces ruled out Bill's proposal, but there was little doubt that the Canadians would have been far happier had they been fed on their accustomed diet of fresh meat, green vegetables, salads, fruit juices and ice cream. They regarded the British diet as an uninspiring assortment of tough meat, compo rations, Brussels sprouts, more Brussels sprouts and suet puddings, and voiced their views in no uncertain manner.

My visit was rudely interrupted by the roar of powerful engines and the whine of an aircraft in a steep dive. This was followed by several explosions. As we ran out of the mess tent, we were in time to see the unfamiliar, sleek silhouette of a Messerschmitt 262 climbing steeply away after its dive-bombing attack. A cloud of smoke rolled into the air and I drove quickly to the scene. The bombs dropped by the enemy aircraft were of the canister type, and the containers burst at a pre-selected altitude a few feet above the ground. Small fragmentation bombs were then scattered over a wide area, and these had found their mark in 416 Squadron's dispersal. Some wounded airmen were being tended by the doctors, but five airmen were beyond all human aid. One Spitfire was burnt out and a quantity of burning petrol and exploding ammunition handicapped the efforts of the rescue squads. Two pilots, McColl and Harling, distinguished themselves when, despite the danger from the ammunition, they jumped into two adjacent Spitfires and taxied them back to safety.

During the following days we were often attacked by the 262s, and more airmen were killed and more Spitfires damaged. The enemy jets came in very fast from the east, and in order to protect our airfield we carried out standing patrols at the favourite attacking height of the intruders. But our Spitfires were far too slow to catch the 262s, and although we often possessed the height advantage, we could not bring the jets to combat. Suddenly we were outmoded and out-dated. Should the enemy possess reasonable numbers of these remarkable aircraft, it would not be long before we lost the air superiority for which we had struggled throughout the war.

The complete superiority of the Messerschmitt 262 was well demonstrated to us one evening when we carried out a dusk patrol over Grave. Kenway had told us that the jets were active over Holland, but although we scanned the skies we could see nothing of them. Suddenly, without warning, an enemy jet appeared about one hundred yards ahead of our Spitfires. The pilot must have seen our formation, since he shot up from below and climbed away at a high speed. Already he was out of cannon range, and the few rounds I sent after him were more an angry gesture at our impotence than anything else. As he soared into the darkening, eastern sky, he added insult to injury by carrying out a perfect, upward roll. We were at a loss to know why the enemy pilot did not attack one of our Spitfires, unless he had already used all his ammunition. Later that evening Dal Russel phoned to say that some of his boys had shot down a 262. This was the first time that this type of enemy aircraft had been destroyed, and Dal and his wing were celebrating the event. It was a good thing; but it was an ominous sign that the destruction of a single aircraft should receive such acclaim.

Despite his assurances that we should never see him again on this side of the Atlantic, just after Arnhem we received word that Danny Browne had already passed through England and was on the last lap of his journey to rejoin the wing. We expected him to turn up in time for dinner, and I was anxious to provide him with a decent meal. On some evenings I had seen the flighting mallard, and from my Spitfire had selected a pool where it was more than likely that the duck would alight. That evening, for a few glorious minutes, the mallard swung in thick and fast, and before it became too dark to shoot, Sally had retrieved half a dozen plump birds. On my way back I stopped the jeep, and in the light of the headlamps gathered a suitable quantity of mushrooms which flourished here in great abundance. When I arrived back at the caravan, Danny had already arrived. In addition to his return, it was a suitable evening for a party; on this very day the wing had shot down its 200th enemy aircraft since its formation at the end of 1942.

We walked across the few yards which separated my caravan from the mess tent. Here we met the other squadron commanders, who were delighted to see Danny, and after we had filled our glasses we settled down to hear a highly spiced account of his activities in the States. The tent was crowded with the greater part of our 150 officers, but the buzz of conversation was interrupted by yet another unfamiliar sound in the evening sky which coincided with the bark of anti-aircraft fire. We flung ourselves to the ground as the night was shattered by a very adjacent and extremely loud explosion. Fortunately no one was injured, and investigation on the following morning proved the intruder to be a composite aircraft known as the 'Mistletoe'. This unorthodox contraption consisted of a Junkers 88, well laden with high explosives, on the top of which was mounted a Messerschmitt 109. These two aircraft were so coupled to each other that the 109 pilot could release the unmanned bomber against selected targets. For various reasons only small numbers of these composite aircraft were built, but it was another example of German ingenuity.

Before Bill returned from leave, I was told that Paula had given birth to our first son, Michael. There had been some complications, and she was very ill. It was obvious that I must get home with the utmost speed; but I could not leave the Canadians in Bill's absence. Steps were taken to get him back at once: meanwhile, I had to fret at Grave with little definite news from England. Eventually Bill arrived, and I wasted no time in a fast flight to Norfolk. Happily, Paula was making good progress after her initial setback, but for a few days I stayed close to the nursing-home. It was not until late October that I flew to Tangmere, refuelled and pressed across the Channel to rejoin the wing.

Chapter Eighteen

BRUSSELS

Towards the end of my flight to rejoin the Canadians, I was diverted to Brussels. This could only mean that the wing had been withdrawn from the water-logged airfield alongside the Maas river. When I circled over the Brussels-Evère airfield, I saw the Spitfires of our four squadrons dispersed near the perimeter track. Bill met me and said that the move from Grave had taken place a few days previously. The surface of our late airfield had become so wet that landings and take-offs were dangerous. Besides these hazards, the jet bombers of the Luftwaffe had continued to attack it.

There was plenty of accommodation at Evère, and our Canadian ground crews gladly stowed away their tents and moved into substantial quarters. We were told that we could requisition private houses, provided they had previously been occupied by Germans or Belgian collaborators. Our pilots were soon living in luxurious homes, and Bill found a couple of apartments into which we moved with our batman and dogs. So we gave up our pleasant nomad life under canvas with its gay, buccaneering environment. Now, after the day's operations were over, we returned to an unfamiliar world of hot baths and dinner parties. More often than not our spare bedrooms were packed with pilots on short leave from 'roughing it' on the damp airfields between Brussels and the Rhine.

On most Saturday evenings throughout these winter months, we spent a few hours with our group commander at his pleasant house near Eindhoven. These occasions became something of an institution, and all group captains and wing leaders tried to get there. Some of these officers were no longer in the first flush of youth. One had flown in the Battle of Britain on his fortieth birthday, and another, well over fifty and too old to fly on ops., had won the D.S.O. under shellfire in Normandy. But age was of little account. The very lives we led, surrounded by a hard core of young fighter pilots, kept all of us young in mind and spirit.

For the first half of December the weather was very poor. We had to be content with an occasional sweep and some sporadic attacks against ground targets north of the Ruhr. We saw few enemy aeroplanes, because Galland, now a lieutenant-general and holding a staff appointment, was holding them for his 'Big Blow'. Galland's doctrine was to build up his fighter strength so that at a chosen time, and under favourable weather conditions, he could throw great packs of mixed fighters against the American heavies and their strong fighter escort.

In his autobiography, Galland tells us of his plans for the Big Blow. Some 3,000 German fighter aeroplanes were ready for what was meant to be the largest and most decisive air battle of the war. To begin with, more than 2,000 fighters would be sent up against the Americans in gaggles of about sixty aeroplanes. A further 500 fighters would take off on a second mission, and night fighters would patrol the German borders to cut off any crippled bombers heading for Sweden or Switzerland. The object of this tremendous operation was to shoot down between 400 and 500 bombers. Galland figured that he would lose about the same number of his own pilots, but many would live to fight again.

Galland tells how this great force was kept waiting for suitable weather, until he was stunned by an order to release a large part of it to take part in the forthcoming Ardennes offensive. But he fails to mention several important occasions during November when very large formations of Luftwaffe fighters clashed with the Americans. These air battles were very significant, for the German fighters were driven off with heavy losses; they undoubtedly forecast the fate of the Big Blow, had it taken place. This operation would have resulted in the fiercest and bloodiest air battle of the war. It would also have witnessed the final destruction of the Luftwaffe, for the Germans persisted in the wrong fighter tactics when they still tried to assemble their large mixed formations of Focke-Wulfs and Messerschmitts. These could be spotted from a great distance and made easy targets for the ranging American fighters.

At this time, the average German fighter pilot was not sufficiently well trained to fight on equal terms against either his British or American opponent. Apart from their veteran and dangerous leaders, the rank and file of enemy fighter pilots were no match for either the close-in tactics of the British or the long-range style of the American fighting. The German pilots, too, showed a marked tendency to avoid flying in bad weather, and the day bombers attacked Germany for weeks without fighter opposition. When the weather cleared, the Luftwaffe would attack in force, and then become completely dormant again. But an air defence system cannot wait for clear skies before it operates, otherwise it becomes a token force of no real value.

The number of victories claimed by the leading enemy fighter pilots was very high. Their top-scorer, Hartmann, was credited with 336 victories, and there were a number of others who claimed more than 200. Nevertheless, we should remember that the very character of a confused mêlée in the air means that all fighter pilots tend to overclaim.

After they began to fight on two fronts, the Germans introduced a points scheme in connection with their awards for gallantry in the air. This system meant that on the western front a single-engined fighter destroyed counted as one point, a twin-engined bomber rated two points, and a four-engined bomber scored three points. Senior formation leaders were credited with a number of points which varied according to the total points obtained by the pilots they led. Kills at night were acknowledged as double those of day fighters, so that a pilot who shot down a Lancaster at night received six points. Like us, the Luftwaffe fighter pilots did not count aeroplanes destroyed on the ground by strafing attacks.

Towards the end of the war, a fighter pilot with twenty points, on the western front, qualified for the award of the Knight's Cross or the Iron Cross. On the eastern front, however, the number of points required for the same decoration was very much higher, and this alone is a fair indication of the great difference in the intensity of the air fighting on the two fronts.

After the war, when we heard of the huge German scores, I suspected that we were confusing points with victories. But experienced German pilots, with whom I have discussed this interesting subject, insist that their official scores were all absolute victories. There can be no doubt that the German fighter pilots had far more opportunities to accumulate higher scores than either ourselves or the Americans. During the initial phases of the air war on the eastern front, the German pilots certainly destroyed a very large number of Russian aeroplanes. On the western front, especially from 1943 to the end of the war, they faced great odds but still brought down many Allied aeroplanes. Moreover, the Luftwaffe had developed the mobility of their combat units to a high degree. Fighter squadrons were switched, at short notice, from one front to another, as the occasion demanded, and their pilots were seldom far from the great air battles.

I have found it possible to make a detailed check of some of the claims of a well-known German who has been called 'the unrivalled virtuoso of the fighter pilots'. His greatest day in the Western Desert was on 1st September 1942, when he claimed seventeen victories, eight of them in the space of ten minutes. But our own records show that, on this day, we lost a total of only eleven aeroplanes, including two Hurricanes, a type which the German pilot did not claim. In fact, some of our losses occurred when he was on the ground.

Greatest of all living German fighter pilots was the able and fearless Adolf Galland, whom I have already mentioned several times, for he was associated with their fighter arm throughout the war. During his interrogation at the end of the war, Galland told us that because another famous fighter ace, Werner Mölders, had been grounded by Hitler at one hundred victories, he 'stopped counting his victories after the ninety-fourth'.

Galland was constantly at odds with the outmoded Göring, who, as a result of his achievements in the First World War, still regarded himself as a tactician and an expert on fighter affairs. The history of the enemy fighter arm is one of a series of disagreements between Galland and Göring which were reflected in the force itself, for the former had a following of young leaders who were devoted to him. This disunity was graphically illustrated by an incident in 1943 when, at a conference of fighter leaders, Göring insulted the fighter pilots and accused them of cowardice. Göring went on to say that many pilots with the highest decorations had faked their combat reports, whereupon Galland tore his Knight's Cross from his collar and, with a dramatic gesture, flung it on the table.

Despite their poorly trained fighter pilots, the Luftwaffe were still capable of delivering some hard blows, as the Americans discovered to their cost on one particular operation. A force of Fortresses, escorted by Mustangs, had bombed a target in Germany and then landed on Russian airfields. Unknown to the Americans, they had been shadowed by a Heinkel and shortly after midnight the Luftwaffe bombers went into action. American and Russian aeroplanes were bombed and strafed, and great damage was done. No German aircraft was lost and the strike was brilliantly successful. Just after the war, a high-ranking American airman told Göring that this was the best air attack ever made against the Americans. Göring's eyes sparkled, and he said to his captors: "Those were wonderful times!"[1]

On 16th December 1944, von Rundstedt launched three armies on a wide front. The main axis of the armoured thrusts lay through the hilly country of the Ardennes, and the weather, which was still against us, grounded our reconnaissance patrols. Unhampered by the attentions of our air forces, von Rundstedt was able to average a daily advance of slightly more than twelve miles. Just before Christmas the clouds lifted and we were able to get into the air. Within two days the enemy's advance had been halted.

Once again we flew in squadron strength and patrolled Malmedy, St Vith and Bastogne. Our job was to hold off the Luftwaffe fighters, while our fighter-bombers strafed columns of enemy vehicles on the few good roads in this part of the Ardennes. One day Danny Browne and I flew a two-man patrol over the battle area. Our squadrons were operating to a strict time-table, and we had not intended to fly. But it was a grand day, with sparkling sunshine and unlimited visibility. Soon we were over the snow-covered, hilly terrain, flying fairly low but above the enemy's light flak.

Danny guarded the rear of our two Spitfires and I concentrated on searching ahead and below. For we were after the low-flying Focke-

[1] *The Army Air Forces in World War II,* Vol.III, p.314.

Wulfs, which were active again. Three miles above, vapour trails made intricate filigree patterns and, below, the hills were clothed in a concealing, white blanket of frozen snow. Navigation was far more difficult than usual, for the highways and railroad merged into the surrounding countryside and only the unfrozen rivers and the country towns gave some clue to our position. From above, our grey-green Spitfires could easily be seen by an alert enemy pilot, as they were conspicuous against the backcloth of virgin snow. Every few seconds I yawed my Spitfire with coarse rudder so that I could help Danny search behind. Suddenly my Spitfire was rocked by an explosion. I heard the ugly crunches of heavy flak. Several bursts bracketed the Spitfire, and when I had zoomed away from the danger zone I dropped a wing and saw the guns below.

"Johnnie, you O.K.? That looked darned close to me."

"I'm all right, Danny," I said. "Let's see what's going on below."

We climbed our Spitfires high into the shielding sun, then stall-turned into a fast dive towards the shoulder of the wood where I had pin-pointed the flak positions; but they had drawn our attention to something far more important. On the far side of the wood was a long column of enemy vehicles, including tanks, self-propelled guns, staff Volkswagen and half-tracks. Doubtless it was a spearhead of a *Panzer* army. We climbed back a few thousand feet so that our radio transmissions would reach our ops. room.

"Greycap to Kenway. Over Houffalize and have spotted enemy transports. Suggest you send two squadrons. I'll brief and head them to the target. Over."

"Kenway to Greycap. Will do. One of your squadrons has just taken off. We'll divert it and follow up with another. How long can you stay there?"

"Greycap to Kenway. We're good for another thirty minutes. Tell the chaps to hurry. Out."

Presently the squadron commander broke the radio silence:

"Greycap from green leader. Understand you have some trade for us. What's the form?"

"Greycap to green leader. Rendezvous over Houffalize at 8,000 feet. I'll take you to the target."

Our fourteen Spitfires were soon formed together, and I led the formation to where the enemy still crouched along a narrow road which meandered along the edge of the wood. The twelve Spitfires fell to their work and for a few minutes Danny and I watched the scene from above. Some flak opposed the first few attacks, but the guns were quickly silenced and the strafing continued almost at leisure. It was a sombre setting. Falls of thick black smoke curled upwards from the doomed column, making a strange contrast with the white hills, whose ice-bound peaks glittered in the sunshine of the late afternoon. The hungry Spitfires plunged downwards with short, accurate bursts of cannon fire, then soared away to manoeuvre for another attack. Seizing an opportune moment, Danny and I strafed some half-tracks. Then we climbed away and set course for Evère, as our petrol was running low. Before darkness fell, the enemy column had been written off – a half mile of blazing, ruined vehicles.

It was not a great occasion. Nothing like the destruction and carnage of the Falaise gap. But it was a fine example of the flexibility of our fighter-bomber squadrons and the speed with which we could concentrate our fire power in any particular section. Not more than a few minutes had elapsed between the time I called for assistance and the moment when the first squadron made its appearance.

We saw an unusual accident at Evère when young Tegerdine, of 403 Squadron, took off on an armed reconnaissance. He was easing back his throttle and trying to pick up squadron formation when, at a height of only a few hundred feet, his engine cut dead. He was too low to bale out, and since he was over a densely built-up area he tried to stretch his glide to a small patch of open ground. Losing height, and at a dangerously low forward speed, Tegerdine realised that he did not have enough height to make his crash landing. A turn would have been fatal, but he kept his head and held the Spitfire on a straight course. The sinking aeroplane struck the roof of a block of apartments and some three tons of metal skidded across the concrete and struck a small parapet wall on the far side of the roof. For a moment the Spitfire rocked to and fro along its axis, like a child's see-saw, before it finally settled on the roof. Our pilot was unhurt but, unhappily, he had to bale out over Germany a few days later.

Our group commander, Harry Broadhurst, also had a lucky escape at Evère. One day Bill and I met him and had a few words together before he drove into Brussels. It was late afternoon when he took off for the return flight to Eindhoven. The little Storch took its usual short run and sprang into the air. Rocking in the stiff breeze, the pilot began to climb to a few hundred feet for his journey. When the Storch was but a few feet above some buildings, the engine stopped. Bill stood rooted to the ground as he watched the drama. Broadhurst tried to get down on the roof of a hangar, but unfortunately the hangar was practically gutted; all that remained of the once flat roof were a few charred beams. The little Storch bounced on these beams. Then it fell to the ground below. An ominous pall of dark smoke rose into the air. A few minutes later the Storch was little more than a pile of debris, but, miraculously, the group commander stood alongside it, shaken but unhurt.

The fighter pilots of the Luftwaffe did not take part in the usual celebrations of New Year's Eve. Instead, they were briefed for Operation *Hermann* (planned by Göring himself) and forbidden to take part in any parties. The strike was to take place on the following morning, and aimed at the destruction of the maximum number of Allied aircraft where they lay on our crowded airfields. The attack had been planned for some time, and should have been the prelude to the Ardennes offensive. But already the German soldiers had felt the chill wind of defeat and had walked on Belgian soil for the last time.

Elaborate measures were taken by the Luftwaffe to make sure that their large force, including jets, reached their targets. The flight from Germany took place in four great waves of fighters. Squadrons attacking targets in the Brussels area flew over the southern part of the Zuider Zee. Those formations attacking airfields near Eindhoven flew from the north over the Zuider Zee, and the remaining two waves struck from the east. The fighters were led by Junkers 88s to assist in navigation, and although these turned back near the Rhine, their assistance was invaluable to the less-experienced fighter pilots. Various visual aids were employed to help the fighters, including flares called 'golden rain', coloured smoke and searchlights. Despite these measures, some of the German aeroplanes were fired upon by their own flak.

Strict radio discipline was enforced and no tell-tale conversations were heard which would have alerted our defending fighters. The German squadrons flew at the lowest possible height over the bare, snow-sheeted landscape: whenever the terrain permitted, they flew up the valleys to escape our radar detection. At all costs, Göring wanted complete tactical surprise, and this the Luftwaffe achieved.

Our four Canadian squadrons at Evère each possessed fourteen Spitfires, and upwards of sixty fighters were dispersed about the eastern half of the airfield. Except when it was frozen hard, the ground was soft and treacherous, and our Spitfires were packed close to the perimeter track. The western portion of the airfield was occupied by a miscellaneous collection of Fortresses, Austers, Ansons, Prince Bernhard's Beechcraft and a luxurious Dakota. The camouflage nets which we had used to cover our Spitfires in Normandy had long since been withdrawn, for there was little point in concealing our fighters when conspicuous transport aircraft lay scattered about the airfield. The heavy anti-aircraft guns had been taken away and the defence of Evère was vested in a handful of light guns. There must have been upwards of a hundred aeroplanes on our airfield, while at Melsbröek, three miles away, dozens of bombers were packed in straight lines, wing-tip to wing-tip.

There had been a sharp frost during the night. Then it had rained, and the frozen surface of the single runway at Evère was dangerous both for take-offs and landings. Accordingly, the early-morning patrols which usually went off at first light were delayed until the runway was sprinkled with grit. Kenway was anxious for us to carry out two weather reconnaissance flights over different sectors, and shortly before nine o'clock two Spitfires of 403 Squadron, led by Steve Butte, took off. Steve called up our airfield controller to say that the runway was all right, providing pilots did not use their brakes harshly: another section of two Spitfires was sent off and 416 Squadron was called to readiness.

Dave Harling was the leader of 416 Squadron, and a few days

previously we had been present at a pleasant ceremony in Brussels when Dave's sister, an attractive Canadian nurse, was married. After briefing his pilots, Dave led the twelve Spitfires along the slippery perimeter track. He reached the junction of the perimeter track and the runway; with eleven Spitfires packed behind him, he began a slow turn on to the runway itself. Meanwhile Butte's section was returning and the other pair of Spitfires had reached their patrol line. This was the setting at Evère when, without warning of any description, a mixed bunch of about sixty Focke-Wulfs and Messerschmitts appeared on the circuit.

I heard the noise of a large number of aeroplanes, but paid little attention, since large formations of American fighters often flew over Evère. Flying along the western boundary of the airfield, the leading elements turned left and the first four Messerschmitts came low over the boundary in loose formation. The cannons belched; the three aircraft behind Harling's Spitfire were badly hit. The pilots jumped from their cockpits and scrambled for shelter. Dave roared down the runway with wide-open throttle. Alone he turned into the enemy fighters and shot one down. But the odds were far too great; our brave pilot was killed before his Spitfire had gathered combat speed.

From our reasonably safe positions on the ground Bill and I took stock of the attack. The enemy fighters strafed singly and in pairs. Our few light ack-ack guns had already ceased firing; later we found that the gunners had run out of ammunition. The enemy completely dominated the scene, and there was little we could do except shout with rage as our Spitfires burst into flames before our eyes.

At the end of the runway stood a small caravan which provided an office for our airfield controller. Despite the continuous strafing attacks, the officer remained at his post and warned our two airborne Spitfire sections to get back at their fastest speed.

Our small clutch of operations caravans were grouped together in a disused dispersal bay, with steep sides. This site was well protected and camouflaged; so far the enemy pilots had not spotted it. In one of the caravans the phone rang. Frank Minton, our short, plump Spy – who owned a dairy back in Canada – eased himself from his prone position on the floor. A staff officer spoke urgently:

"Large gaggles of Huns near your airfield. Get your Spits off."

Frank, who did not lack a sense of humour, replied:

"You're too late. If I stick this phone outside you'll hear their bloody cannons!"

The attack had already lasted about ten minutes. Many enemy fighters flew directly over us and their speed seemed to be very slow – not more than 150 m.p.h. Their marksmanship was very poor, for several Spitfires still remained in one piece. Some pilots wasted their ammunition by spraying the hangars instead of concentrating on more profitable targets.

Suddenly our Spitfires arrived back over Evère and the highest Messerschmitts and Focke-Wulfs curved to meet the threat. Three of our pilots shot down six of the attackers; Steve Butte got three. But they were too few to drive off sixty Germans, and after using all their ammunition the Spitfires took to their heels.

The Luftwaffe withdrew as abruptly as they had appeared, and we were left to our burning airfield. The first thing was to get a strong formation of Spitfires into the air to beat off a follow-up attack. After arranging the details, Bill and I looked at the damage. One airman was killed and another nine wounded. Eleven of our Spitfires were written-off and twelve damaged. On the west side of Evère some transport aeroplanes still blazed, including the Beechcraft and the luxurious Dakota; others, whose undercarriages had collapsed, obstinately refused to burn and lay on the ground like tired cattle; We had escaped lightly. Not one Spitfire should have remained undamaged at Evère.

Operation *Hermann* was a bold stroke, but we saw for ourselves that the average German fighter pilot was not equal to the task. Thanks to the assistance of the bombers, the various formations were able to find their targets. Owing to their low-level tactics and their radio silence, they achieved complete surprise. But once over the crowded airfields, they were unable to exploit their advantage. The shooting was atrocious, and the circuit at Evère reminded us more of a bunch of beginners on their first solos than pilots of front-line squadrons. The time factor was badly planned, for the basis of the strike should have been a sharp, concentrated attack. As it was, the long time spent over our airfield meant that we were able to scramble fighters from secure airfields and divert those already in the air. Both sides suffered about the same losses in aeroplanes, but the enemy lost far more pilots as he was operating over our territory. Strategically the operation was carried out at the wrong time; it should have been the prelude to the Ardennes offensive. Tactically, the attacks were well planned, but poor flying was their undoing.

For the last time during the war, the group captains and wing leaders were summoned to group headquarters. On this occasion Harry Broadhurst's briefing dealt with the crossing of the Rhine, Operation *Varsity*, which would take place in a few days' time.

Our group commander discussed the various tasks of his wings in great detail; these fell under five main headings. Primarily, and most important, the fighter wings were to make sure that the air space over the dropping and landing-zones was kept clear of enemy aircraft. Rocket-firing Typhoons and light bombers would deal with the flak defences, an unenviable and dangerous job. More fighters would provide close escort to the American and British transport aeroplanes. Typhoons would also supply close support to the troops, for which purpose contact cars would be provided in some gliders. Finally, all enemy ground movement into the battle area would be harassed by armed reconnaissance operations and bombing of selected communication centres. It was a good plan, and we felt that it could not fail.

The day before *Varsity* we saw some Typhoons in action. Coming out of Germany after a fighter sweep, we crossed the Rhine fast and fairly low. Looking up-river, near Wesel, I spotted three pairs of aircraft some distance away. Turning towards, them, they were soon recognised as six rocket-firing Typhoons.

The Typhoons were on an anti-flak patrol and for a few minutes we watched their technique. The three sections were separated by distances of about 1,000 yards; when the flak opened up at the leading pair, the next pair spotted the flashes on the ground and went down in a shallow rocket attack. Sometimes other guns fired at the second pair; these were dealt with by the last section of Typhoons. After an attack, the leader circled his small force to assess the damage and then the procession down the Rhine was resumed. These pilots had plenty of guts, and we admired them.

The dawn was driving in from the east when we took-off on our first *Varsity* mission. As the Merlin engine lifted my Spitfire into the air, with the Canadians streaming behind, the rising curtain of light revealed the flat fields below. On the far horizon, silhouetted against the pastel back-cloth of the early morning sky, a great pall of smoke rose into the still air, marking the recent visit of Bomber Command to Wesel.

On our second flight of the day we flew over the parallel streams of transport aircraft and gliders when they approached the Rhine. The American force was far greater than our own and took more than two hours to pass a position on the ground. Danny, who was flying alongside me, could not resist the temptation to sing out: "Greycap. You can see Uncle Sam is on the ball today!"

Unfortunately, the leading British transports and gliders arrived over their dropping zone ahead of the planned zero hour, before the Typhoons had neutralised all the flak batteries. Weaving between the slow Dakotas, the fighter-bombers pressed home their rocket attacks, even after the first parachutes had spilled open. We were horrified to see several bursts of heavy flak explode among the paratroopers as they swung helplessly from their sinking parachutes.

Except for the failure to silence all the flak, *Varsity* was a complete success. Before we turned in for the night, we heard that the situation on the far bank of the Rhine was well under control. This final thrust, which was to lead to unconditional surrender in six weeks' time, had got off to a good start.

Early the next morning Harry Broadhurst phoned. My days with the Canadians were over. I was to go to Eindhoven and take over command of 125 Wing from David Scott-Malden. The group commander wanted to move the wing, with their latest Spitfire 14s, to the first available airfield east of the Rhine. He was confident that there would be more air fighting before the end of the war. So I was to put up my fourth stripe. He congratulated me on the promotion, not forgetting to stress the fact that I should lose it and revert to a junior rank once the fighting was over, and, on this encouraging note, rang off.

While Varley packed our clothes and rounded up the Labrador, I drove to the four squadron dispersals to say goodbye. It was more than two years since I had first led the Canadians, and some of the more senior pilots had flown with me many times. There existed between us that bond of comradeship that only those who have served and fought together are privileged to know. I had a look at my old Spitfire, which, during the previous twelve months, had carried me on nearly 200 operations. She was far more battered and weathered than when I had selected her at Digby, but she was good for many more flights. The patch on the wing root, which marked my fight with the Messerschmitts over the Seine, still held firm. Finally, I shook hands with my ground crew. As we sped up the cobbled road to Eindhoven I realised that this was the end of a memorable period in my life.

Chapter 19

THE FATED SKY

A dozen Spitfire 14s wheeled over Eindhoven as Varley and I drove on to the airfield. When the fighters taxied past the jeep, we could see that most pilots had fired their guns, and I soon learnt that these boys of 130 Squadron had just knocked down seven Focke-Wulfs. This was the finest possible welcome, and promised well for those last dramatic weeks of the fighting.

My wing leader was the Canadian George Keefer, who had flown with the Kenley Wing some time ago. George was as slim and fit as ever, and we had a long chat about the activities and personalities of his three squadrons – 41, 130 and the Belgian-manned 350. George said:

"I suppose you'll want your own Spit, just the same as when you were a wing leader?"

"That's right, George," I answered, for I knew what he was driving at. "Pick out a good Spit for me and get my initials painted on. I'll have a crack with you tomorrow."

George looked down his nose at this, so I got up, clapped him on the back, and explained:

"We can only have one wing leader, and that's you, George. But I can't free-wheel on the past and I must fly two or three times a week to keep up to date. Besides, the chaps won't respect me unless I keep my hand in. You generally operate in squadrons, so I shan't be taking your job. When we fly as a wing, you'll do the leading and I'll lead a section or a squadron."

"That's fine, sir," replied the Canadian. "I'll go and give your new Spit a whirl round."

"All right, George," I said. "There's just one thing, though. I'm leading the first show over Berlin as soon as we're in range!"

"That's a deal," laughed George. "And I'll fly alongside you on that day!"

Four days after the crossing of the Rhine, I was told that a grass strip was ready for us. I was to have a look at it, and, if suitable, the wing was to move in immediately.

I took a fairly strong reconnaissance party with me. After swaying across the river on a very temporary wooden bridge, we drove through what remained of the little town of Wesel. Bomber Command had hammered this place a few hours before the assault and now it smouldered and stank in the warm sunshine. Here and there little groups of dubious, sullen young men stood at the street corners. We suspected that, not very long ago, they had worn different clothes, but we had important things to do and left them to their own devices.

The new airfield, at a place called Damme, was quite unsuitable, the ground being badly drained and water-logged. We could never operate our Spitfires from this site until it had thoroughly dried out, so I phoned the group commander and said that it wasn't on.

"Never mind," he said. "The army have just captured a far better place. Twente, in Holland, and very close to the German border. Get your wing there at once."

We struck camp and pressed on to Twente. The airfield had been used by the Luftwaffe, but the brick runway had been bombed many times, and, although it had been patched up, odd bricks lay all over the place and the surface looked uneven and dangerous. A fine looking strip of grass lay alongside a wood on the east side of the airfield. The surface seemed reasonably dry and I thought it would make a far better runway than the crumbling bricks.

I circled Twente in my Spitfire that afternoon. I had a careful look round to clear my tail before making the final approach to our grass strip, for we were very near to the front and I didn't want to get bounced with wheels and flaps down. I landed safely, and an airman waved me to a dispersal point near the central building. I switched off and heard the usual tinkling of the engine as it cooled. The airman bent over the cockpit to lend a hand with the straps.

"Well, how do you like…" I began, and looked up as a lean, grey Messerschmitt roared a few feet over our heads.

The Hun had seen us, and over the far side of the field began to turn for his strafing run. I tore a finger-nail on the Sutton harness.

Then I scrambled out of the cockpit with the parachute still strapped on, tumbled down the easy slope of the wing root, fell to the ground and grovelled under the belly of the Spitfire. We could hear the Messerschmitt boring in. What a bloody way to buy it, I thought. After five years and just made a group captain!

We heard two crumps in quick succession above the noise of the engine, then a large explosion when the Messerschmitt hit the deck. The two of us scrambled to our feet: on the far side of the field a column of dark, oily smoke rose into the calm spring air. The boy and I slapped the dirt from our uniforms and laughed together. I said:

"Fill her up, son. I want to take off in half an hour."

Someone produced a jeep, and I drove across the Twente airfield to thank the crew of the Bofors gun who had undoubtedly saved us from a nasty smack. They belonged to the R.A.F. Regiment, and now, in their shirtsleeves, busied themselves about their gun. I shook hands with each one and congratulated them:

"A magnificent piece of shooting," I said. "Absolutely first class! I'll send you a crate of beer over as soon as I can get my hands on one."

"Excuse me, sir," said the young corporal, "but would you confirm the 109 for us?"

I looked puzzled and pointed to the smouldering wreck about a hundred yards away.

"Surely that's all the confirmation you want," I replied.

"Well, sir," explained the corporal, "they'll never believe the Regiment has shot down an enemy kite with only a couple of rounds."

"All right," I laughed. "I'll ring up Colonel Preston at 83 Group and tell him there's no doubt about this one."

We only remained at Twente for a few days. Our grass strip remained serviceable, but only because of constant attention from the rollers, pulled by teams of sweating airmen and officers. Whenever there was a lull in the flying, out came the rollers: everyone enjoyed it, as long as we kept the Spitfires in the air. The troops knew they were on the last lap and soon they would be back at home. You could see it shining from their eager, happy faces. Then we were told to get our three-tonners, trailers and caravans on the road again for what proved to be our last move of the war. This time we were to go to the peace-time Luftwaffe airfield at Celle, which lies a few miles north of Hanover. There was some doubt as to whether the landing-strip would be long enough for our Spitfire 14s, so George and I flew there together and guarded each other on this low-level flight deep into Germany. As we taxied over the grass towards the hangars, a dozen Bofors guns began their fast chatter and the shells burst round four Focke-Wulfs which streaked over Celle at high speed and disappeared over the far horizon.

The two of us were driven round the airfield by a young infantry officer from the Scottish unit which had captured the place a day or two previously. All the various buildings were undamaged. We saw magnificent, centrally heated messes and barrack blocks for the men, well-built hangars and technical workshops alongside a railway siding, a spacious, well-appointed cinema and a large swimming-pool. Finally, we inspected the officers' mess, which would be our new home. It stood discreetly apart and was a most pleasant building with a fine, lofty dining-room, a minstrel's gallery and bronze busts of Göring and Hitler in the hall. Downstairs was a spacious beer-cellar, whose walls were covered with beautiful murals depicting the clandestine birth and progress of the Luftwaffe. It was all there – the gliders, the uniforms, pilots training in secret sections of the commercial flying schools, well-developed fräuleins and the bombs raining down on Spain. Obviously, the Germans were proud of the manner in which they had fooled the rest of the world. George summed up our thoughts when he growled:

"We could paint in one or two pictures to complete the story!"

Next door to the beer-cellar was a lavatory with the usual conveniences; but there was something which puzzled us for a few moments. There was a line of porcelain basins about three feet apart and smaller than the usual hand-basins. These basins had large outlets and no plugs, and on either side were chromium handles which were obviously meant to be gripped by the hands.

"What the hell are those things?" demanded George.

"Don't know," I answered as I gripped the two handles. "Surely they can't be to vomit…"

"They are, you know," exclaimed our knowledgeable Scot. "The Krauts called them *Brechbecken*. When they got full of beer they staggered in here and got rid of it. The Romans used to do the same after tickling their throats with a feather! Very handy, you know!"

"And then staggered back for more," I said.

"I've seen everything now," said the Canadian.

I thought that we should never fully understand the mentality of the people who deemed such things necessary in an officers' mess. But if Celle was a typical example of the German forces' pre-war standard of comfort and living, we could fully understand how Hitler had swung the generals to his cause.

We moved the wing to Celle and began a stirring bout of fighting which was a fitting climax to the war. What remained of the Luftwaffe operated from a complex of airfields east of the Elbe, and these squadrons were gradually being squeezed into impotence by ourselves and the advancing Russians. But the enemy still possessed ample supplies of aeroplanes, from the latest sleek jets to light communications types, and during these last two weeks we gave them no respite, harrying them from dawn till dusk.

For us, the war in the air suddenly became a more personal affair than before. Previously, we thought of the destruction of an enemy aeroplane in the same terms as a strafing attack against an armoured car or a strongpoint. When you sent a Messerschmitt spinning down out of control, the pilot either got out or he didn't. If he baled out, then the rule which we followed throughout the war was that he should be allowed to drift down to earth without being riddled with cannon fire. It was an act of chivalry which we had inherited from our forebears of the previous war; and despite accounts to the contrary, I never knew of a pilot who was shot at as he drifted helplessly to the ground. But when the Messerschmitts hit the ground and burst apart, we had no thought for the fellow inside.

Now we began to see it from a different angle, because we lived in Germany and saw something of the Germans. We visited the concentration camp at Belsen, for this dreadful place was but a few miles from Celle, and saw the ghastly ovens and the long, filthy corridors of the wooden huts where we could not distinguish between the dead and the dying. We saw the bulldozers at work as they pushed hundreds of corpses into the square, mass graves.

There were accounts from our own prisoners of war who, liberated by the advancing Russians, swarmed across Germany and made their way in thousands to Celle. They arrived in vehicles of all makes and descriptions, from supercharged Mercedes to horses and carts, so that my airfield looked like a second-hand junkyard, and every pilot seemed to have his own car. It was an easy matter to get these men home to England, for numerous Dakotas landed daily with petrol supplies, and instead of returning empty, we filled the transports with the ex-prisoners.

One day, I was going to my room before lunch when Varley met me and whispered:

"There's a squadron leader in your room, sir. He's one of these prisoners and wants to see you. He's about had it!"

I went silently into the bedroom. The young squadron leader was asleep on my bed. His battledress was torn and threadbare, his face gaunt and heavily lined, and he twisted in his fitful sleep. Soon he awoke and told me that he must get to the Air Ministry that very afternoon. Didn't I remember the mass escape from Stalag Luft 3, when many Allied airmen tunnelled their way to freedom? And had I forgotten how fifty of those chaps had been recaptured and then shot in the back? Well, he had some vital information about the brutes responsible for this outrage, and the sooner he got to London the better.

The attitude of the local inhabitants to all these things simply infuriated us. A strapping bevy of fräuleins reported to our airfield each day to scrub and clean the various messes. Some twenty of them were employed in our mess, and it was quite obvious that they weren't averse to these duties; they twittered amongst themselves whenever a bunch of my pilots walked by. Of course, they knew nothing of Belsen and what had taken place in the big ovens! Their elders subscribed to the same story, although the place was but a few miles away and the infamous blonde guard, Irma Grese, and the commandant, Kramer, both of whom were subsequently hanged, often visited the local town. I took the necessary steps to ensure that some of the local populace went to Belsen to bring their political education up to date.

We found a lot of Huns during this latter half of April. We took off before first light to get at them, and the last patrols landed on the flare path. We destroyed fighters, bombers, transports, Stuka dive-bombers, those once dreaded peregrines of the Blitzkrieg, trainers and a bunch of seaplanes we found floating on a lake. We could not catch the jets in the air, but we knew they were operating from Lübeck, on the Baltic coast. We paid special attention to this airfield, shooting them down when they took off or came in to land. Some of the enemy leaders showed flashes of their old brilliance, but the rank and file were poor stuff.

I led the wing on the Berlin show at the first opportunity. For this epic occasion our first team took to the air. George led a squadron and Tony Gaze flew with me again – the first time since we flew together in Bader's wing. We swept to Berlin at a couple of thousand feet above the ground, over a changing sunlit countryside of desolate heathland, small lakes and large forests, with the empty, double ribbon of the autobahn lying close on our starboard side.

We shall not easily forget our first sight of Berlin. Thick cloud covered the capital and forced us down to a lower level. The roads to the west were filled with a mass of refugees fleeing the city. We pressed over the wooded suburbs, and Berlin sprawled below us with gaping holes here and there. It was burning in a dozen different places and the Falaise smell suddenly hit us, the corrupting stench of death. The Russian artillery was hard at it: as we flew towards the east, we saw the flashes of their guns and the debris thrown up from the shells. Russian tanks and armour rumbled into the city from the east. Tony said:

"Fifty-plus at two o'clock, Greycap! Same level. More behind."

"Are they Huns, Tony?" I asked, as I focused my eyes on the gaggle.

"Don't look like Huns to me, Greycap," replied Tony. "Probably Russians."

"All right, chaps," I said. "Stick together. Don't make a move." And to myself I thought: I'm for it if this mix-up gets out of hand!

The Yaks began a slow turn which would bring them behind our Spitfires. I could not allow this and I swung the wing to starboard and turned over the top of the Yaks. They numbered about a hundred all told.

"More above us," calmly reported Tony.

"Tighten it up," I ordered. "Don't break formation."

We circled each other for a couple of turns. Both sides were cautious and suspicious. I narrowed the gap between us as much as I dared. When I was opposite the Russian leader I rocked my wings and watched for him to do the same. He paid no regard, but soon after he straightened out of his turn and led his ragged collection back to the east.

We watched them fly away. There seemed to be no pattern or discipline to their flying. The leader was in front and the pack followed behind. Rising and falling with the gaggle continually changing shape. They reminded me of a great, wheeling, tumbling pack of starlings which one sometimes sees on a winter day in England. They quartered the ground like buzzards, and every few moments a handful broke away from the pack, circled leisurely and then attacked something in the desert of brick and rubble. In this fashion they worked over the dying city.

(I was to remember this experience when, little more than five years later, I was serving in Korea with the United States Air Force and the first squadrons of well-trained, well-disciplined Mig 15s made their appearance over the Yalu river. The Communists had learnt a lot during those few years.)

We were not allowed to fly over Berlin again; and perhaps it was just as well, for there could easily have been an unfortunate clash between the Russians and ourselves, especially during bad weather with poor visibility. A high-level decision was made to halt our armies on the Elbe, and once again we patrolled the area between Celle and the Baltic coast.

The German flak was as accurate as ever and their gunners did not seem short of ammunition, for the stuff came up at us every time we were within range. In those last few days of the war we found that the enemy had not forgotten how to decoy unsuspecting fighter pilots with nasty flak-traps.

We received orders to pay special attention to enemy shipping off the Baltic coast. One day the Belgian squadron, led by their English C.O., Terry Spencer, found a fat petrol tanker lying in Wismar Bay. The flak burst round the twelve Spitfires, so Terry left two sections circling at height and led his section to strafe the tanker at mast height.

The Belgians watching from above saw their leader's Spitfire burst into flames when it roared over the tanker. The wings and fuselage fell into the shallow water of the bay, but the engine continued to soar through the air and fell with another explosion on the far shore. The eleven Spitfires returned to Celle, and the senior pilots came to me with the story. Even allowing for their colourful and dramatic description of the incident, there seemed to be no hope for Terry. We felt his loss keenly, for he was a most attractive personality and a natural commander for the Belgians, who, in turn, were devoted to him.

One evening, George led one of the squadrons on a sweep round the far side of the Elbe and I led a finger-four down-sun from him. We were after the jets and we intended to visit the maximum number of Luftwaffe airfields.

We swung towards an airfield which lay neatly camouflaged in the midst of some thick woods. The heavy flak reached up and bracketed us and the soot bags followed us through the sky when George led us into the cover of the low sun. Before we turned away, I scanned the airfield below and saw a squadron of Messerschmitts with churning propellers about to take off. The leader and his wingman were already stacked alongside each other on the runway and the remainder were packed closely behind on the perimeter track. I called George:

"A dozen 109s below, George. About to take off."

"O.K. I've seen them, Greycap. We'll come back in a few

minutes."

Five minutes later we returned in a fast dive from the sun. The 109s were still there, but there was no fooling the Huns for the gunners were ready and waiting and hundreds of light flak guns joined the heavy barrage. The Germans had developed this type of defence to a fine art, and sometimes they succeeded in holding us off with the flak whilst their own aeroplanes made their approach to land through special safety lanes.

My heart sank when I saw the flak. Probably we were all thinking the same things. The war that could only last a few more days. The 109s below whose pilots had probably left their cockpits, for their engines had stopped. What were the chances of getting through the flak, now that the gunners were thoroughly roused? I reckoned this was about fifty-fifty. George said:

"Greycap, I'm going in with my number two. Cover us, will you?"

I wanted to say – "Is it worth it George?" or "The army will probably capture this place tomorrow" but I only muttered:

"O.K., George."

I reefed my Spitfire into a tight turn and watched the pair of Spitfires hurtle down towards the junction of the runway and the perimeter track. George was making his strafing attack parallel to the perimeter track to destroy the greatest number of Messerschmitts, and didn't have the benefit of the sun.

The two Spitfires got smaller and smaller as they went down in a fast dive. Their grey-green camouflage merged into the spring greenery of the trees below and for a second or two I lost them. But the gunners on the ground still saw them, and the whole airfield seemed to sparkle with the flashes from the guns. Heavy guns and light guns. Single barrels, double barrels and quadruple barrels; firing from all angles and from the hangar roofs, the control tower and even the tops of trees. A thick bed of explosions filled the air space below us. Yellow flak, black flak, white flak and strings of flak.

We saw them again when they streaked over the boundary of the airfield. We saw the cannon shells from George's Spitfire flashing and bouncing on the concrete perimeter track, and I shouted into my microphone:

"Up a bit George, you're under-deflecting!"

Then his shells ripped into the last Messerschmitt in the line and we saw the winking explosions on the rest. The rear Messerschmitt caught fire, its ammunition exploded in the heat, and the cannon shells slammed into the next 109. In a matter of seconds the whole lot were blazing and a great spiral of white smoke curled up from the airfield.

"You all right, George?" I said.

"Fine, Greycap. Am climbing up."

"Red two?" I asked.

"I've been hit, sir, but she's flying O.K.," replied the wingman.

"Lead him home, George, and we'll cover you," I instructed.

I twisted my neck for a final look at the airfield. All the Messerschmitts were still burning fiercely and the smoke was already up to our height of 6,000 feet. It was the best strafing attack I had ever seen. It was certainly the bravest.

"Nice work, George," I said. "You got the bloody lot!"

"How many were there, Greycap?" asked George.

"Exactly eleven. I counted them," I told him.

We tried to get the record bag of one hundred Huns in a month, but after the final patrol on the last day of April we were three short. During these spring days the wing flew a record number of missions, and apart from the Luftwaffe we had damaged or destroyed well over a thousand pieces of transport and more than a hundred trains. We had sprayed a number of tanks with our cannon with doubtful results, sunk barges and tugs on the rivers and canals, and beaten up the enemy troops wherever we found them. It was quite a month.

There was a lot of talk about the cease fire, but our operations continued into May. One evening a belt of fine rain finished our patrols somewhat earlier than usual and George recalled our Spitfires. After they were all safely down, George and I walked into the bar for a drink before dinner. Suddenly a tremendous party developed, as they sometimes did. This one was really our end-of-the-war celebration, for this could only be a matter of days or even hours. There was nothing official or planned about this thrash. It just happened. The Belgians started to sing, the champagne corks began to pop and the beer cellar was jammed with pilots and ground officers in their working dress. Suddenly the singing stopped, the clamour ceased and a great shout went up from the Belgians. George yelled in my ear:

"It's Terry Spencer!"

His face was burnt. He limped badly and walked with the aid of a stick. We thrust a glass of champagne into his hand, and when I had restored order he told us his story.

"I remember going in to attack that tanker at mast height, about forty feet. There was a fair amount of light flak and the next thing I knew was hitting the water with the parachute collapsing on top of me. I saw the tail of my Spit crash alongside and then I struggled from underneath the 'chute. I thought it would suffocate me."

Terry broke off and began to laugh.

"Go on," we said. "What happened then?"

"Well, I got rid of the 'chute and struck out for the land. The shore looked a long way off, and I didn't think I'd make it. But suddenly my foot touched the bottom and I found myself standing in four feet of sea!"

We all roared with laughter at the scene he described so well. Terry continued:

"The Hun gunners were as surprised as I was. They saw the Spit explode and the parachute stream out, but I was so low they didn't see me on the end of it. They took me to the local hospital at Wismar and here I am! Where's the champers?"

I went to a quiet room and telephoned the group commander. Harry Broadhurst had personally selected Spencer to lead the Belgians and would be delighted with my news. He said:

"You recommended him for the D.F.C. just before he went missing?"

"Yes sir," I said.

"And this is the second time he's been shot down and walked back to our lines?"

"Yes sir. He came back the first time about a month ago," I said.

"Right," said the group commander. "Then I'll fix an immediate D.F.C. for him. When you tell him, give him my congratulations and say I'll confirm it by signal tomorrow."

I ran back to break the good news to Terry, but I was too late. His injuries, the journey back, the excitement and the wine all combined against him, and under George's supervision he had been carried to bed by his faithful Belgians. In the bedroom I told them about the gong. Someone produced a bit of coloured ribbon and another a piece of cardboard. George hacked the cardboard into the form of the cross and I scrawled on it, 'Immediate D.F.C.' Then we switched off the light and went back to our party.

Soon afterwards, we flew our last operation of the war. We were told to patrol south of Kiel until 8 a.m. and then return to Celle. When we saw any enemy aeroplanes, we were to escort them to a British airfield and see that they landed. If they acted hostile, we were to take the usual steps.

A lone twin-engined transport was soon spotted by my pilots. The enemy aeroplane took evasive action, turned back to the north and paid the full price. Then the Spitfire pilots spotted four Focke-Wulfs. The Huns waggled their wings, dropped their undercarriages and generally behaved in a nervous manner. The Spitfires flew on either side and eventually this strange little gaggle set course for our lines. My boys chattered to themselves about their prospects of acquiring Luger automatics and Leica cameras. But the 190s landed at the first British airfield they saw and left the frustrated Spitfire pilots circling above.

The next morning we were not awakened by the powerful song of our Spitfires being run-up on the pre-dawn checks. We realised then that the war was really over.

A few weeks later, I was lunching with three or four Danish businessmen who were interested in flying. For a long time we talked of aeroplanes, of flying and of the recent war in the air. By the way, asked Borge Moltke-Leth, had I seen the results of the wonderful bombing by the Mosquitoes when, in March of this year, they had attacked the Gestapo headquarters in Copenhagen? Inside the building were a number of Danish resistance personnel and the bombs were placed with such skill that many of them escaped without injury. No, I answered, I hadn't seen it, but I would welcome the opportunity. Good, after lunch we would drive to Shell House, the late Gestapo Headquarters, and inspect it.

The bombing was a splendid example of the type of precision work often carried out by 2 Group. The leader, Bob Bateson, had led his eighteen Mosquitoes to Copenhagen at tree-top height, and although Shell House was gutted, the surrounding buildings were practically unscathed. We had heard various accounts of this raid: we knew that the legendary Basil Embry had flown on this mission, and indeed many more, under an assumed name.

As we walked round the empty fabric of Shell House, the Danes fell silent and I sensed an atmosphere of uneasiness. Some of my hosts had resorted to their native tongue and shrugged their shoulders in expressions of despair. I asked what the trouble was.

For a moment or two they avoided the issue, and then one of them blurted out the story. During the low-level run across Copenhagen, one of the Mosquitoes from the leading formation struck a flagpole and crashed into a convent school. Worse was to follow, for the building caught fire, and other Mosquitoes, approaching at high speed just above the roof-tops, bombed it instead of Shell House. Many children were killed and some were maimed for the rest of their lives. But, concluded the Dane, these things happen in war.

The right words of sympathy and understanding sounded dreadfully inadequate. I made a mental note to let Basil Embry know of this misfortune, for I knew he would find the time to fly to Copenhagen and console the relatives and nuns, which he did soon afterwards.

On the drive to Kastrup the Danes enquired several times whether it would be possible to hold an open day on the airfield so that the air-minded public could have a close look at our Spitfires. Many people would visit the airfield for such an occasion.

I brooded over this question. Why not? And better still, why not put the aircraft into the air? A vic of Spitfires for formation aerobatics. A Meteor to show the paces of a jet. A few Typhoons to fire their rockets into the Baltic which lapped the eastern boundary of the airfield. A fly-past by the wing. Perhaps Basil Embry would let Bateson's Mosquitoes carry out a dummy low-level attack against Kastrup. And why not charge a small entrance fee, say two kroner (about four shillings) and put the proceeds into an endowment fund for the crippled children?

The Danes were flat out for the scheme. They would look after the publicity, tickets and the collection of all monies. The Air Display Committee was formed there and then. All I had to do was to obtain Harry Broadhurst's approval, produce more aircraft, check the safety regulations, and persuade Basil Embry to participate! I was on the phone to the group commander soon afterwards, telling him about Shell House, the maimed children and the enthusiasm of the Danes. He said guardedly that perhaps it was a good idea. But he had some experience of pre-war air displays and they required careful handling. I was to watch my step.

Planning went ahead. The show would be an informal type of affair – a sort of country flower-show with a band and tea was what we had in mind.

Rehearsals took place and targets were assembled for the Typhoons; these were Blohm and Voss seaplanes moored to the edge of the tideless Baltic. The Mosquitoes would put in an appearance, and Bob Bateson would lead them. Basil Embry, who would also fly, had arranged for the Danish commander-in-chief to sit in his aircraft. We all hoped that the general's spurs wouldn't get caught up in the controls. The Committee expected about 50,000 people to turn up, which would produce a not inconsiderable sum for the children.

The Air Display was scheduled to take place on a Sunday afternoon. On the previous day the telephone rang in my office. It was a call from the royal palace. A lady-in-waiting to the queen of Denmark would like to speak to me. Eventually she came to the phone. The queen had heard of the Air Display at Kastrup. She was very interested and would like to see the affair. Would this be possible? I explained that it was only a small show. Just a few aeroplanes. Everything would be most informal and hardly suitable for the queen. Perhaps the weather would wash out the show altogether. I was thanked graciously for this information. She would appraise the queen and call me back. I replaced the receiver and tried not to visualise dreadful complications.

She phoned within a few minutes. The queen appreciated the fact that the show was of an informal nature and had been laid on at short notice. However, she was determined to see the display and, accompanied by the Crown Prince, would arrive at Kastrup a few minutes before it was scheduled to begin.

It was Saturday afternoon. We had less than a day to revise the arrangements so that the Royal Air Force could fittingly welcome the queen of Denmark. Fortunately, I had already arranged for the W.A.A.F. Band, who could play the various national anthems. A guard of honour could be provided by my R.A.F. Regiment squadron. A small child would present a bouquet of flowers to the queen. But what about diplomatic procedures, protocol and the like? A mere group captain – and a very temporary one at that – could hardly welcome the first lady in the land. Higher authority must be informed at once. I called the group commander on the telephone and explained the latest development. He listened in silence and was then rather rude about the whole affair. He thought he had told me not to let the affair get out of hand. Obviously it had. He would call our commander-in-chief and phone me back. The whole thing might have to be cancelled. I shuddered at this suggestion, for more than 100,000 tickets had been sold and many more Danes would pay their entrance fee tomorrow. Our local machinery was in top gear. I could hardly throw a spanner in the works at this late stage.

Harry Broadhurst phoned back within the hour. The commander-in-chief had said that we could carry on. An officer of air rank would be imported to Copenhagen to receive the queen and make sure that all was well. It had better be. Good-afternoon!

All was well. The sun shone. The little Waafs played valiantly.

The bouquet was charmingly presented and the guard of honour inspected. 41 Squadron's three Spitfires looped and rolled in tight formation. The Typhoons sank the seaplanes and Tony Gaze belted a Meteor above the runway as only he could. Dark clouds gathered on the horizon when Bob Bateson's Mosquitoes climaxed the afternoon with a low-level run across the airfield, which brought home to the quarter of a million spectators the object of the display.

The money was audited and a sizeable cheque was ready for the children. Yet another ceremony was to be enacted, but this time I kept well clear of the planning. The commander-in-chief flew up personally from Germany and handed the cheque to the King of Denmark. In this fashion the future care of the children was secured, and that, perhaps, is a fitting note upon which to end my story.

INDEX